# About This Book

## Why is this topic important?

As at no time in recent memory, the quality of our business leaders has been thrust into the public's collective awareness. As a nation, we have been obsessed with the myth of the senior executive and the power of these individuals to overcome any obstacle and achieve outstanding results no matter what situation they face. But given recent events, we are forced to ask whether our leaders have the capability to meet the challenges of today's competitive environment. The news is full of stories of senior executives who have failed to meet the expectations of Wall Street, stockholders, and employees. The dramatic missteps of some of our most venerable companies, such as AT&T, Lucent, Xerox, and Conseco, as well as the questionable behavior of leaders who ended up destroying more than they built, like those at Enron, Global Crossing, Adelphi, Worldcom, and Tyco, have caused us to take another look at common assumptions about what it takes to be an effective leader in today's competitive world.

## What can you achieve with this book?

Our book differs from other leadership books in several important ways. We provide a more comprehensive model that incorporates what has been learned about effective leadership in more than half a century of research. Our model of flexible leadership builds on earlier leadership theories, and it incorporates ideas from related areas of study, such as organization theory, strategic management theory, traditional management theory, and theories of change management. Our model also includes insights provided by practitioner books and books about famous leaders, but these insights are incorporated into the theoretical framework. The model has a much broader range of leadership behaviors, including some often regarded as examples of managing rather than leading. We explain how management programs, systems, and structural features are relevant for effective leadership in organizations.

We explain the key processes that determine organization performance and what leaders at all levels can do to influence these processes and enhance performance. The roadmap it provides will help leaders analyze their situations, identify the leadership challenges, and understand what can be done to achieve the desired results. Our model describes specific leadership behaviors that can be used to influence people and indirect forms of leadership, such as improvement programs, management systems, and changes in the formal structure of an organization.

## How is the book organized?

In the first chapter we review some of the myths of leadership and introduce a model of flexible leadership. The book has a separate section for each of the three performance determinants. Section I (Chapters 2 through 4) deals with efficiency and process reliability. Section II (Chapters 5 through 7) deals with innovation and adaptation. Section III (Chapters 8 through 10) deals with human resources and relations.

The first chapter in each section explains the underlying processes, describes the conditions that make the performance determinant especially important, provides examples of companies that have been successful or unsuccessful in improving the performance determinant, and introduces ways leaders can directly and indirectly influence it. The second chapter in each section describes the direct leadership behaviors that are relevant for influencing the performance determinant and includes examples of what these behaviors look like, both when they are done well and when they are done poorly. The third chapter in each section describes indirect forms of leadership that are relevant, such as programs, management systems, and structural arrangements. The leader's role in implementing these processes and making them successful is also discussed.

The last section of the book has two chapters to integrate the different components of the model. Chapter 11 explains how the three challenges are interrelated, the tradeoffs among them, and how their absolute and relative importance can change. This chapter also describes other competing demands that make it important for the leader to be flexible. Chapter 12 provides guidelines on how to be flexible and adaptive in balancing the performance determinants and dealing with the other tradeoffs and competing demands. This final chapter also has examples of individuals who were successful in meeting these challenges.

# Flexible Leadership

## Creating Value by Balancing Multiple Challenges and Choices

Gary Yukl

Richard Lepsinger

JOSSEY-BASS
A Wiley Imprint
www.josseybass.com

Published by Jossey-Bass
An Imprint of Wiley
989 Market Street, San Francisco, CA94103-1741   www.josseybass.com

For additional copies/bulk purchases of this book in the U.S. please contact 800-274-4434.

Jossey-Bass books and products are available through most bookstores. To contact Jossey-Bass
directly call our Customer Care Department within the U.S. at 800-274-4434, outside the
U.S. at 317-572-3985 or fax 317-572-4002 or www.josseybass.com.

Jossey-Bass also publishes its books in a variety of electronic formats. Some content that
appears in print may not be available in electronic books.

ISBN: 0-7879-6531-6

**Library of Congress Cataloging-in-Publication Data**
Yukl, Gary A.
  Flexible leadership: creating value by balancing multiple challenges and choices /
Gary Yukl, Richard Lepsinger.
     p.; cm.
  Includes bibliographical references and index.
  ISBN 0-7879-6531-6 (alk. paper)
     1. Leadership. I. Title: Creating value by balancing multiple challenges and choices.
  II. Lepsinger, Richard, 1948- III. Title.
  HD57.7.Y848 2004
  658.4'092—dc22                                                          2003024759

Acquiring Editor: Matthew Davis
Director of Development: Kathleen Dolan Davies
Editor: Rebecca Taff
Senior Production Editor: Dawn Kilgore
Manufacturing Supervisor: Bill Matherly
Printed in the United States of America
Printing   10   9   8   7   6   5   4   3   2   1

# Contents

Acknowledgments      ix

Preface      xi

The Authors      xv

1. The Nature of Effective Leadership      1
   Leadership: Fact and Myth    3
   Model of Flexible Leadership    11
   Origins of the Model    19
   Overview of the Book    22
   Conclusions    23

   **Section I: Efficiency and Process Reliability**      25

2. The Challenge of Improving Efficiency and
   Process Reliability      27
   Examples of High Efficiency and Process Reliability    30
   Conditions Affecting Efficiency and Process Reliability    34
   Ways to Improve Efficiency and Process Reliability    36
   Conclusions    37

3. Leadership Behaviors to Enhance Efficiency
   and Process Reliability      39
   Operational Planning    39
   Clarifying Roles and Objectives    45
   Monitoring Operations and Performance    51
   Solving Operational Problems    58

Relationships Among the Behaviors    60

Conclusions    62

4.  Programs and Management Systems for Improving
Efficiency and Process Reliability                        63

Quality and Process Improvement Programs    63

Cost Reduction Programs    67

Management Systems and Structural Forms    70

Recognition and Reward Programs    74

Conclusions    76

**Section II: Innovation and Adaptation            79**

5.  The Challenge of Adapting to the External
Environment                                            81

Conditions Affecting the Importance of Adaptation    82

Examples of Failure in Adaptation    84

Examples of Successful Adaptation    87

Reasons for Success and Failure    89

Ways to Enhance Adaptations    96

Conclusions    98

6.  Leader Behaviors to Enhance Adaptation            99

Monitoring the Environment    99

Strategic Planning    102

Envisioning Change    106

Building Support for Change    109

Implementing Change    111

Encouraging Innovative Thinking    115

Facilitating Collective Learning    118

Relationships Among Change-Oriented Behaviors    120

Conclusions    121

7.  Programs, Systems, and Strategies for
Enhancing Adaptation                                123

Intrepreneurship Programs    123

External Benchmarking    125

Programs for Understanding Customers    127

Reward and Recognition Programs   129

Collective Learning Practices   130

Knowledge Management Systems   131

Structural Forms to Facilitate Innovation   133

Mergers, Acquisitions, and Strategic Alliances   135

Conclusions   140

**Section III: Human Resources and Relations   141**

8.   The Challenge of Managing Human Resources   143

Conditions That Affect the Importance of
   Human Resources   144

Implications of Strategy for Human Resources   146

Examples of Good Human Relations   147

Examples of Human Relations Problems   150

Ways to Improve Human Resources and Relations   152

Conclusions   153

9.   Leader Behaviors for Enhancing Human Resources   155

Supporting   155

Recognizing   158

Developing   162

Consulting   166

Empowering   169

Team Building   171

Relationships Among the Behaviors   173

Conclusions   174

10.   Programs and Management Systems for
Enhancing Human Resources   175

Human Resource Planning Systems   175

Employee Development Programs   178

Empowerment Programs   181

Recognition, Award, and Benefit Programs   185

Quality of Work Life Programs   187

Orientation and Team-Building Programs   189

Conclusions   190

**Section IV: Finding the Right Balance**     191

11. Multiple Challenges and Tradeoffs for Leaders     193
     Tradeoffs Among the Three Performance
       Determinants    193
     Changes in Performance Determinants    201
     Examples of Effective Balancing    203
     Other Tradeoffs for Leaders    207
     Conclusions    215

12 The Path to Flexible Leadership     217
     Guidelines for Effective Leadership    217
     Competencies for Effective Leadership    228
     Conclusion: The Essence of Flexible Leadership    236

Notes     239

Index     263

# Acknowledgments

This book presents an integrated model of leadership that includes a wide range of direct and indirect leader behaviors. Our work would not have been possible without access to the thinking of the many academics and practitioners who came before us. Although there are too many to mention here, we hope that they have been adequately acknowledged in the text and references.

It would be impossible to write a book of this type without the help and support of many people. We would like to thank Jim Appleton, Lee Bellarmino, Janet Castricum, Patrick Crotty, Kelly Fitzgerald, Daniel Greaves, Julia Huang, Pierre Jauffret, Gie Kauwenberghs, Laree Kiely, Drew Lambert, Terri Lowe, Toni Lucia, Chris Pierce-Cooke, Roger Smitter, Dennis Taylor, Stuart Walkley, Steve Wall, Thaddeus Ward, Alicia Weisser, Gail Wise, and Donna VanAlstine for their willingness to read many pages of our early drafts. Their comments and suggestions were invaluable in helping us clarify our message and organize our thoughts.

We thank Evelyn Toynton for her contribution in shaping several sections of the book, for her reminders to eliminate the endless lists, and her encouragement to find more interesting ways to present the information. We also want to acknowledge the contributions of Max Wolf, musician and researcher extrordinaire, who was able to find an example or reference for any subject we provided.

Finally, we want to thank our wives, Maureen and Bonnie, for their encouragement to do the book, and for their patience and ready willingness to give up many consecutive weekends.

# Preface

As at no time in recent memory, the quality of our business leaders has been thrust into the public's collective awareness. As a nation, we have been obsessed with the myth of the senior executive and the power of these individuals to overcome any obstacle and achieve outstanding results no matter what situation they face. But given recent events, we are forced to ask whether our leaders have the capability to meet the challenges of today's competitive environment. The news is full of stories of senior executives at some of our most venerable companies who have failed to meet the expectations of Wall Street, stockholders, and employees. Even worse are the stories of CEOs who ended up destroying more than they built, as did those at Enron, Global Crossing, Adelphi, Worldcom, and Tyco. These failures have caused us to take another look at common assumptions about what it takes to be an effective leader in today's competitive world.

The daily lives of millions of people are affected by the actions of business leaders and the quality of their leadership. If you picked up this book, you must have at least a passing interest in the topic of leadership. Yet with all the books currently available on this topic, you must be wondering if there is anything more to be said about it.

We believe there is much more to be said. Although much progress has been made in learning about effective leadership, most of the academic research and theory has a narrow focus on one or two aspects of leadership. The theories are usually about motivating individual followers and are unable to explain how leaders can influence the financial performance of a business corporation. Another limitation of currently popular theories is the assumption that one type of leadership can be used for all situations. These theories do not provide the guidance needed by leaders confronted with new types of challenges and changing situations. Today's organizations operate in a turbulent, highly competitive environment and need flexible leaders who are able to adapt their own leadership behavior as well as the organization's structure, programs and management systems to different situations and conditions.

The leadership books written for practitioners usually have a more strategic focus, but few are based on solid research. The authors examine descriptions of events in successful companies to see what leadership practices are used, and in a few cases successful companies are compared to unsuccessful ones. These authors usually provide a list of guidelines based on subjective judgments about relevant aspects of leadership behavior, but they do not provide a coherent theory to explain how the guidelines are related to each other and to organizational processes that determine success or failure. Many of the guidelines in these books may be helpful, but they are presented without concern for aspects of the situation that determine when the guidelines are relevant. Also, the emphasis on newly discovered "leadership secrets" in many of the books usually means that little or no effort has been made to relate the guidelines to prior theory and research.

Books about a celebrity leader, such as a CEO, general, or politician, have even greater limitations. These books are based on the leader's recollections of earlier experiences and events, and it is difficult to determine their accuracy. Even when past events can be remembered clearly, they are likely to be filtered by the celebrity leader's desire to make a favorable impression. The description of events will be questionable unless verified by other people who have firsthand knowledge and can be trusted to describe the events objectively. Finally, it is difficult to derive "best practices" or "lessons learned" from the experiences of a single leader, however famous or successful. Some of these books provide useful insights, but without a coherent theory it is difficult to determine how useful they will be for other leaders in different situations.

Our book differs from other leadership books in several important ways. We provide a more comprehensive model that incorporates what has been learned about effective leadership in more than a half-century of research. Our model of flexible leadership builds on earlier leadership theories, and it incorporates ideas from related areas of study, such as organization theory, strategic management theory, traditional management theory, and theories of change management. Our model also includes insights provided by practitioner books and books about famous leaders, but these insights are incorporated into the theoretical framework. The model has a much broader range of leadership behaviors, including some often regarded as examples of managing rather than leading. We explain how management programs, systems, and structural features are relevant for effective leadership in organizations. However, even though the model is more comprehensive than earlier ones, it does not deal with all aspects of managing a business. This book is about leadership, not management subjects such as finance, marketing, and accounting,

We will explain what it takes to be a flexible leader and how to enhance individual and organizational performance. The model presented in this book describes the key processes that determine organization performance and what leaders at all levels can do to influence these processes and thereby enhance performance. The roadmap it provides will help leaders identify and understand the leadership challenges they face, and what can be done to achieve desired results. The model describes specific leadership behaviors that can be used to influence people and indirect forms of leadership, such as improvement programs and changes in the formal structure of an organization.

A common tendency in leadership books written for managers is to oversimplify the process by making leadership seem to be nothing more than conscious rational choices from a list of guidelines and best practices. However, effective leadership also requires intuition, insight, experimentation, and learning from experience. Just as possessing a set of good tools will not make someone a skilled carpenter, understanding the potential uses and benefits of different leadership practices will facilitate but not ensure success as a leader. To become more effective it is necessary to apply the model and learn from experience what forms of direct and indirect leadership work best in various situations. Over time, applying the insights and behavioral tools we provide can help a reader to become a more effective leader.

This book is relevant for people at all levels of an organization, from the CEO to a team leader or department head. We emphasize effective leadership in business organizations, but the book can be useful for understanding leadership in other types of organizations as well. The book will be especially useful for human resource professionals and consultants who are responsible for the training and development of effective leaders in their organizations.

# The Authors

**Gary Yukl** received a B.A. in business administration from Occidental College in 1962 and a Ph.D. in industrial-organizational psychology from the University of California at Berkeley in 1967. He is currently a professor of management at the State University of New York in Albany. He was department chair from 1985 to 1991. His current research and teaching interests include leadership, power and influence, and management development.

Dr. Yukl is a Fellow of the American Psychological Association, the Society of Industrial-Organizational Psychology, the American Psychological Society, and the Academy of Management. He was a consulting editor for the *Academy of Management Review* and has served on the editorial boards of various journals, including the *Journal of Applied Psychology, Journal of Organizational Behavior Academy of Management Journal,* and *Leadership Quarterly.*

Dr. Yukl has written ten books, including *Leadership in Organizations* (5th ed.) (Prentice-Hall, 2002). This widely acclaimed leadership book has been used in many major universities in the United States and other countries. Dr. Yukl is also the author of many book chapters and invited reviews, including contributions to the *Handbook of Industrial-Organizational Psychology* and the *Annual Reviews of Psychology.* He has published articles in many professional journals, including the *Journal of Applied Psychology, Academy of Management Journal, Personnel Psychology, Journal of Management, Journal of Organizational Behavior, Organizational Behavior and Human Performance, Leadership Quarterly, Group and*

*Organizational Management, Decision Sciences, Journal of Personality and Social Psychology, Journal of Social Psychology,* and the *European Journal of Work and Organization Psychology.*

Dr. Yukl has received many honors for his research, including the best article award from the Organizational Behavior Division of the Academy of Management in 1983; the OB Division's best paper award for the Academy of Management meetings in 1978; the best paper award at the Eastern Academy of Management Meetings in 1991; the best article in *Group and Organization Management* for 1993; and the award for excellence in research from SUNY.

Dr. Yukl has been invited to lecture about leadership and management development at many companies and universities in the U.S. and other countries. He has consulted with a variety of business and public sector organizations, and he collaborates with Right Management Consultants to design and deliver management development programs on leadership skills for middle managers and executives in many Fortune 500 corporations. Dr. Yukl's consulting experience includes several projects to improve leadership or training and leadership development in the United States Army and Navy.

**Richard Lepsinger** is managing vice president of Right Management Consultants, a global organization that specializes in helping businesses implement their strategies successfully. He has been a consultant in the areas of management and organization development for over twenty years. He has served as a consultant for leaders and management teams at the Coca-Cola Company, Goldman Sachs, Siemens Medical Systems, Conoco, PeopleSoft, Northwestern Mutual Life, GreenPoint Bank, KPMG Peat Marwick, Lehman Brothers, the New York Stock Exchange, Prudential, UBS, Subaru of America, Bayer Pharmaceuticals, Pfizer Inc., and Pitney Bowes, among others.

Lepsinger has extensive experience in formulating and implementing strategic plans and in developing and using feedback-based technology to help organizations and managers identify their strengths and weaknesses. He has addressed executive conferences and made presentations on the topics of strategic leadership, strategy formulation and implementation, 360-degree feedback and its uses, and developing and using competency models to enhance organizational effectiveness.

Lepsinger also co-authored *The Art and Science of 360° Feedback* and *The Art and Science of Competency Models* with Toni Lucia. He is the author of several book chapters, including "Performance Management and Decision Making" in *The Handbook of Multi-Source Feedback* and "The Art and Science of Competency Modeling" in *What Smart Trainers Know*, as well as numerous articles on getting the most out of 360-degree feedback and effectively integrating the process with human resource and performance management systems. He also developed two business simulations: Tower Insurance and Plasco, Inc., and is the co-author with Stephen Wall of the article "Surveying the Scene," which discusses the challenges facing cross-functional teams and appeared in the British journal *Best Practice*.

*Chapter 1*

# The Nature of Effective Leadership

Within any industry some companies consistently outperform other companies with similar opportunities and constraints. Even when industry conditions are poor, some businesses are able to remain profitable while others barely survive. Dell Computer and Southwest Airlines are two examples of companies that have been more successful than their competitors in the same industry in both good and bad times.

Many factors could explain why companies like Dell and Southwest are able to produce consistently superior performance. One factor is *competitive strategy*. Dell decided to sell directly to the consumer without the additional cost of an intermediary distribution network. Southwest focused on short-haul flights that were point-to-point rather than the hub-and-spoke model that is used by other major airlines. Another factor is *operating costs*. Dell developed an efficient production process that makes it possible to build computers to a customer's specifications and maintain very low inventory. Southwest uses only one type of aircraft, the Boeing 737, which is more economical to fly and enables them to maintain lower inventory and maintenance costs. Unlike their competitors, Southwest mechanics only have to learn and be certified on one aircraft and only have to stock parts for one type of plane.

However, even after taking into account competitive strategy and operating costs, companies like Dell and Southwest Airlines have significantly better performance than their competitors. Why these factors alone do not explain the superior performance of Dell and Southwest can be seen by comparing each company with a similar but less successful company in the same industry.

Dell and Gateway Computers provide one such comparison. Founded within a year of each other, they both use the same business model—taking orders directly from customers, building PCs according to their specifications, loading the software, then shipping the machines directly to the purchaser. Both companies have been confronted with the commoditization of their product and a slowdown in demand. Yet Dell has consistently outperformed Gateway on all key measures of performance. Dell's return on assets (ROA), return on equity (ROE), and return on investment (ROI) as of July 2003 were 15.44 percent, 47.78 percent, and 35.9 percent, respectively, while the figures for Gateway were –15.44 percent, 31.58 percent, and –24.91 percent.[1] Dell had a 109.3 percent inventory turnover rate for the twelve months ending July 2003; Gateway's was 34.0 percent.[2]

Southwest Airlines and America West provide another comparison. Both airlines operate in the same market, having entered it at roughly the same time. Both airlines fly only Boeing 737s. Both airlines fly point to point, instead of on the more expensive hub-and-spoke routes used by other major airlines. In the beginning, America West looked as though it might outperform Southwest. The airplanes it used were newer, its ticketing and payment system was more convenient for passengers, and there were assigned seats (Southwest had open seating only). Yet year after year, Southwest's profits have been higher, its on-time record has been better, and it has had many fewer cancellations. Southwest has also been the industry leader in customer satisfaction.[3]

Why are Dell and Southwest more successful than competitors confronted with the same opportunities and constraints? Is it merely a matter of good luck? We believe the key factor in explaining the difference in company success is the *quality of leadership* and how effectively it responds to a set of industry and competitive conditions. Clearly some companies have leaders who demonstrate greater flexibility. They adapt to changing situations, maintain efficient and reliable operations, provide products and services that customers want, and maintain high levels of employee morale and productivity. These leaders assess the situation, identify key determinants of performance, and find a way to balance the tradeoffs involved in meeting these challenges.

What leaders actually do to enhance the survival and prosperity of companies such as Dell and Southwest has long been a subject of interest to scholars and practitioners. In this chapter we will examine some popular myths about leadership and then introduce a model that can provide a better explanation of the ways leaders can influence organizational processes and performance.

## Leadership: Fact and Myth

To say that leadership is important for the success of a company does not mean that a chief executive can single-handedly determine the fate of the company, as suggested by some journalists and leadership gurus. Consider these headlines from the business press:

- Pat Russo's Lucent Vision: The new CEO must turn Lucent around in the midst of a brutal storm. Can she deliver?[4]
- Work your magic, Herr Dirmann; ABB faces meltdown— so this CEO isn't wasting time[5]
- Meet Mr. Nissan—is Carlos Ghosn a savior?[6]
- Can Jamie Dimon restore Bank One's lost luster?[7]
- Ingram Micro's future lies in new CEO's hands.[8]
- The King of Storage—After fixing EMC's service problems, Michael Ruettgers put the company on a stellar growth path and built it into an industry powerhouse.[9]
- Prada Goes Shopping: Patrizio Bertelli transformed Prada from a stuffy family company into a fashion powerhouse. And he's just warming up.[10]

By now we are so used to seeing corporate leaders described in such terms that we hardly even notice anything odd about it. But when you stop to think about it, there is something a little askew about the assumption behind these headlines and countless others like them. Is it really Pat Russo alone who is going to turn Lucent around? Did Patrizio Bertelli really transform Prada all by himself? Does Ingram Micro's future really depend entirely on the new CEO? If you work in an organization yourself, you know that any transformation, any turnaround, depends on many people. The future of a large organization does not depend on a single leader, however powerful, clever, and visionary.

## The Myth of the Heroic Leader

Organizations are complex social systems of patterned inter-actions among people. In their effort to understand the causes, dynamics, and outcomes of organizational processes, people interpret results in simple, human terms. Stereotypes, implicit theories, and simplified assumptions about causality aid people in making sense out of events that would otherwise be incomprehensible. One especially strong and prevalent explanation of organizational events is to attribute causality to the influence of individual leaders.

Depicting a senior executive as a heroic individual is a dramatic, romantic notion of leadership, similar to that of other stereotyped heroes in our culture, such as the lone cowboy who single-handedly vanquishes the bad guys or the secret agent who acts alone to save the world from nuclear destruction by terrorists. These images have particularly strong appeal to people in a culture of celebrity like our own. They also make excellent copy in the business press. There is something satisfying about the fairy-tale character of the knight on the white horse who will slay the dragon and thereby ensure triumphant victory for the organization. But like any fairy tale, this heroic conception of leadership does not quite align with reality. It greatly exaggerates the influence of a single leader on organization performance, and it has some negative consequences.[11]

One negative consequence is overreliance on the heroic leader to make decisions and solve important problems. Because no single leader has the necessary knowledge and expertise to solve difficult problems for an organization, it is essential to involve other people with relevant knowledge and diverse perspectives. However, members are unlikely to become involved if they believe the leader has superhuman abilities to singlehandedly find the right path. Nor is high involvement likely to be encouraged by a leader with an exaggerated self-image who wants to appear to have all the answers. If there is strong reliance on the chief executive and the culture reinforces obedience to directives from the top, then the organization will be less likely to respond successfully to events in the environment. As a result, it is not uncommon for an organization with a string of earlier successes to suddenly experience a major disaster.[12]

It is by no means clear that today's employees really want to be led by a figure on a white horse, except perhaps in a dire emergency that requires a decisive leader who knows how to prevent a looming disaster. Many commentators have observed that people born after World War II are much less willing to follow orders or accept someone else's ideas on how they should be doing their jobs. As an article in *Business Week* puts it, "Saying 'just do it' no longer works because a new generation of workers has been groomed to think instead of react. The new CEOs, baby boomers themselves, understand that."[13] A survey conducted by the Families and Work Institute, a New York-based research institution, would seem to support the idea that employees prefer more empowerment. The study showed that workers' perceptions of control over their jobs increased significantly between 1977 and 1997. During those twenty years, the percentage of workers who said they had the freedom to decide what they do on the job increased from 56 percent to 74 percent.[14]

One commentator goes so far as to declare that, nowadays, "Leadership is about following."[15] That assertion may be a slight exaggeration, but it seems clear that the old, paternalistic concept of leadership, with the leader as the strong father figure, needs to be replaced. In today's world, a model of leadership in which leaders guide the organization through enlisting cooperation and consulting with others, rather than making unilateral decisions, may be more appropriate. Lee Iacocca, who embodied the old ideal of the charismatic, paternalistic CEO, was widely viewed as a great leader until his much more accessible and consultative successor, Bob Eaton, got dramatically better results at Chrysler. While Iacocca was effective in leading the company through the immediate crisis, his style of leadership was not the best one for rebuilding the company and preventing a similar crisis in the future.

## The Myth of the Born Leader

One of the dangers of viewing senior executives as heroic leaders is that it makes leadership sound like a mystical quality, something innate to certain special people, rather than anything people simply *do*. The business press frequently encourages this idea by telling us, for example, that the "e-factor" (short for executive factor) is a "neuropsychologically determined propensity to lead."[16]

We are often told about the importance of that indefinable leadership quality called charisma, as though some people are literally born to lead others. The importance of having "the right stuff" is an idea that many corporate leaders also appear to accept. The Yale School of Management and the Gallup Organization recently surveyed 130 prominent chief executives and found that 26 percent of them felt that "great leaders are born and not made."[17]

For decades now, leadership scholars have been trying to define exactly which traits are associated with effective leadership. Some of the attributes that have been cited as prerequisites to great leadership include unflagging energy, uncanny foresight, and great persuasive skill. But despite hundreds of studies over the past seventy years comparing more and less effective leaders, researchers have failed to identify any specific traits that guarantee leadership success.[18,19] Moreover, studies of successful chief executives find that most of them do not have the type of personality characteristics or superhuman image usually associated with charisma.[20,21]

Although a charismatic figure at the top can help to enlist enthusiastic support for a necessary change, it may be counterproductive to think of leadership in those terms. How do you acquire charisma or become visionary? What does a visionary leader do to inspire others, and what makes the vision compelling? To understand the reasons for effective leadership, inherent traits and abilities are much less useful than observable behavior and concrete knowledge. A trait theory of leadership emphasizes inherent qualities that are difficult to change, such as needs, temperament, energy level, emotional stability, extroversion, and intelligence. In contrast, a behavior theory emphasizes specific types of behavior that, however difficult, can be learned by most people who desire to become better leaders. When the focus of research is on what leaders actually do, it is easier to understand the situational nature of leadership and the importance of flexible leadership. We are not saying that personality traits and inherent abilities are irrelevant for understanding why some people want to become leaders or which people are most likely to be successful as leaders, only that traits are less useful than concrete behaviors for understanding what leaders must do to be effective in a given situation.

## The Myth of the Celebrity Leader

The cult of personality is so pervasive in depictions of organizations that, according to a recent survey, CEOs now represent 45 percent of a company's reputation.[22] According to a study conducted in 2001 by consulting firm Burson-Marsteller, 90 percent of Wall Street analysts and institutional investors said they were more likely to buy or recommend a stock based on a good CEO reputation. That figure was up from 70 percent five years before.[23] How powerful is the impact of a celebrity CEO? Several examples over the years would indicate that investors put a great deal of faith in the CEO as savior. In 1996 shares of Sunbeam went up by half in a single day when Al Dunlap was hired. In 1997, $3.8 billion was added to the value of AT&T's stock when C. Michael Armstrong was brought on board. In 2002, shares of Tyco International increased 46 percent the day after a respected Motorola executive, Ed Breen, was hired to lead the troubled company.[24]

However, in a company with a celebrity leader, a single highly publicized mistake or misdemeanor by a senior executive can have a catastrophic effect on a company's profits. The case of Martha Stewart, who built a lifestyle empire that includes magazines, cookbooks, television shows, designer sheets, and endorsements of other domestic products, is a perfect example. When it was learned in December 2001 that an insider-trading charge was being brought against her for selling her shares in another company, her own company's stock plunged by 54 percent and profits declined by 45 percent in the third quarter of the fiscal year.[25]

Fortunately, there are not many high-profile cases of companies spiraling downhill after their famous CEOs are accused of wrongdoing. A more common problem is unrealistic expectations for the CEO. When a celebrity leader is appointed the CEO for a troubled company, expectations (and stock prices) are dramatically raised, only to be rapidly deflated if no miracles occur shortly afterward. Consider what happened when Gary Wendt was selected to be the new CEO of the insurance company Conseco after a successful tenure running GE Capital. When the appointment was announced, Wendt was hailed as a savior for Conseco, and its stock price rose by almost 50 percent. The stock rose even more dramatically when he started issuing upbeat reports to investors. However, just over two years later, Wendt stepped down, having failed to rescue Conseco from its doldrums. The stock sank by more than 99 percent from its high, and Conseco was left with the burden of paying Wendt millions of dollars per year for the rest of his life.[26]

The idea that leadership is something provided only by those at the top is dangerous for another reason. In today's volatile business environment, the need to be responsive to rapidly changing conditions is too urgent to wait until all the information possessed by people at different levels of the organization filters up to the senior executives and penetrates the cocoon in which many such figures live. In an increasingly dynamic, competitive environment, it is essential to understand what customers need, what competitors can do, and how potential customers view a company's products and services. Front-line personnel and lower-level managers will obtain much of this essential information long before it arrives in the senior executive's office. If people depend entirely on top management to identify emerging problems or threats or to recognize promising opportunities, it may not be possible to make a timely, successful response.

### The Myth of Leaders and Managers

Many scholars and practitioners view leadership as a different and more important process than management. Some writers[27,28] contend that the two processes are mutually exclusive and cannot occur in the same person, because the values and personality traits essential for leadership are incompatible with those essential for management. Managers value stability, order, and efficiency, whereas leaders value flexibility, innovation, and adaptation. Managers are concerned about how things get done, and they try to get people to perform better. Leaders are concerned with what things mean to people, and they try to get people to agree about the most important things to be done. The idea that leaders and managers are different kinds of people is taken to an extreme by writers who offer a very negative stereotype of managers that portrays them as controlling, micro-managing, "bean-counting" bureaucrats.

Other scholars[29,30,31,32] view leading and managing as distinct processes or roles. Although this perspective does not preclude the possibility that leading and managing can be done by the same person, the two processes have some incompatible elements that are difficult to reconcile. As noted by Kotter,[33] strong leadership can disrupt order and efficiency, and strong management can discourage risk taking and innovation. The popularity of books about leadership suggests that practitioners consider leading a more inter-esting and relevant process than managing. The omission of effec-tive managerial behaviors from the currently popular leadership theories suggests that the theorists do not consider this process nec-essary for understanding effective leadership.

A broader perspective is needed to understand how leaders can influence organizational processes and outcomes. We agree with Kotter,[34] who proposed that both processes are necessary for the suc-cess of an organization. Strong management alone can create a bureaucracy without purpose, but strong leadership alone can cre-ate change that is impractical. To be effective, managers must also be leaders, and leaders must manage. Misconceptions about leading and managing have impeded progress in understanding how to inte-grate the two types of processes and balance the inherent tradeoffs.

### The Myth of Easy Answers

An astounding number of books about leadership sold each year indicate the importance of this subject to people. Most of these books take a relatively narrow approach to the subject, and few of them are based on solid research. The best-selling books usually offer simple answers for complex problems, such as "one minute" actions or a list of "leadership secrets" that can be applied in any situation. Books written by celebrity leaders (and their ghostwriters) also sell well. Readers probably assume that, "If it worked for a famous leader, it will work for me also." The popular-ity of leadership books seems to indicate a widespread belief that a few best practices or secret remedies can easily transform the reader into an effective leader. The appeal is not unlike many products and services that promise to make people attractive, healthy, and happy with minimal effort.

A similar situation can be found in fads surrounding the use of management programs over the past three decades. Examples of these programs include management by objectives, profit sharing plans, quality circles, self-managed teams, re-engineering, multi-source feedback, and outsourcing. Every few years we see a new set of programs that vendors and consultants claim will help managers deal with important problems. The millions of dollars companies spend each year on such programs with little or no proof they are relevant suggests a strong belief in easy answers. The popularity of the programs and other "remedies" such as downsizing and reorganization may also reflect the desire of worried leaders to appear as if they are dealing with the problem. Unfortunately, most management programs and structural changes are difficult to implement and require a significant investment of time and effort to have any hope of success. Although some companies report success with these programs or changes, in a majority of companies they fail after a year or two and are abandoned, only to be replaced by the next faddish remedy.

The reality is that there are few, if any, easy answers. Leadership is difficult and demanding, and leaders need to be flexible because the situation is constantly changing. What worked well last year may no longer be successful. Problems that appear to have been solved often reappear again in new form. Solutions to one problem can create another that is much worse. What seems a minor problem may be only the tip of a deadly iceberg. The number of problems is endless, and they seem to appear out of nowhere, like waves crashing on the shore. And like waves, they can drag you under if you disregard them or underestimate the danger. Best practices, improvement programs, and other remedies can be useful, but they are only tools, not solutions. To be successful, leaders must understand the challenges they face and the relevance of different ways to meet these challenges. A good leadership model can be immensely helpful to improve understanding and guide action.

## Model of Flexible Leadership

The model of flexible leadership featured in this book provides a comprehensive explanation of the challenges facing leaders and the requirements for effective leadership. The core of the model is an explanation of the organizational processes that determine the success of an organization and an explanation of the ways leaders at all levels in the organization can influence these processes. The emphasis is on behavioral aspects of leadership that can be learned, not on mysterious gifts that only a few heroic leaders possess. Key themes are (1) flexible leadership in response to continually changing situations, (2) the need to find an appropriate balance among competing demands, and (3) the need for coordinated action by leaders across levels and subunits. The model does not offer easy answers, but it can help leaders understand complex challenges confronting them and how to deal with them more effectively.

The different components of the model are depicted in Figure 1.1. The first component is organization performance, which can be measured in a variety of different ways. Some examples of performance indicators include net earnings, profit margin, growth in profits, increase in stock price, return on investment, or equity and debt ratios. The second component is composed of three determinants of organizational performance: (1) efficiency and reliability of work processes, (2) timely adaptation to changes in the external environment, and (3) strong human resources and relations. Each type of performance determinant provides a unique leadership challenge.

Indicators of efficiency include employee productivity, direct cost of operations, cost of sales, and return on assets (ROA). Indicators of process reliability include number of product defects caused during production, errors or omissions in providing products or services, avoidable delays in production or delivery of products or services, customer complaints, and accidents or injuries to employees or customers. Indicators of adaptation include sales growth, market share, customer satisfaction, percentage of sales from repeat customers, research discoveries (e.g., patents, inventions), number of new products and services, and percentage of sales from new products or services. Indicators of human resources include employee skills, job satisfaction, loyalty and commitment to the organization, absenteeism, turnover, grievances or lawsuits initiated by employees, and employee theft or sabotage.

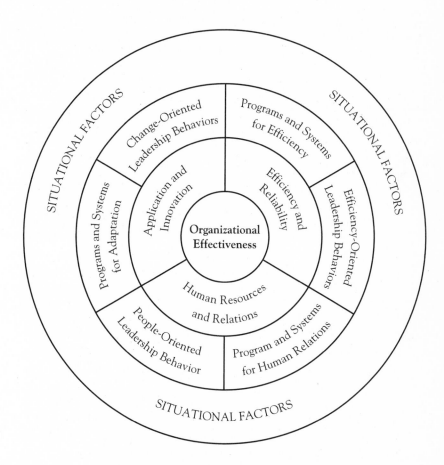

Figure 1.1.  Model of Flexible Leadership

The third component of the model consists of the situational variables that determine which challenge or challenges are most important to the organization at any given time. Examples include environmental uncertainty and the nature of the competition. The last component consists of the direct and indirect forms of leadership used to influence the performance determinants. Each component of the model will be explained in more detail.

## The Performance Determinants

The effectiveness of an organization depends on the three performance determinants identified earlier, which we regard as distinct leadership challenges. *Efficiency* involves the use of people and resources to carry out essential operations in a way that minimizes cost without sacrificing established standards of quality and safety. *Process reliability* involves the production and delivery of products and services in a way that avoids unnecessary delays, errors, quality defects, or accidents. *Adapting to the external environment* involves responding in appropriate ways to threats and opportunities resulting from changes in technology, competitor actions, and changes in customer needs and expectations. Adaptation also involves finding ways to acquire necessary materials and resources and doing things to increase the sale of products and services to customers. *Human relations and resources* involve recruiting, developing, and retaining people with the skills and commitment to do their jobs effectively and maintaining mutual trust and cooperation in the performance of collective work.

## Direct Leader Behavior

The three types of direct leadership behaviors are differentiated by their primary objective, namely efficiency, adaptation, or human resources. The behaviors are listed in Table 1.1. The "task-oriented" behaviors are concerned primarily with improving efficiency and process reliability. These behaviors include planning

## Table 1.1.  Direct Leadership Behaviors

*Task-Oriented Behavior*

- Plan short-term operations
- Clarify roles and objectives
- Monitor operations and performance
- Solve operational problems

*Relations-Oriented Behavior*

- Provide support and encouragement
- Provide recognition for achievements and contributions
- Develop skills and confidence among unit members
- Consult with relevant people when making decisions
- Empower unit members to take initiative in doing their work
- Build mutual trust, cooperation, and identification with the organization

*Change-Oriented Behavior*

- Monitor the external environment
- Identify a competitive strategy relevant to core competencies and the environment
- Articulate an appealing vision of what can be accomplished
- Build internal and external support for necessary change
- Implement necessary changes in the organization
- Encourage innovative thinking
- Facilitate collective learning

how to use personnel and resources to conduct operations, clarifying responsibilities and task objectives, monitoring operations and performance, and taking decisive action to identify and resolve problems that disrupt operations. The "change-oriented" behaviors are concerned primarily with adaptation to the external environment. These behaviors include monitoring the external environment to identify threats and opportunities, strategic planning, initiating and leading change, encouraging innovative thinking, and facilitating collective learning. The "relations-oriented" behaviors are concerned primarily with improving human relations and resources.

These behaviors include developing individual skills and confidence, providing recognition for contributions and achievements, involving people in decisions that affect them, empowering people to do their work better, and providing the support needed to make the job satisfying to people.

Although each leader behavior can be categorized according to its primary objective to improve efficiency, adaptation, or human relations, a behavior can have implications for more than one of these performance determinants. For example, clarifying behavior may have a positive influence on employee task commitment as well as on efficiency. Sometimes a leader behavior will influence all three types of performance determinants. For example, when a leader consults with team members about the action plan for a project to be done for an important client, the possible benefits may include more individual and team commitment to the project (human relations), better use of available personnel and resources (efficiency), and more effort to find innovative ways to satisfy the client (adaptation).

The relevance of each behavior at any given time depends on the leadership situation and the extent to which a performance determinant can be improved. Some of the specific types of behavior are more useful than others in a particular situation. The relevance of the behavior also depends on the type of leadership position. For example, some of the change-oriented behaviors are used more by higher-level leaders than by lower-level leaders.

### Indirect Leadership

Leaders can indirectly influence the performance determinants with the use of formal programs, management systems, and aspects of formal structure. Table 1.2 lists programs, management systems, and structural features that have been widely used to influence each performance determinant. CEOs and leaders of major subunits often have the authority to implement such programs, but low-level leaders seldom have this option. As with the specific types of

## Table 1.2.  Formal Programs, Management
## Systems, and Structural Forms

*Efficiency and Reliability*

- Goal setting programs (for example, MBO, zero defects)
- Quality and process improvement programs (business process improvement, reengineering, TQM, Six Sigma)
- Cost reduction programs (downsizing, outsourcing, just-in-time inventory)
- Performance management systems (goal setting, feedback, appraisal)
- Structural arrangements (functional specialization, formalization, standardization)
- Recognition and reward systems (focused on reinforcing efficiency and reliability)

*Human Resources and Relations*

- Human resource planning (talent management, succession planning, recruiting and selection programs)
- Employee development programs (training, education subsidies, mentoring program, 360-degree feedback, assessment centers)
- Empowerment programs (employee ownership programs, self-managed teams, employee councils)
- Recognition and benefit programs (focused on reinforcing loyalty, service, skill acquisition)
- Quality of work life (flextime, job sharing, child care, fitness center)
- Orientation and team-building programs (socialization and assimilation programs, company events and celebrations, systematic use of symbols, rituals, and ceremonies)

*Innovation and Adaptation*

- Innovation programs (intrepreneurship programs, formal goals for innovation and commercialization, budgets for research and new product development)
- Programs for understanding competitors (comparative product testing, external benchmarking of competitor products and services)
- Programs for understanding customers and markets (market surveys, focus groups, customer panels, customer relations teams)
- Knowledge acquisition (hiring consultants, joint ventures, importing best practices from other organizations)

*(Continued)*

Table 1.2.  (Continued)

---

- Collective learning programs (controlled experiments, after-activity reviews)
- Knowledge management systems (expert directories and networks, best practices forums, knowledge sharing data bases and groupware)
- Recognition and reward systems (focused on reinforcing innovation and adaptation)
- Structural arrangements (small product/client divisions, product managers, cross-functional project development teams, design of facilities and work sites, R&D departments)
- Growth and diversification strategies (acquisitions, strategic alliances, foreign subsidiaries)

---

leadership behavior, these formal programs and systems are likely to have consequences for more than one type of performance determinant. Some programs may improve more than one performance determinant simultaneously. For example, a well-designed incentive system may improve reliability, innovation, and employee satisfaction. However, some programs used to enhance one performance determinant can adversely affect another performance determinant. For example, downsizing programs may improve efficiency at the expense of employee satisfaction and commitment. Ensuring that different programs are mutually compatible is another challenge facing top-level leaders in organizations.

### Balancing Competing Demands and Tradeoffs

Talking about leadership in terms of what effective leaders do rather than what they are is a good beginning, but it is not enough. It is important to remember that what works in one situation may be less effective in a different situation or when circumstances change. For that reason, leaders at all levels should determine what types of behavior, programs, management systems, and structural forms are relevant at any given time. Leadership has sometimes been defined as "doing the right thing"; but a better definition is "doing the right thing at the right time." Deciding to use a particular type of behavior or approach because it proved successful in the past, or has proved successful for others, may not lead to the desired results. Instead, it is crucial to assess each situation on its own merits and act accordingly.

The key to flexible leadership is the ability to balance the competing and sometimes contradictory demands related to the performance determinants. A leader who puts too much emphasis on efficiency and reliability may make adaptation more difficult to achieve, and vice versa. An overemphasis on motivating employees may adversely affect operational efficiency and increase costs. The most effective leaders understand that flexible leadership starts with knowing what to do, how to do it, and when to do it. Effective leadership requires skills in diagnosing the situation, evaluating the challenges, balancing competing demands, and integrating diverse leadership activities in a way that is relevant for meeting the challenges.

## Origins of the Model

The model of flexible leadership reflects decades of research and the convergence of related discoveries in several distinct areas of study. In this section we will briefly describe the origins of the model, how it evolved, and sources of supporting evidence.

A major obstacle to progress in learning about effective leadership has been the narrow perspective taken in much of the theory and research. Most leadership theories try to explain how a leader can influence direct reports to be enthusiastic about the work and accomplish more than they initially expected. Motivating direct reports is important, but so too are aspects of managing, such as selecting and developing capable employees, organizing and coordinating work processes, obtaining necessary resources and approvals, monitoring operations and performance, tracking changes in the external environment, and finding a good competitive strategy. To understand effective leadership in organizations requires a model that incorporates relevant aspects of both leading and managing.

Another obstacle to understanding effective leadership behavior has been a lack of agreement about how to classify behavior into separate categories. In the past half-century there has been a bewildering proliferation of models of leadership behavior, making it difficult to compare results from different studies. Sometimes different terms have been used to refer to the same type of behavior, and at other times, various theorists have defined the same term differently. Key concepts in one model are absent from another. The many different models that have emerged from the research on leading and managing make it difficult to translate from one set of concepts to another. One way to reduce the confusion is to find broadly defined "meta-categories" or "underlying dimensions" that can be used to sort and classify specific types of behavior in a way that is relevant for explaining effective leadership.[35]

The two meta-categories involving task-oriented and people-oriented behavior were identified in the 1950s,[36,37] but something important was still missing. The two meta-categories did not include behaviors directly concerned with encouraging and facilitating innovation and change. By the 1980s, change-oriented behavior was implicit in some theories of charismatic and transformational leadership, but it was still not explicitly recognized as a separate dimension or meta-category. That discovery was made independently in the 1990s by researchers in Sweden[38] and the United States.[39] With the three meta-categories, it was now possible to classify most leading and managing behaviors into a hierarchical taxonomy.[40] The meta-categories make it easier to find general relationships between leadership and organizational processes (to "see the forest for the trees"), but using them does not mean that the specific behaviors can be ignored. Much of the research on leader effectiveness indicates that for a given situation some of the specific behaviors in a meta-category are more relevant than others. Thus, to determine what form of leadership is appropriate in particular situation, it is still necessary to study the specific behaviors rather than merely looking at the meta-categories.

Having a better way to view leadership behavior was not sufficient to explain how leaders can affect organization performance. Two more things were needed to clarify this connection. First, it was necessary to understand the internal processes and external events that determine whether an organization will survive and prosper. Second, it was necessary to understand how leaders are able to influence these processes in a significant way. Insights about these issues were provided by literature on organization theory,[41,42] change management,[43,44,45] strategic management,[46,47,48] and strategic leadership.[49,50,51,52] These distinct but overlapping areas of research provided support for three key propositions of the model: (1) efficiency, adaptation, and human relations are distinct but interrelated determinants of organization performance; (2) events in the external environment can affect the importance of these performance determinants; and (3) leaders at all levels can have a significant influence on the performance determinants. When the different types of variables were considered together, it became apparent that most of the direct leadership behaviors affect one performance determinant more than the others and are more relevant in some situations than in others. A similar pattern was found for formal programs, management systems, and structural features.

Although the entire model is difficult to test in a single study, evidence for the proposed relationships can be found in hundreds of relevant studies conducted by scholars over the past half-century. In addition, the model incorporates insights provided by our own research and consulting over the past thirty years. Interacting with teams and individuals in working sessions, feedback workshops, and training programs has yielded useful insights about effective leadership, and we have incorporated these insights into the book as well. At various times we have analyzed data from the behavior description questionnaires and behavior importance ratings used in the feedback workshops, and these studies provide additional support for some of the proposed links between leader behavior and effectiveness.[53,54,55,56,57] Finally, many of the insights, guidelines, and best practices found in practitioner books on effective leadership also appear consistent with the theory.

## Overview of the Book

In this first chapter we reviewed some of the myths of leadership and introduced a model of flexible leadership. In the chapters that follow, we will look in detail at each type of leadership challenge, explain when it is most important, and offer practical guidance on the specific processes and leader activities that are most useful in meeting the challenge effectively. Examples of effective and ineffective behavior are used throughout the book to illustrate key points. These examples come from industry and trade journals as well as over thirty years of our own consulting work with a wide variety of businesses in a range of industries.

There is a separate section for each of the three performance determinants, and the organization of the three chapters in each section is similar in terms of what is covered. Section I (Chapters 2 through 4) deals with efficiency and process reliability. Section II (Chapters 5 through 7), deals with innovation and adaptation. Section III (Chapters 8 through 10), deals with human resources and relations. The first chapter in each section explains the underlying processes, describes the conditions that make the performance determinant especially important, provides examples of companies that have been successful or unsuccessful in improving the performance determinant, and introduces ways leaders can directly and indirectly influence it. The second chapter in each section describes the direct leadership behaviors that are relevant for influencing the performance determinant and includes examples of what these behaviors look like when they are done well and when they are done poorly. The third chapter in each section describes indirect forms of leadership that are relevant, such as programs, management systems, and structural arrangements. The leader's role in implementing these processes and making them successful is also discussed.

The last section of the book has two chapters to integrate the different components of the model. Chapter 11 explains how the three challenges are interrelated, the tradeoffs among them, and how their absolute and relative importance can change. We also describe other challenges that make it important for the leader to be flexible, such as the need to balance short-term and long-term objectives, stability and change, control and empowerment, and competing demands from different stakeholders. In Chapter 12 we provide guidelines on how to be flexible and adaptive in balancing the performance determinants and dealing with the other tradeoffs and competing demands. This final chapter also has examples of individuals who were successful in meeting these challenges.

## Conclusions

Despite the many years of research devoted to the study of leadership, there is still a lack of consistency in how effective leadership is defined. Among the many myths associated with the subject is the belief that leaders are born not made, the belief that a single heroic individual determines the fate of an organization, the belief that leadership and management are mutually exclusive processes, and the belief that effective leadership can be easily attained with a few secret remedies. We believe that all of these myths are incorrect.

The model of flexible leadership we present in this book focuses on behavioral aspects of leadership that can be learned. Key themes are that flexible leadership is a response to continually changing situations, that leaders need to find an appropriate balance among competing demands, and that leadership must be coordinated and consistent across levels and subunits. The model is comprised of four components: organizational performance, performance determinants, situational variables, and direct and indirect forms of leadership. Effective leaders understand what must be done to facilitate performance by the organization. They use an appropriate pattern of direct and indirect leadership, and they find ways to balance competing demands and adjust to changing situations.

# Section I

# *Efficiency and Process Reliability*

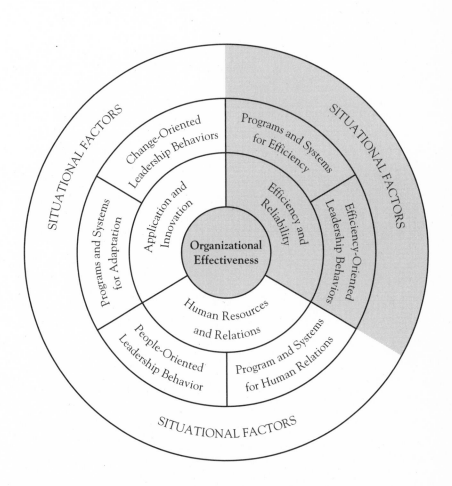

## Chapter 2

# The Challenge of Improving Efficiency and Process Reliability

The quality of a company's products or services depends to a greater extent on process reliability. Quality will suffer unless production and delivery occur without defects, errors, or delays. A writer for one of the leading business journals recently interviewed forty top business leaders for a book he was working on, and not one of them mentioned quality as a major strategic challenge.[1] These forty business leaders may have felt that, instead of thinking about reliability and efficiency, they should be formulating an exciting vision, creating a dynamic culture for their organization, negotiating lucrative acquisitions, or reaching new markets at warp speed. In the past decade, maintaining reliable, efficient processes to minimize costs and ensure high quality of products or services has increasingly come to be seen as responsibilities for "mere" managers rather than for leaders.

The lack of interest in the efficiency and reliability of production processes as a strategic issue may reflect the belief that it is no longer a problem. Roger Ackerman, chairman and CEO of Corning Inc., feels that quality has now become so deeply embedded in corporate processes that we no longer even have to talk about it.[2] Clearly there is a widespread feeling that the technical problems that plagued manufacturing not so long ago have largely been solved.

The assumption, however, that quality problems have been solved seems premature even for the manufacturing sector. Several examples can be found in the automotive industry. Ford recalled nearly one million Focus Taurus/Sables early in the fourth quarter of 2002.[3] It also had to retrofit 350,000 Crown Victoria police cars with reinforced fuel tanks in an attempt to prevent more accidents of the

27

kind that burned to death at least ten police officers.[4] Both Firestone and Goodyear have had highly publicized problems with defective tires that caused grisly accidents and resulted in costly lawsuits.[5]

Even companies that manufacture products for the most vulnerable members of the population—babies—have been plagued with quality disasters. In January 2001, for example, a leading manufacturer of highchairs recalled about one million chairs following reports that a number of babies had been injured when the chairs collapsed or the restraints gave way.[6] Then there were the stuffed kittens containing contaminated water that could make babies ill,[7] toys that contained metal pieces and sewing needles in their stuffing, jumper seats with springs that were likely to break, and mobile walkers that had to be recalled because they were dangerous.[8]

The problems are not limited to manufacturing. America is primarily a service economy—80 percent of GDP is service,[9] and, as many consumers are willing to testify, the quality of service continues to decline. The American Business School's American Customer Satisfaction Index (ACSI), which measures the perceived quality of U.S. economic output, has recorded consecutive annual declines in service satisfaction since 1994. Airlines, banks, department stores, fast-food outlets, hospitals, hotels, and phone companies all have below national average customer satisfaction ratings.[10] Mystery shoppers hired by McDonald's to make unannounced visits found that restaurants were meeting speed of service standards only 46 percent of the time and cited complaints of rude, unprofessional, and inaccurate service.[11] PC World's annual survey of 29,000 subscribers also reveals growing frustration with service quality. Overall, less than half the respondents said their problems were resolved within five days, and only 53 percent said their problem was resolved the first time they called.[12]

The problems involving process reliability have not received adequate attention in the management literature. As Larry Bossidy and Ram Charan, co-authors of Execution: The Discipline of Getting Things Done, observe, "The real problem is that execution just doesn't sound very sexy. It's the stuff leaders delegate. Do great CEOs and Nobel Prize winners achieve their glory through execution? Well, yes, in fact, and therein lies the grand fallacy." Fortunately there are signs that some companies are beginning to appreciate the importance of improving reliability in work processes.

In March 1999, Chung Mong Koo became CEO of Hyundai Motor Co., a company that had a reputation for poor quality, including problems that could be avoided easily, such as doors that did not fit properly and frames that rattled. Within months of taking over, Chung established a quality control unit and appointed a quality control Czar. These efforts have met with considerable success. In 2001 J.D. Power & Associates reported that Hyundai's quality increased 28 percent over the previous four years compared to 14 percent for the industry overall.[13]

Similarly, there seems to be a growing recognition in some quarters that efficiency of organizational processes is also a worthwhile concern for leaders. A recent article in *American Banker* criticized senior executives at major U.S. financial firms for not having established any standards or benchmarks for measuring and evaluating productivity, pointing out the fallacy (and danger) of the notion that such measures are only relevant in manufacturing industries.[14] Another recent article, this time in the *Harvard Management Update*, cited a study of forty Fortune 500 firms conducted by the Center for Effective Organizations at the University of Southern California and the management consulting firm Booz Allen Hamilton. One conclusion was that "the CEOs whose companies are best weathering the recent downturn are practicing old-fashioned, pragmatic management by the numbers." The same article also quoted management expert Jim Collins and others as saying that the most successful leaders are those who tend to such nuts-and-bolts aspects of the business rather than leading through charisma and vision.[15]

An article in the *Journal of Leadership & Organizational Studies*[16] argued even more forcefully for pragmatic management: "Many outstanding leaders get along quite well without charisma by focusing on the fundamentals of management. For the past two decades or so, executives produced impressive bottom-line results, even under conditions of intense competition, by creating lean and efficient organizations through reducing the size of staff departments, de-layering hierarchies, outsourcing activities that can be carried out more efficiently by vendors, and continually improving processes and practices through re-engineering." The message is becoming clear: leaders of business organizations need to be concerned about management issues such as efficiency and reliability. To be a good leader, one must also be a good manager.

## Examples of High Efficiency and Process Reliability

To better understand the importance of efficiency, it is helpful to look at some companies for which these factors have been a major determinant of successful performance. For these examples, and all the examples in this book, we do not suggest that meeting a specific challenge at a particular point in time is the only reason for a company's success, just that it is an important one. Nor do we suggest that the company will continue to be successful in the future. As we have said before and will explain in more detail in later chapters, continued success requires leaders who consistently and accurately assess the situation and take appropriate action.

### Sterling Autobody Centers

Sterling Autobody Centers has achieved success by doing for auto repair what Home Depot did for hardware. Sterling brought both efficiency and reliability to an industry that is famous for lacking both those elements. The inspiration for Sterling's revolution came when its founder, Jon McNeill, experienced the typical frustrations of being a collision-repair customer. A neighbor had backed into his wife's Volkswagen Jetta in the summer of 1996. When McNeill set out to have the car repaired, his insurance company demanded estimates from three different body shops. At the shop that wound up doing the $1,600 repair job, delays were such that it was a full two months after the accident before the McNeills finally got their Jetta back. McNeill, a former Bain & Co. consultant, was smart enough to recognize an opportunity when he saw one. In 1997, along with Bill Haylon, a former Bain colleague, and longtime body-shop owner Bob Thompson, they founded Sterling Autobody Centers.[17]

When Thompson converted his shop into the original Sterling Autobody Center, he and the Sterling team analyzed the repair process to identify the ways technicians could work both smarter and faster. Their cycle time was about fifteen days, which was about average for the industry. Not surprisingly, the biggest hold-up came in waiting for car parts. Every time a part had to be ordered it added 2.9 days to a job. Thompson decided that to minimize delays it would be necessary to make the damage estimates more accurate. Rather than basing estimates on visible damage, which is what repair shops usually do when insurers ask for multiple quotes, Sterling adopted a policy of "tearing down the car." A damage-analysis manager removes all the damaged parts and decides what can be repaired and what needs to be replaced. When technicians have a clear sense of the extent of the damage, unexpected repairs are much less likely to be needed once the process is underway, and it is easier to predict when the repair work will be finished. Sterling now averages less than one reorder per repair and is able to guarantee the delivery date for completion of a repair job. "Before, our on-time delivery was about 68 percent," says Thompson. "Now we're at 95 percent."[18]

Technicians are encouraged to improve the workflow continually and to share their ideas with the other shops in the chain. Rather than focusing on individual productivity, the staff's goal is to get more cars out the door faster, which makes for happier customers and happier insurers. "We're not doing anything fancy," McNeill says. "We're doing what Henry Ford did one hundred years ago. I've told our guys that in five years, I want to be able to have the bulk of our repairs done in one day. You can't do that by just showing up and doing things the same old way."[19]

## Dell Computers

Dell Computers has become a byword in its industry for efficiency and reliability and is one of the great American success stories. The founder, Michael Dell, spent his time in college cutting classes and building PCs in his dorm room. When he started marketing his computers, the competition regarded him as just another cut-price reseller. However, his build-to-order model and elimination of the retailer revolutionized the business. Manufacturing PCs that had already been purchased and eliminating virtually all inventory enabled him to unseat such giants as Digital and Compaq from the top of the heap.

The Dell model of dealing with customers directly through the Web or on the telephone saves both money and time. Costs are further reduced by the company's inventory practices. Dell has no warehouses to store parts; instead parts are delivered straight to the factory only when needed to fill specific orders. Because each PC or other product is assembled by one person, direct accountability helps to keep quality high. Finally, Dell spends much less than its competitors on product research and development—a mere $440 million a year, compared to Hewlett-Packard's $4 billion. Dell's many patents tend to be for manufacturing processes, which is an indication of the importance placed on both efficiency and process reliability.[20]

The production, distribution, and marketing practices at Dell have provided a 10 percent cost advantage over competitors, enabling it to make a profit on far slimmer margins than competitors. Even in lean times, when all its competitors were suffering, the company could keep its prices low and still make money. While Dell competes primarily on the basis of price, the made-to-order marketing strategy in combination with flexible manufacturing techniques also makes it possible for customers to satisfy their varying needs.[21]

## Southwest Airlines

A significant part of Southwest Airlines' success can be attributed to stressing efficiency in its operations. As we noted earlier, the company operates one type of plane, which reduces training, maintenance, and inventory costs, increases efficiency in crew and flight scheduling, and speeds up pre-flight checks and ground crew preparation. The airline does not offer hot meals, so no time is wasted on the ground loading pre-cooked meals onto planes. There are no seat assignments, which reduces cost and enables quicker boarding. At several airports Southwest installed underground fueling systems at its gates so that workers would not have to use fuel trucks to transport fuel to airplanes. These changes reduced labor costs and turnaround time for aircraft at the gate. As a result, Southwest has been able to fly its planes about 15 percent more than the industry average. The increased use of aircraft reduced Southwest's fleet size relative to competitors, thereby lowering its capital requirements.[22]

Another major difference between Southwest and other carriers is that Southwest has many more direct flights to destination cities, rather than relying so heavily on transfers at a hub airport. As a result, fewer gates are needed and operating costs are lower. Labor costs were reduced by paying less than industry average and including stock options as part of the compensation package for regular employees. Southwest pilots also fly more hours per week than do pilots for most other airlines, which increases productivity and reduces labor costs.[23]

Southwest also makes use of technology to increase efficiency and process reliability. The airline gets more than half its customer revenue from its online booking site, which makes the cost of sales lower than that for most other airlines. Southwest also uses technology to enhance its maintenance operations. Southwest uses computer programs to keep track of scheduled maintenance for the carrier's 390 planes, which eliminates the huge paper trail each airplane repair creates and minimizes the time required to enter and sort through reams of data. In addition, there are required checks and inspections depending on the time each plane spends airborne. Because Southwest is able to readily access data on the scheduled maintenance for each plane, checks and maintenance can be coordinated to avoid unnecessary visits to the hangar.[24]

## Wal-Mart

In 2002, Wal-Mart had $217.8 billion in sales and employed 1.3 million people, making it the largest company in the world. Sam Walton started Wal-Mart with one store in 1962, and today the company has over 3,500 stores worldwide. By holding fast to the founding principles of customer satisfaction and low prices, Wal-Mart has ascended to one of the top-ranked companies in the world.

Wal-Mart focuses on the efficient operation and execution of strategy in every facet of the business. Walton's growth-oriented strategy of placing stores in areas that were a few miles outside of towns and allowing suburban expansion to come to the store, described as "stretch out and back fill," allowed Wal-Mart to save money on startup costs. As it grew larger, Wal-Mart upgraded its technology to stay organized and efficient. By linking inventory in stores across the nation to suppliers, manufacturers can plan production and delivery schedules, allowing efficient and reliable supply to the Wal-Mart stores. The application of technology has been vital to the survival of the ever-growing company.[25]

In addition, since Wal-Mart controls such a huge portion of the retail market, it has gained the ability to press suppliers for the best possible prices to uphold the "everyday low prices" promise. Wal-Mart asks its vendors to help reduce costs so that they can be passed on to the consumer. When Wal-Mart began selling groceries in the mid-1990s, its ability to lower prices made it possible to quickly capture a large share of this market. Although the margins on food sales are low, by offering substantially lower food prices, Wal-Mart attracts new customers who buy more of Wal-Mart's higher-priced items while shopping for food.[26]

## Conditions Affecting Efficiency and Process Reliability

It seems self-evident that no business can ever afford to ignore the matter of efficiency and reliability in its operational processes. Yet, although both are important objectives, their relative importance for any given business will depend on specific situational factors such as the type and nature of the business, its competitive strategy, and the conditions faced in the external environment.

Efficiency is especially important when the competitive strategy of the organization is to offer its products and services at a lower price than competitors. This strategy is most common for products and services that are viewed as commodities (steel companies, paper companies, supermarket chains, airlines, consumer electronics products). Efficiency is also important for businesses that compete in industries that experience downward price pressure due to market share wars (beer producers, fast food restaurants), a high degree of cyclicality creating a mismatch of supply and demand (petrochemical companies), or the demands of a few large customers that dominate the market.

Although it is desirable for all organizations to keep costs low, it is relatively less important when high costs will not affect the net earnings of an organization, because it is able to pass the costs along to customers by increasing prices. Examples include companies that have cost-plus contracts with a sole client, such as the federal government, to provide a unique product or service and organizations that are the exclusive provider of a product or service customers cannot do without. Likewise, an organization that is highly subsidized by government or a wealthy patron has less need to maintain a high level of efficiency.

Reliability in the processes used to provide products and services is especially important when it can affect the health and safety of employees (injury or death from accidents or exposure to harmful substances), it can result in financial loss (mistakes in contracts, stolen or misappropriated funds), or it can result in damage to expensive equipment or other property. Process reliability is also more important when the quality of a product or service is dependent on the procedures used to provide it, and quality defects or mistakes can have serious consequences for the health and safety of customers or can result in costly lawsuits. Obvious examples of organizations for which service reliability is crucial include hospitals, medical labs, airlines, nuclear power plants, financial services companies, and auditing firms.

The impact of unreliability cannot be overemphasized, and the most dramatic examples can be seen almost daily on the news, such as the teenage girl who died after surgeons mistakenly transplanted a heart and lung with the wrong blood type. "This particular incident is as horrendous an error as one can imagine," said Thomas Murray, president of the Hastings Center in Garrison, New York, a medical ethics think tank. "I was quite shocked to know that there were not multiple independent checks of things as critical as blood type before organs were accepted for transplant."[27]

In another example, John Moares, the director of nuclear generation support at British Energy, criticized the company's operational record, pointing to a high loss of functionality. Unplanned station shutdowns for BE were at 12 percent of capacity, as compared to only 2 percent for the most efficient companies in the world. He also criticized the company's poor systems for checking the equipment in nuclear stations and claimed that BE does not have a full picture of safety risks needed to guide the maintenance of plants.[28]

Then there was ConAgra's recall of 18.6 million pounds of meat in July of 2001 because of concern about E. coli. Health officials in several states blamed the recalled meat for forty-seven illnesses and one death.[29]

## Ways to Improve Efficiency and Process Reliability

Leaders can affect efficiency and reliability in a number of different ways. One approach is with the use of direct leadership behaviors. Behaviors that are most likely to be useful in improving efficiency and reliability of an organization's operational processes include operational planning, clarifying roles and objectives, monitoring operations, and solving operational problems in a timely way. Like most leadership behaviors, they may take different forms, depending on whether they are being used by a senior executive, a middle manager, or a manager of front-line employees such as customer representatives or sales people.

Leaders can indirectly affect efficiency and process reliability through the design, implementation, and support of improvement programs, management systems, and structural features. Examples of quality and process improvement programs include business process improvement, re-engineering, total quality management, and Six Sigma. Examples of widely used cost reduction programs include downsizing and outsourcing. Examples of management systems include performance management systems and reward systems. Examples of structural features to facilitate efficiency and reliability include formalization of rules and procedures, and standardization of facilities, technology, and processes.

## Conclusions

High levels of efficiency and process reliability are relevant for the continued success of any organization, and we believe that paying attention to efficiency and reliability is an important responsibility for leaders at all levels in an organization. Efficiency is especially important for a business that provides products or services that are basic commodities and has a competitive strategy that requires minimizing costs and keeping prices low. Process reliability is especially important for organizations when product defects and poor customer service will strongly affect sales, or when mistakes and accidents can endanger the health and lives of employees, customers, or other people. Many products continue to have defects caused by unreliability in the production processes, and poor customer service can often be attributed to inadequate practices and procedures. Direct and indirect forms of leadership that can be used to improve efficiency and process reliability will be described in the next two chapters.

*Chapter 3*

# Leadership Behaviors to Enhance Efficiency

As we saw in Chapter 2, some leader behaviors are primarily concerned with organizing and facilitating work to improve the efficiency and reliability of operations. These task-oriented behaviors include operational planning, clarifying roles and objectives, monitoring operations and performance, and solving operational problems. In this chapter we will examine these behaviors in more detail and provide guidelines for using them more effectively.

## Operational Planning

Operational planning includes determining short-term objectives and action steps for achieving them; determining how to use personnel, equipment, facilities, and other resources efficiently to accomplish a project or initiative; and determining how to schedule and coordinate activities among individuals, teams, and work units. Planning can improve efficiency by facilitating the organization and coordination of related work activities, preventing operational delays and bottlenecks in work processes, avoiding duplication of effort, and helping people to set priorities and meet deadlines. By identifying and addressing potential problems that could lead to accidents, errors, and erratic performance, planning serves to increase reliability of work processes.

Operational planning is especially useful when the work unit is carrying out large, complex projects over a period of months or years; when there is a need to meet difficult deadlines and stay within tight budgets; when the work unit performs several different types of tasks; and when interdependent work units need to ensure close coordination. The more initiatives you have to manage, and the more complex they are, the more essential planning becomes. Operational planning increases a leader's ability to manage several initiatives simultaneously, especially when they involve shared use of facilities, equipment, and personnel.

Systematic planning is necessary to manage complex activities, but leaders frequently rely on an informal approach limited primarily to their own subunit or area of responsibility. An informal approach may work for smaller projects that are confined to one work unit, but it is almost never effective for handling complex initiatives that require coordination among different people in the same unit, or between activities in different units. For example, when a large New York-based mutual insurance and financial services company reorganized and became a publicly held company, it soon became obvious to the senior management team that they would not meet their mid-term performance targets or the expectations of Wall Street analysts. To help improve the organization's performance on two key measures—return on investment and operating income—each division head focused on cutting expenses for his or her own division. However, because of recent acquisitions and reorganization, each manager began this work without really understanding how other parts of the organization would be affected. Attempts to save money included recommendations to eliminate certain support services that were in fact critical to another division's success. As a result, the other division would have had to obtain the services themselves, and there would be no actual saving to the company.

The advantage of a systematic approach to operational planning can be seen in the events involving the relocation of a car rental company. Soon after the car rental company was acquired by a holding company that owns several travel-related businesses, the decision was made to relocate its headquarters from New York to New Jersey. During the transition, the goal was to maintain morale and productivity so that the field offices (the car rental stations in airports and hotels) and customers would receive uninterrupted service during the move.

The vice president of human resources was charged with planning and coordinating both the physical move to New Jersey and the separation and outplacement of employees who decided not to relocate. It soon became apparent that there was no plan specifying the necessary action steps or the timing of key events. As a result, decisions were being made incrementally, and potential problems were not being identified in advance. For example, when the person responsible for the relocation was ready to announce the schedule for the move, it was discovered that the person responsible for the outplacement plan was not prepared to communicate the details of that plan. Clearly, these two events had to be coordinated. Once the lack of internal coordination was identified, the solution was straightforward. The vice president of human resources and other key stakeholders came together and developed a broader, integrated plan that aligned the key milestones of both initiatives. This broader plan was then used to guide the more detailed plans for each initiative.

As this example illustrates, when there are several interrelated projects or initiatives, it is important to ensure that they are mutually supportive and carefully coordinated. During the initial planning stage, the people who are accountable for these projects should meet to jointly review their plans and ensure that interrelated activities are scheduled in appropriate ways and shared resources (e.g., people, equipment, facilities) will be available when needed.

In addition to ensuring compatibility in the early stage of the planning, work activities must also be coordinated during implementation. The early completion of a project or activity, a missed deadline, or the inability to complete an activity successfully, may cause problems for another team and require revisions of their plan. For example, during a merger of two large pharmaceutical companies, the research and development unit had plans for a reduction in force and a reorganization. When there was a delay in the merger announcement, both plans had to be adjusted and realigned. In addition, decisions about resource allocation may also need to be revised as plans unfold.

Even the most detailed and thoughtful plan will encounter unanticipated problems that threaten its successful completion. By definition, plans deal with an unknown future state. When developing them, we make assumptions about a set of future conditions and determine actions based on those assumptions. As plans are implemented, we learn more about actual conditions and the accuracy of our assumptions. Not having a plan causes activities to be fragmented and incremental, but having a plan that is too rigid is just as bad. Because they are oriented toward an unknown future, effective plans need to be used as flexible guidelines and should be adjusted in response to new information or changing conditions. Table 3.1 outlines the components of effective operational planning.

Although action plans are generally recognized as a primary tool for operational planning, it is surprising how many leaders do not use this tool regularly. Sometimes they feel that the project is too small to warrant developing a plan, or that things are moving too fast, or that there are too many uncertainties to make a plan feasible. All these explanations miss the point; action planning is a necessary process for determining how to implement a strategy or carry out a project in an effective manner, regardless of the conditions under which the plan is being implemented. In addition, the availability of computer software planning tools that facilitate and simplify the development, monitoring, and revision of complex plans makes excuses not to develop detailed action plans even harder to justify. Table 3.2 outlines the steps for developing

### Table 3.1.  Guidelines for Operational Planning

- Ensure the efficient use of facilities, equipment, and personnel
- Determine the appropriate allocation of resources across projects and initiatives
- Ensure plans are compatible across projects, units, and levels
- Review operational plans at appropriate times and revise them as needed

### Table 3.2. Key Steps for Action Planning

- Develop an implementation goal and project standards
- Identify the sequence of necessary action steps for a project
- Estimate the time needed to carry out each action step and develop a schedule
- Determine accountability for each action step
- Estimate the cost and necessary resources for each action step
- Identify potential problems and determine how to avoid or minimize them

high-quality action plans that can be used to monitor projects and ensure deliverables are provided on time and on budget.

### Operational Planning at Different Levels

Although it may look somewhat different, operational planning is as important for a senior executive as it is for a first-line supervisor. The crisis period of the New York-based mutual insurance company mentioned earlier provides an example of operational planning at the senior level. Part of the problem was that, although individual departments and work units had developed specific objectives, they were unaware of the objectives and priorities for the overall company. This lack of context made it difficult for the leaders to develop operational plans that were compatible across the organization or to coordinate the day-to-day activities required to achieve overall business objectives. To resolve this problem, the CEO worked with his executive team to develop performance targets for the overall business and identify cross-organizational initiatives that were priorities for the entire company. A broad overview, including objectives, resource requirements, and key milestones, was developed for each cross-organizational initiative. Then each divisional leader identified the specific goals and initiatives for his or her division that would support the achievement of corporate objectives and initiatives. The person who was assigned accountability for each divisional initiative took responsibility to ensure that a specific action plan was in place for it. The divisional objectives and plans were then reviewed by the CEO and his leadership team to ensure they would be mutually supportive and compatible.

An example of operational planning at the middle level can be found at Dow Chemical Company, which developed a planning process specifically designed to control costs in a highly cyclical industry. Dow's "bottom-of-the-cycle planning" is geared to reduce processing costs by increasing capacity utilization, cutting layers of management, and eliminating unnecessary staff. Since prices in the chemical industry are extremely volatile, annual performance is not an accurate reflection of how well a business is controlling costs. Dow focused instead on the bottom of the next cycle. A return-on-assets target was established for each business, to be achieved at the next bottom; and that figure is used to drive targets for annual cost reductions. Managers are not asked to predict the timing of the next bottom; they are only expected to forecast what the price will be at that new low, something they feel fairly confident about being able to do. In its initial stages, the plans cut processing costs by 30 percent. Planning and implementation efforts are overseen by Dow's corporate manufacturing function, which sees to it that operations managers remain focused on cost control and that their annual improvement plans are sufficiently demanding to produce real results. To reflect Dow's capital-intensive cyclical businesses, the measure of profitability on which the plans are based is economic profit, a measure that incorporates the cost of capital in each business and discourages managers from bringing processing costs down by making excessive capital investments.[1]

For lower-level managers, operational planning is usually focused on developing and implementing action plans for a specific project. For example, as part of their strategy to enhance their worldwide consulting practice, a global human resource consulting firm, headquartered in Philadelphia, decided to provide a standard set of consulting processes and solutions throughout the entire organization. For the initiative to have the intended impact, field consultants would need to have a high degree of commitment and ownership of results. Therefore, rather than trying to implement the initiative at the corporate level, the head of each field office was asked to take responsibility for the development of specific action plans for each element of the initiative, including training consultants to use and deliver the solutions, ensuring that local salespeople were familiar with each solution so they could align them with client needs, and developing marketing plans. In this way, the unique needs of each location could be taken into account and the timing of events could be coordinated with other activities that were already planned for that location.

## Clarifying Roles and Objectives

Clarifying is the communication of responsibilities, role expectations, and performance objectives to direct reports, peers, and outsiders who make an important contribution to work unit performance. Clarifying behavior includes setting specific task objectives, explaining duties and responsibilities, explaining priorities among different tasks or objectives, describing expected results, setting clear standards against which performance will be compared, setting specific deadlines for completion of a task, and explaining standard procedures that must be used and when they are appropriate. At higher levels of management, clarifying of expected results tends to emphasize the performance of the direct report's unit rather than aspects of his or her individual performance. Table 3.3

**Table 3.3. Guidelines for Clarifying
Work Roles and Responsibilities**

- Clearly explain an individual's duties and responsibilities
- Agree on expectations for activities involving shared responsibilities
- Set priorities among different responsibilities
- Clarify rules and standard procedures that should be followed
- Confirm understanding and agreement about work responsibilities

provides guidelines that are relevant for clarifying work roles and responsibilities.

Research on leadership indicates that clarifying is an important leader behavior because it improves employee satisfaction and performance by removing ambiguity related to roles and priorities.[2] Clarifying also improves results, motivation, and commitment by ensuring that people know what to do and how to do it to meet expectations. Clarifying helps people understand how their work supports the organization's goals and relates to the work of others. To perform at a high level, people need to clearly understand their responsibilities and roles, their performance goals, the expected results for a task, and when it should be completed. People also need to know and understand the relative priority of the different tasks and activities for which they are responsible.

In today's complex, rapidly changing business environment, success often depends on cooperation and coordination among people and across teams and organizational subunits. The team does its work more efficiently and the output is of higher quality when people are clear about who should be involved in decisions and activities and the nature of that involvement. Inadequate clarification can result in conflicts among team members or departments and key responsibilities that "fall through the cracks" because each party believes that the other party is responsible for them.

Clear policies, rules, and standard operating procedures are sometimes necessary to ensure that people understand how to keep their actions consistent with contractual agreements, legal requirements, quality standards, mandated procedures, and ethical practices. Policies and standard procedures may also be needed to help people understand when and how to involve others appropriately to get the work done efficiently. For example, to help turn Hyundai Motor's quality problems around, Kim Sang Kwon, the quality control Czar, and his team produced a quality control manual that clarified who is responsible for each manufacturing step, what outcome is required, and who checks and confirms performance levels.[3]

Clarifying is especially useful when the work is complex, multiple performance criteria are involved, and people are confused about what is expected of them. Such confusion is more likely when the nature of the work or technology is changing, when there is a crisis and people do not know how to respond, and when employees are new to the job and lack relevant prior experience. Clarifying is more important when work unit operations are frequently affected by changes in policies, plans, or priorities determined by higher management or clients. Since clarifying is a way to communicate plans, the situations where planning is especially important also apply to clarifying, for example large, complex tasks performed by multiple individuals or teams. Finally, clarifying is important for avoiding accidents or mistakes that are likely to have serious consequences in terms of product quality, customer satisfaction, injuries to people, and lawsuits against the company.

There are several reasons for the lack of adequate clarifying. One is the common assumption that others will understand what you want to have done without a detailed explanation. Another reason is the fear of insulting a person's intelligence or of looking stupid by stating what is already obvious. Some leaders may think they are too busy to spell things out, without realizing the possible consequences of failing to do so. This attitude can lead to unfortunate misunderstandings that are often costly for the organization.

### Examples of Effective and Ineffective Clarifying

General Motors is a good example of a company in which employees are given a clear sense of the company's goals and their role in achieving them. At GM, an ambitious employee communications initiative aims to ensure that every employee will understand where he or she fits into the automaker's long-term strategy, as well as how goals and targets for each plant are specifically designed to meet the demands of the highly competitive automotive marketplace. Says Steve Harris, GM's vice president of communications, "It's all about giving our employees a context of where their jobs relate within GM, within the auto industry, and within the global economy. It's a dialogue we never had with our employees until now, and it's a way to provide meaning to GM's overall strategy so each person can understand his place within that strategy."[4]

Unfortunately, not all companies provide employees with adequate clarity about their responsibilities and how they relate to business objectives. In the early 1990s, Sears, Roebuck & Company experienced a rash of complaints about its automotive service business in over forty states. The company was accused of misleading customers and selling them unnecessary parts and services, from brake jobs to front-end alignments. What had happened was that Sears had tried to boost flagging revenues by establishing new goals and incentives for its auto center employees. Minimum work quotas were increased, and productivity incentives were introduced for mechanics. The automotive service advisers were given product-specific sales quotas—sell so many springs, shock absorbers, alignments, or brake jobs per shift—and paid a commission based on sales. Since failure to meet the new quotas could lead to a transfer or a reduction in work hours, the pressure on employees to produce was intense, and some desperate employees resorted to unethical practices. As one commentator put it, "Management's failure to clarify the line between unnecessary service and legitimate preventive maintenance, coupled with consumer ignorance, left employees to chart their own courses through a vast gray area, subject to a wide range of interpretations." The total cost of settlements with consumers was estimated at $60 million.[5]

In another example, a U.S.-based, wholly owned subsidiary of a Japanese pharmaceutical company found its growth objectives threatened because of role ambiguity and the resulting conflicts among members of its R&D function. When the company was smaller, each therapeutic head had been able to carve out a comfortable niche for his or her area, a practice that continued as the company grew larger. Each manager acted as if his or her development projects had the highest priority. As a result, they frequently competed for scarce resources, ignored a colleague's request or decision if they disagreed, and seldom worked with colleagues to coordinate activities that required shared resources, such as clinical trials and the timing of regulatory submissions. As a result, many projects were behind schedule and the leaders in Japan were losing confidence in the teams' ability to deliver on their commitments. Although individual conversations were held with each member of the R&D team to encourage more cooperation, there remained a fundamental difference of opinion about appropriate roles and responsibilities. The solution was to hold a meeting during which the managers listed the goals, decisions, and activities for which they shared accountability. Using that list as a starting point, the managers discussed and agreed on the authority and degree of involvement each person needed to have in making key decisions to ensure work was done efficiently, on time, and in a high-quality manner. The agreements were then documented and distributed to each manager's department so the behavior of direct reports would be consistent with the agreements reached by the managers.

### Goal Setting

Setting specific performance goals or task objectives is also an important form of clarifying for leaders, and it is a subject about which there has been extensive research. Specific, challenging objectives offer several benefits. They focus on important activities and responsibilities; they encourage people to find more efficient ways to do the work; and they facilitate constructive performance evaluation by providing a benchmark for comparison. Performance improves because specific objectives guide effort toward productive activities, and challenging objectives tend to energize a higher level of effort. Table 3.4 outlines guidelines that are relevant for clarifying work objectives.

A common problem is clarifying objectives for easily measured aspects of the work such as quantitative outputs or sales, but not for important aspects that are more difficult to measure, such as service quality or customer satisfaction. To set objectives for less tangible

### Table 3.4. Guidelines for Clarifying Objectives

- Ensure objectives are set for primary responsibilities and tasks
- Ensure objectives are specific, challenging, and realistic
- Confirm an individual's understanding and acceptance
- Ensure objectives are compatible and coordinated across projects, levels, and units

aspects of the work, remember that although some goals may be difficult to quantify, all goals can be verified. For example, the extent to which service quality goals are being met can be verified by comparing actual service to an agreed-on set of standards that define quality service (e.g., responsiveness, handling of problems, on-time performance, availability of products).

When the objectives of one person or group are at odds with the objectives of another, efficiency and reliability will suffer. Picture the likely conflicts and inefficiencies when one group is working toward reducing costs while another group is focused on bringing state-of-the-art products and services to market. These objectives can coexist, but it will not happen easily if things are left to run their own course. Compatible and mutually supportive objectives need to be developed in a thoughtful and explicit manner. One approach is to develop a set of broader, collective objectives for a team or work unit, review the task objectives for specific individuals or groups, and ensure that they are consistent with and mutually supportive of the collective objectives.

For example, to set the stage at the beginning of the year, the chief technology officer of a large brokerage firm and his boss identify the ten critical objectives for the organization as a whole. These are goals that reflect the mission of the organization and are necessary for the overall success of the business enterprise. The extended management team briefly reviews the goals, and then in-depth work is done to ensure that each will be accomplished. Cross-functional teams discuss the goals in concurrent sessions to clarify, fine-tune, and determine what it will take to ensure their accomplishment, including key deliverables, required assistance, mileposts, key stakeholders, and so on. Following these discussions, the individual with primary accountability for a particular goal reports on the overall plan, identifies areas that require problem solving, and explains how progress and success will be monitored and communicated throughout the year. After all the goals have been discussed, possible overlaps, synergies, tradeoffs, and barriers are highlighted and resolved. The process results in clarity among members of the extended team on priorities, resource allocation, and role expectations.

## Monitoring Operations and Performance

Monitoring involves gathering information about work activities, checking on the progress and quality of the work, and evaluating individual and unit performance. Monitoring can take many different forms, such as following up to make sure a request has been carried out, walking around to observe how the work is going, checking on the quality of the work (inspecting it, monitoring quality reports, reviewing complaints from customers or clients), meeting with people to review progress on a task or project, checking work progress against plans to see if it is on target, and evaluating how well a major activity or project was done.

Few people will argue with the statement that a leader needs timely information about work unit operations and performance. Simply said, leaders must know what is happening in their units and how well it is performing its mission. Internal monitoring is the way leaders gather information about the operations of the work unit, the progress of the work, the quality of products and services, the success of projects and programs, and the performance of individuals. Appropriate monitoring makes it possible to identify potential problems early, prevents disruptions in work-unit activities and service to customers, and ensures that people are accountable for the quality of their work. This information is then used to formulate and modify objectives, strategies, policies, and procedures. In addition, monitoring provides the information needed for problem solving and decision making, for evaluating task performance, recognizing achievements, identifying performance deficiencies, assessing training needs, providing assistance, and allocating rewards such as pay increases or promotions.

The appropriate degree of internal monitoring depends on aspects of the situation such as the nature of the work and the people doing it. Monitoring is most important when employees are inexperienced or apathetic about the work. Monitoring is also important when the operations are prone to accidents or disruptions of the workflow caused by equipment breakdowns, materials shortages, or personnel shortages, and leaders need to detect emerging problems quickly to deal with them effectively. Likewise, monitoring is essential when mistakes or delays have serious consequences for the success of a project and must be quickly remedied. Tight deadlines and difficult contractual obligations increase the need for monitoring, as do interdependent tasks that need to be closely coordinated. In this type of situation, the failure to meet deadlines or achieve goals would seriously disrupt the activities and results of others.

Over the past decade, the emphasis on empowerment has led some people to conclude that monitoring, with its connotations of command and control, is no longer an essential leader behavior. Ironically, empowerment actually brings with it the need for *increased* monitoring. People are taking on new roles and responsibilities; they are using new skills and working in new arenas; and they are making and implementing decisions that can have a powerful effect on an organization's success. When monitoring is done appropriately, it is not like micromanaging. The primary purpose is not to increase control but to facilitate performance of the work by others. For all the talk about how people need to be coached instead of supervised, it is difficult to know when to offer coaching or what type of coaching is required without analyzing and evaluating their performance. A key to effective monitoring is to involve people in developing meaningful measures of performance and progress, then show people how these measures can be beneficial to them as well as to the organization.

### Examples of Effective and Ineffective Monitoring

Inadequate monitoring is a major reason for some costly disasters at organizations. For example, failure to carefully monitor the activities of the rogue trader Nick Leeson brought about the complete collapse of the distinguished, long-established Barings Bank. Operating out of Barings' Singapore office, the relatively junior Leeson built up almost unbelievable trading obligations in his employer's name. When the balloon finally burst and Barings was forced into bankruptcy, Leeson had outstanding futures positions of U.S. $27 billion, whereas Barings' actual capital totaled only $615 million. Leeson hid many of his unauthorized trades in an errors account—he sold $7 billion worth of Nikkei options, for example, without the knowledge of Barings London—but just as many of his transactions were included in published data. As one commentator put it, "Theoretically Leeson had lots of supervisors, in reality none exercised any control over him."[6]

A more recent example of inadequate monitoring is provided by The New York Times, America's most prestigious newspaper, which published hundreds of fraudulent stories by staff writer Jayson Blair. Using a cellular phone and a laptop computer to obscure his actual whereabouts, Blair sent dispatches that purported to be from the scene of significant events all over the United States, when in fact he was most often at home in New York, either concocting scenes or plagiarizing stories in other newspapers and wire services. Blair's pattern of deceit could have been detected by senior editors had they monitored his performance and behavior. During five months as a national correspondent, Blair filed articles claiming to be from twenty cities in six states, yet he did not submit a single receipt for a hotel room, rental car, or airplane ticket. After "covering" the October 2002 sniper attacks in the Washington area, where he had supposedly

collected hot "scoops" in interviews with area law enforcement officials, Blair submitted receipts from New York for dates when he
should have been in Washington. As the *Times* itself reported after
Blair's pattern of fabrication was finally discovered: "Five years'
worth of information about Mr. Blair was available in one building,
yet no one put it together." As a result of its neglect in proper monitoring and the ensuing scandal about its reporter's fraudulent jour-
nalism, the paper now suffers what *Times* publisher and chairman
Arthur Sulzberger, Jr., calls "a huge black eye."[7]

### Monitoring Operations

Guidelines for monitoring operations are outlined in Table 3.5.
The performance indicators that are most relevant will depend on
the nature of the work and the factors that determine success. It is
a common mistake to focus on a single indicator when information
about other indicators is essential to evaluate overall effectiveness.
Examples of potentially relevant indicators for efficiency and reliability include employee productivity, operational costs, inventory
turnover, customer complaints, time required to respond to customer requests, on-time deliveries, total availability of systems,
downtime of equipment due to unplanned maintenance, and number of quality defects.

The processes used to produce outcomes should be measured as
well as the outcomes themselves. By measuring essential steps in
operational processes, a leader can gain a better understanding of

### Table 3.5. Guidelines for Monitoring Operations

- Identify and measure key indicators of performance
- Monitor work processes as well as the outcomes
- Assess performance relative to previous levels and similar units
- Develop independent sources of information
- Observe operations directly when feasible

the causal relationships that determine efficiency and reliability. For example, quality problems can be dealt with more effectively by identifying the critical steps in the production or service process where most defects and mistakes occur. Continuous measurement of those processes makes it easier to eliminate common mistakes, detect deficient materials before they are used, and correct any defects immediately. Measures of the personnel, equipment, and resources involved in each step in the production process make it easier to analyze the processes and find ways to simplify procedures, avoid delays, and reduce unnecessary costs.

There are two primary sources of standards for evaluating the performance of an activity. *Prior performance* of the same type of activity by an individual or unit provides a basis for setting standards for future performance under similar conditions. However, even when performance by a unit improves, it may remain well below the performance of similar units in competing organizations. Thus, a second source of standards is the *performance of similar units* within or outside the organization. When information about the performance levels of competitors is not available, it is often possible to develop standards of performance based on customer expectations of service and quality, safety and other government regulations, generally accepted standards of conduct (ethical behavior, fairness, respect for individuals), and internal standards of quality and effectiveness.

## Monitoring Performance

In addition to monitoring the overall operations of the work unit, it is also important, in most cases, to monitor the performance of direct reports and people you depend on to carry out key support activities for your unit. Guidelines for monitoring performance are shown in Table 3.6.

A common method for monitoring progress on assignments and projects is to obtain an update or status report from the person who is performing the task or is responsible for managing the

### Table 3.6. Guidelines for Monitoring Performance

- Determine appropriate reporting requirements for a task or project
- Conduct progress review meetings at appropriate times
- Measure progress against plans, target dates, and budgets
- Ask specific questions about relevant aspects of the work
- Encourage reporting of problems and mistakes

project. The type of information and level of detail in progress reports should be agreed on when a new project is initiated or a new assignment is made. Establishing clear reporting requirements in advance is also a form of clarifying, and it helps managers avoid monitoring too closely and thereby communicating a lack of trust. The frequency and nature of the follow-up will depend on the complexity of the task or project; more detail is appropriate for a complex, important task than for a simple, short one. The reporting requirements should also reflect the experience and capability of the individual or group responsible for the result. More frequent reporting is appropriate for people who are inexperienced or unreliable. Follow-up and reporting could take the form of written reports and formal progress review meetings, or they could be more informal discussions.

Although you can obtain information about the operations of the organization with reports and progress review meetings, there is no substitute for direct observation. Walking around to observe operations and talk with employees is essential, especially for middle managers and senior executives, who tend to become isolated from day-to-day activity. If the visit to a work site is announced in advance, people will try to make a good impression and it will be difficult to obtain accurate information about the way things are normally done. If the leader brings a group of assistants with notepads, employees at the site are likely to be intimidated about what they say. The visit should begin with observations of whatever operating employees are doing at the time, and the leader should ask employees what they are doing and why. A meeting with the facility manager should occur last rather than first. Starting at the operating level shows employees that the leader recognizes their importance.[8]

Soon after Chung Mong Koo took over as CEO of Hyundai Motor Co., he paid a surprise visit to one of the plants. Employees at the plant were not only surprised to be visited by the CEO (employees rarely saw any of Hyundai's previous CEOs), but were also surprised when Chung walked onto the plant floor and demanded a look under the hood of a Sonata sedan. Hyundai was having quality problems at the time and Chung did not like what he saw—loose wires, tangled hoses, bolts painted different colors. Chung ordered immediate changes, telling his plant chief that the company had to get back to basics and raise their quality to the level of their key competitors.[9]

The success of monitoring depends on getting accurate information from people who may be reluctant to provide it. For example, people may be hesitant to inform their boss or a senior manager about problems, mistakes, and delays. It is difficult to obtain the information needed to execute effectively if people withhold or distort information about problems. Even a person who is not responsible for a problem may be reluctant to report it if concerned about becoming the target of an angry outburst (the "kill the messenger" syndrome). Therefore, it is essential that the reaction to information about problems be constructive and non-punitive. For example, a leader can express appreciation for accurate information even if it is negative, respond quickly to a problem with specific actions to deal with it, and help people learn from mistakes rather than punish them.

Effective leaders also use their knowledge about technology, products, services, and procedures to ask specific questions and obtain vital information about the work when observing operations or holding progress review meetings. Questions should be open-ended and non-evaluative to encourage people to respond and provide a more complete picture of the situation. The questions should communicate the leader's concerns and expectations to people, in addition to obtaining information from them.

## Solving Operational Problems

Solving operational problems involves identifying work-related issues, analyzing them in a systematic but timely manner, and acting decisively to implement solutions. Problem solving occurs in response to an immediate disturbance of normal operations, such as equipment breakdown, a shortage of necessary materials, a customer with a complaint, a mistake in the work, an accident, an unusual request by higher management, or direct report or colleague actions that jeopardize the success of a mission. The solution to an operational problem may or may not involve innovative ideas, but any changes are incremental rather than major.

As with operational planning, problem solving involves processing information, analyzing, and deciding. However, there are some important differences between the two leadership behaviors. Problem solving often involves crises or disturbances that cannot be ignored, in contrast to planning, which is more likely to be stimulated by the discovery of an opportunity to be exploited, or by the anticipation of a future problem to be avoided. Problem solving is a reactive behavior with a short-term perspective, whereas planning is a proactive behavior with a longer-term perspective. Just as the time perspective varies, so does the typical duration of the decision process. Due to the pressure of time, problem solving typically occurs more quickly than planning. Some information seeking, analysis, and consultation may occur, but there is usually much less than with planning.

Leaders face an endless stream of problems and disturbances in their work, and solving operational problems was found to be related to leader effectiveness in many survey studies.[10] The descriptive research on leader effectiveness suggests that effective leaders take responsibility for dealing with problems in a timely way. In contrast, ineffective leaders attempt to avoid responsibility for a problem by ignoring it, by trying to pass the problem off on someone else, by involving more people than necessary in making the decision to diffuse responsibility, or by delaying the decision for as long as possible (e.g., form a committee to study the problem and write a detailed report, send an invention or new product back for more testing).[11]

Research on crisis management suggests that effective leaders quickly identify the cause of the problem and take decisive action to direct the work unit's response to it.[12,13] In a situation where normal operations by the organization are disrupted (e.g., by a serious accident in the workplace, a natural disaster, severe weather, electrical power failure, a terrorist incident, or a labor strike in a related industry), people will be anxious and will want their leaders to explain what has happened and what is being done to deal with the situation. In the absence of timely and accurate information, harmful rumors are likely to occur, and people may become discouraged and afraid. A leader can help prevent unnecessary stress for people by interpreting threatening events and emphasizing positive elements rather than leaving people to focus on the negatives. When feasible, it is helpful to provide short, periodic briefings about progress in efforts to deal with the crisis. Steps to help guide leaders in effectively solving operational problems and dealing with a crisis situation are presented in Table 3.7.

Because there are always more problems than a leader has time to address, it is important to look for relationships among them

### Table 3.7.  Guidelines for Solving Operational Problems

- Take responsibility for identifying problems that need attention
- Make a quick but systematic diagnosis of a problem before acting
- Identify connections among related problems
- Deal with problems in a confident and decisive manner
- Keep people informed in a crisis situation
- Develop contingency plans for predictable emergencies and rehearse them

rather than assuming they are distinct and independent. A broader view of problems provides better insights for understanding them. Relating problems to each other and to strategic objectives makes it easier to recognize opportunities for dealing with several related problems at the same time. Finding connections among problems is facilitated if the leader is able to remain flexible and open-minded about the definition of a problem and actively consider multiple definitions for each problem.[14]

It is also important to seek a balance between careful analysis of the problem and quick, decisive action to solve it. Effective leaders move quickly to deal with an immediate threat or problem. Nevertheless, it is essential to make an accurate diagnosis of the problem and to identify relevant remedies. Kepner and Tregoe[15] found that many leaders implement solutions that are ineffective because they fail to use a systematic, logical analysis to identify the cause of a problem. Solving the wrong problem can make things worse instead of better. To facilitate a rapid, effective response when there is a predictable accident or disruption, it is useful to have contingency plans prepared in advance. To ensure that people understand how to execute procedures for coping with an emergency that could result in serious injuries or loss of life, leaders should conduct periodic rehearsals with employees.

## Relationships Among the Behaviors

As you have probably realized already, operational planning, clarifying, monitoring operations, and problem solving are closely intertwined and should be used together in mutually supportive ways. Monitoring provides much of the information needed to formulate and modify objectives, plans, policies, and procedures. Clarifying is an essential process for communicating plans to others. Operational plans help determine what work processes need to be monitored and provide guidance for evaluating progress by indicating when key action steps should be initiated or completed. Problem solving helps ensure that operations are not disrupted for too long and that the implementation of plans stays on track.

An example that illustrates the interrelationship of the efficiency-oriented behaviors involves a Japanese-owned pharmaceutical company that developed a blockbuster drug targeted to deal with problems associated with aging. The high demand for this drug put tremendous strain on the company's manufacturing facilities. The vice president of operations realized that it would take a highly organized effort to ensure that enough of the drug was available to meet the aggressive sales projections coming out of the field. The vice president worked with his leadership team to set specific productivity and quality goals for the year and to identify the actions required to make those goals a reality. The team recognized the importance of establishing detailed production schedules so that everyone understood what to do, why it had to be done, and when it had to be done. After the goals and plans were formulated for the operations unit, they were translated into specific actions for each department and reviewed to ensure interdepartmental coordination. The people in each department set their own individual targets for the year, aligning them with the department's and the company's overall objectives. Periodic meetings were held to review progress, solve problems, and identify opportunities for the continuous improvement of production and work processes. Production quality and quantity were monitored on a daily basis to ensure targets were being achieved. If any deviations from established standards were discovered during these daily meetings, the team mobilized immediately to identify the cause and develop solutions to get production or quality back on track. The vice president of operations also kept in constant contact with the sales organization, to ensure he had the most recent forecasts and organizational commitments. In this way, adjustments to production levels and quality could also occur on a planned basis.

## Conclusions

The four leader behaviors that have the greatest impact on efficiency and reliability are operational planning, clarifying roles and objectives, monitoring operations, and solving operational problems. Although these behaviors are often described as examples of managing rather than leading—recent events at companies like Ford, *The New York Times*, and K-Mart, to name a few, have shown us the danger of ignoring these behaviors. A challenge for leaders is to determine the appropriate mix of the task-oriented behaviors to enhance efficiency and reliability. In doing so, leaders must also determine how to use both direct and indirect approaches in a complementary way. The indirect approaches will be described in the next chapter.

Chapter 4

# Programs and Management Systems for Improving Efficiency and Process Reliability

Efficiency-oriented behaviors can be used by leaders at all levels, but most leaders at the senior level can also implement programs, management systems, and structural arrangements designed to improve efficiency and reliability. The challenge is to determine which approaches are appropriate and how to implement them in ways that will increase the likelihood of success. Widely used programs include quality and process improvement programs, cost reduction programs, formal management systems, structural forms, and incentive programs. Each type of approach will be described and evaluated briefly in this chapter.

## Quality and Process Improvement Programs

Despite the fact that business process improvement (BPI), re-engineering, total quality management (TQM), and Six Sigma techniques have been available for improving operational efficiency and reliability for more than a decade, many leaders are still confused about the differences among them. We will describe each type of program briefly.

### Business Process Improvement

Business process improvement (BPI) is a way to make operational processes more efficient by eliminating unnecessary steps, transactions, and controls. It is effective for gaining incremental refinements and efficiencies with current processes, rather than creating a new process from scratch. For a BPI initiative to succeed, the support of the work unit's leader is essential. This support can be demonstrated by attending the same training as the team, by holding joint project and steering committee meetings, by enforcing strict adherence to the project schedule, and by ensuring resources are available to the project team.[1] In many cases, technology can also be used to enhance the efficiency and reliability of work processes. However, good technology can only do so much for a weak work process. Overlying technological solutions on a poorly designed work process leads to disappointing results, despite large investments of time and dollars.

### Re-Engineering

Re-engineering is about inventing new approaches and new models of organizing work. It involves scrapping old processes and recreating new, more efficient ones. On a larger scale, re-engineering can be an organization-wide transformation that means greater risks and more disruption for the business. In many organizations today, the term carries a negative connotation. Ironically, one of the reasons re-engineering lost its appeal as a management tool was its popularity. In the 1990s, the concept of re-engineering became widely popular for improving operations, but many senior leaders lacked a clear understanding of what re-engineering was and how it should be implemented. Many companies that tried re-engineering were disappointed by the results, and some suffered serious setbacks that have been attributed to a weak, poorly implemented program. Research conducted by IMA Inc. indicates that only 30 percent of firms are successful in implementing a re-engineering project.[2] Hershey, the famous candy maker, was among the companies hardest hit by re-engineering problems during an ERP implementation. The company reported a 19 percent drop in profits year to year in the third quarter of 1999 that Hershey's CEO, Kenneth Wolfe, attributed to lost sales and costly inventory backups due to a failed implementation of new business processes.[3]

Despite these types of failures, when used properly re-engineering can still be an effective tool for organizations striving for greater operational efficiency and process reliability. As leaders have come to understand that implementing enterprise resource planning (ERP) and customer relationship management (CRM) systems are about changing processes, not installing software, re-engineering and business process improvement are once again being seen as processes that can help organizations increase efficiency and reliability.[4] For example, at GE Capital Fleet Services, executives simplified the customer interface and improved the old processes before implementing a CRM system.[5]

So what does it take to ensure that a re-engineering initiative will be successful? As research conducted by McKinsey, the management consulting firm, demonstrates, the leader must play a very visible role. McKinsey identified five factors that contributed to a successful program: (1) set aggressive re-engineering goals that span the entire organization to ensure sufficient breadth, (2) commit from 20 to 50 percent of the chief executive's time to the project, (3) conduct a comprehensive review of customer needs, economic leverage points, and market trends and use this as a driver for the process redesign specifications, (4) assign additional senior executives to spend at least 50 percent of their time on the project during implementation, and (5) conduct a comprehensive pilot of the new design to test overall impact and build enthusiasm for the implementation.[6] Clearly, as with business process improvement, the amount of time devoted to these initiatives and how that time is used are important factors for success.

### Total Quality Management

Total quality management (TQM) has been defined in a variety of ways by various authors and is acknowledged to be a notoriously imprecise term.[7] Like business process improvement and re-engineering, TQM is a program for improving efficiency and reliability. TQM generally means a quest for excellence in efficiency, reliability, and customer satisfaction and involves creating the right attitudes and controls necessary to prevent defects and errors.[8]

TQM is an approach that assumes the most effective means of improvement is to use the people who actually do the job to identify and implement appropriate changes. The quality circle teams at Iowa-based Grain Processing Corporation provide an example. The teams decided to find some way to reduce the high expense of replacing seventy air filters every two weeks in the plant's flash driers. The teams conducted their own research and found that the air filters could be replaced with a permanent self-cleaning unit that would save the company $400,000 in equipment and labor costs over five years.[9]

### Six Sigma

Six Sigma is a disciplined, data-driven approach for eliminating defects in highly specialized manufacturing and service-related processes. For most organizations, the term Six Sigma refers to a measure of quality that is used to reduce variation in performance through the application of process improvement projects. The Credit Division at John Deere applied the Six Sigma methodology to the process used to prepare quarterly budget forecasts in two of its locations, and the cycle was reduced from eighty days to thirty days.[10]

Other companies have used Six Sigma to streamline manufacturing processes and ensure greater reliability of product. For example, the architectural and functional coatings (AFC) unit within the specialty chemicals company of Rohm and Haas was able to streamline its manufacturing processes and technical support processes for an important product line while at the same time increasing consistency. Habib Siddiqui, the Six Sigma manager for the project, reported that they were using older methods that were not very reliable, and without good measurement systems it was difficult to determine whether performance was improving or how it compared to that of competitors. Six Sigma enabled Rohm and

Haas to improve the measurement system and achieve significant cost savings.[11]

Six Sigma programs have been used effectively in many companies. However, like other programs for improving efficiency and reliability, there is no guarantee that one will be successful. While former GE chief Jack Welch, an early champion of the process, cited Six Sigma as the most important initiative GE had ever undertaken, other companies that embraced it in the 1990s have not fared as well. Kodak, Xerox, and Polaroid are three prominent examples of organizations that had little success with Six Sigma.[12]

Programs imposed by chief executives often fail, says Mike Beer, professor of business administration at Harvard Business School. "It is the fallacy of programmatic change," he says. "You don't change a large company all at once. You have to go out unit by unit and get real buy-in from the organization."[13] How, then, can a leader increase the likelihood that Six Sigma, or any quality or process improvement program, will have the intended impact on efficiency and reliability? Dick Smith and Jerry Blakeslee, partners in the Six Sigma practice of PriceWaterhouseCoopers, suggest four things leaders can do to create the cultural conditions that support the effective use of Six Sigma: (1) ensure that all leaders are in agreement about the need to drive the implementation of Six Sigma approaches at all levels of the organization; (2) develop an understanding of statistical analysis and process redesign and cascade that capability to other levels inside the organization; (3) increase employee engagement in Six Sigma projects and practices by using a variety of communication techniques and incentives; and (4) integrate Six Sigma approaches into the organization's business planning and implementation processes.[14]

## Cost Reduction Programs

Downsizing and outsourcing are examples of programs that have been widely used to reduce operating costs in companies and public sector organizations. The focus of a cost reduction program should be to improve operational efficiency and process reliability, not just to reduce employee costs. When used appropriately, downsizing and outsourcing can help an organization achieve these objectives without adverse consequences that exceed the benefits.

## Downsizing

Although no common definition of downsizing has emerged, Freeman and Cameron[15] offer a broad definition: organizational downsizing constitutes a set of activities, undertaken on the part of the management of an organization, designed to improve organizational efficiency, productivity, and/or competitiveness. It represents a strategy that affects the size of the firm's workforce and the work processes used. Downsizing refers to more than the traditional layoffs that have affected workers for decades, particularly in economic downturns. While layoffs are a function of economic or organizational decline, they are often used as a short-term remedy for an immediate problem. In contrast, downsizing can also be an effective tool during times of growth. A downsizing program can be used to improve efficiency by surgically eliminating redundant employees who perform unnecessary functions or who lack the skills and motivation to perform necessary functions.[16]

To slim down successfully, leaders should resist simplistic remedies such as across-the-board layoffs. After firing 12,000 employees, Delta Airlines found itself short of baggage handlers, maintenance workers, and customer-service agents to provide vital services.[17] Rather than randomly dismissing employees from all organizational levels, a company should engage in workforce planning, training, and skills assessment. General Electric, for instance, uses a grading performance system to rank employees. When it comes time to cut, the employees most likely to go are the ones with the lowest performance scores. This approach allows GE to keep talented people and cross-train them to perform important but understaffed functions.[18]

## Outsourcing

Outsourcing refers to the contracting of business processes to an external service provider. Transferring responsibility for a business process to a vendor or supplier makes it possible to reduce operating costs or improve reliability of operations. By turning routine operations over to specialists, a company can fully utilize an external supplier's investments, innovations, and specialized professional capabilities that would be prohibitively expensive or even impossible to duplicate internally.[19]

Companies have started to outsource a wide array of tasks and functions, including manufacturing, human-resources functions, marketing, accounting, sales, building maintenance, machine operators, company cafeterias, payroll processing, the movement of inventory and goods, and help desks. However, despite these trends, the most commonly outsourced activities are still IT services and contract electronics manufacturing. For example, JPMorgan Chase signed a seven-year contract with IBM Global Services (totaling in excess of $5 billion) to outsource major portions of its data-processing-technology infrastructure, including mainframe operations, data centers, help desks, distributed computing, data networks, and voice networks. As part of this relationship, JPMorgan Chase is leveraging IBM's On-Demand Computing to lower costs and improve flexibility.

Companies can also use outsourcing to move many types of risks and unwanted management problems onto suppliers. For example, Gallo, the largest producer and distributor of wines in the United States, outsources the growing of most of its grapes, pushing the risks of weather, land prices, and labor problems onto its suppliers. Argyle Diamonds, one of the world's largest diamond producers, outsources virtually all aspects of its operation except the crucial steps of separation and sorting of diamonds. It contracts all its huge earth-moving operations (to avoid capital and labor risks), its housing and food services for workers (to avoid confrontations on non-operating issues), and much of its distribution (to De Beers to protect prices, finance inventories, and avoid the complications of worldwide distribution). In addition, by outsourcing to best-in-class suppliers, Gallo and Argyle further ensure the quality and image of their operations.[20]

Outsourcing, like any business practice, has potential dangers. Many firms that use outsourcing look primarily at short-term savings from lower costs, not at long-term consequences. The savings from outsourcing can prove illusory when there are unanticipated consequences or when the outsourcing creates expensive new problems. For example, long-term contracts may not include adequate provisions for the possibility of drastic changes in prices. Deloitte & Touche had to help a retail client renegotiate a $170 million contract. The company received a one-time 20 percent cost savings when it signed an information-processing deal, but technology prices then fell so fast that the retailer wound up paying far more than it would cost to do the work in-house.[21] In contrast to American companies, Japanese companies, which pioneered outsourcing, use it primarily to improve long-term quality and efficiency, and this strategy has resulted in bigger cost savings over time.[22]

Another danger of outsourcing is that customers may blame the company for mistakes made by the vendor. Harvard Business School professor Lynda Applegate points out that customers are not able to determine who is responsible when things go wrong, and the company whose name is on the product or service is likely to be blamed for any quality problems. In 1995 when several American and Japanese car manufacturers were forced to recall eight million vehicles, the carmakers took the blame when it was in fact Japan's Takata that had supplied the defective seatbelts.[23]

## Management Systems and Structural Forms

Formal management systems and some types of structural forms are widely used in organizations to improve efficiency and process reliability. Examples include performance management systems, work rules and standard operating procedures, functionally specialized subunits, and standardization of facilities and equipment.

## Performance Management

The primary purpose of a performance management program is to clarify task objectives, ensure individual objectives are aligned with broader business strategies, and help people understand how they are doing relative to performance standards and role expectations. These systems help leaders to coordinate the efforts of people with interrelated jobs, avoid wasted effort, avoid duplication of effort, and ensure that essential functions are not overlooked. The systems also facilitate coordination between different levels of management in an organization, as goals and plans are developed through a cascading process from top to bottom, and then back up again.

Most performance management systems include a formal process for performance planning (which includes setting performance goals), progress reviews, and formal appraisal with performance feedback. Management by Objectives (MBO) is an example of an early performance management system.

Performance management systems have a mixed record of success. All too often, the performance management process degenerates into a bottom-line mentality with exclusive emphasis on costs and profits. The process can easily became an excuse for managers to dictate a series of financial targets to be met by direct reports. In such cases, instead of fostering better communication and problem solving, the performance management process merely becomes another bureaucratic control mechanism that perpetuates and intensifies hostility, resentment, and distrust between a manager and his or her direct reports.[24]

## Work Rules and Standard Operating Procedures

Another approach for achieving efficient, reliable operations is the use of formal rules and standard procedures. They are more effective when used for repetitive operations in which mistakes are likely and for complex, multi-step tasks that are difficult to learn without clear instructions. Rules and procedures are more likely to improve efficiency if they are based on prior lessons learned about effective ways to conduct work operations and avoid mistakes. Examples of standard operating procedures and work rules can be found in the flight preparation and takeoff checklists used by cockpit crews and the procedural checklists used by surgical teams. In addition, standard operating procedures are documented and used in the pharmaceutical industry for a range of complex procedures, from developing new molecules to submitting a filing to the FDA for a new drug.

Rules and procedures are least useful for improving efficiency or reliability when the work involves unique rather than repetitive tasks and when effective performance requires employee initiative and problem solving rather than application of predetermined procedures. For this type of task, guidelines can be helpful for diagnosing causes of a problem, but employees should have more discretion in determining how and when they are used.

Unfortunately, the imposition of new rules and controls is a common way of responding to a prior failure, especially when the paramount concern of leaders is to avoid blame for another failure, rather than finding an effective way to improve reliability. For example, when there was a scandal involving one or two employees who improperly used funds to purchase supplies or services from vendors, New York imposed a tedious reporting procedure on thousands of state employees, including many who did not even have any purchasing responsibility. It was not clear whether this requirement would prevent future incidents of improper behavior, but the agency administrators could claim that they took some action to avoid future incidents.

When rules and procedures are overused, there may be negative side-effects for employee satisfaction and commitment. It is the opposite of empowerment when leaders attempt to control every action of employees by specifying many detailed rules and procedures that must be followed. Complying with excessive control procedures detracts from performance of regular work, and it makes many employees resentful that they are not trusted to do their jobs properly.

## Standardized Facilities and Equipment

An approach that can be used by businesses that have many similar facilities, stores, offices, or operations is to standardize their design. Standardization can reduce costs for the design and construction of facilities, the purchase and operation of equipment, and the selection and training of employees. Retailers, such as The Gap and Best Buy, and fast-food chains, such as McDonald's and Burger King, have long recognized the advantages of standardization. General Motors is creating standardized manufacturing equipment packages for its assembly plants, which will allow the company to buy equipment at higher volumes and save money.[25]

As we explained in Chapter 2, Southwest Airlines gains increased efficiency by flying only one type of airplane, and a trend toward standardization of aircraft is emerging in the airline industry in general. Smaller carriers are banding together to design and purchase identical planes. In the past, carriers avoided fleet standardization, fearing it would dilute their brand. But in today's financial environment, efficiency through cost containment has become an industry priority. When more airlines use the same airplane, there may also be an increase in the resale value.[26,27]

## Functional Specialization

By designing jobs and organizing them into subunits, leaders can indirectly improve efficiency. The benefits of functional specialization have been evident for a long time, and this principle can be applied to the design of jobs and to the grouping of jobs into subunits. In a functionally specialized subunit, the employees may have identical jobs, or they may perform different roles as part of a team that is collectively responsible for one basic step in the production or delivery of a product or service. For example, a manufacturing organization may have functional subunits such as purchasing, engineering, production, distribution, maintenance, sales, and personnel. A hospital may have separate departments for different medical specialties such as internal medicine, pediatrics, anesthesiology, radiology, surgery, psychiatry, gynecology and obstetrics, pharmacy, and medical labs.

Grouping jobs together on the basis of function has several potential advantages. The interaction among similar specialists facilitates mutual assistance and sharing of ideas. There is likely to be more development of individual expertise, more focus on efficient ways to do the work, and a better matching of actual and required skills when making job assignments. Economies of scale can result from having greater specialized personnel perform larger amounts of similar tasks with special-purpose equipment. There may be less duplication of effort and unused resources if similar tasks are performed in one unit rather than being distributed throughout many different subunits of the organization.

However, there are also disadvantages of functional specialization in comparison to other ways to design subunits, such as by product, customer, or location. Members of functional subunits tend to have a narrow focus on issues that are important to their specialization. Members may identify more with their functional specialization and the needs of their subunit than with the needs of customers, other units, or the larger organization. As a result, it will be more difficult to achieve coordination and cooperation among interdependent functional subunits. Moreover, members may resist innovative ideas or changes that would require sacrifices by the subunit to help the organization respond to changes in the external environment.

## Recognition and Reward Systems

Incentive and reward programs are widely used in the United States to improve efficiency and reliability. Many different types of indicators can serve as the basis for determining rewards, including individual productivity, cost management, completion of projects on schedule or under budget, attainment of production or sales goals, accident-free performance, defect-free performance, and having the highest productivity among competing groups. Some awards are based on individual performance, and some are based on team or subunit performance. A common form of efficiency reward is the use of an incentive or bonus based on productivity, the amount of work output for a given time period, or the completion of a defined project on time and under budget. Another type of reward program (sometimes called a Scanlon Plan) consists of a bonus based on reductions in the cost of operations for a unit resulting from higher productivity and improvements in work procedures. The bonus is received by all members of the unit and, unlike with profit sharing, it depends primarily on performance rather than on external economic conditions. Some organizations also use formal rewards to improve process reliability, such as a bonus for error-free performance or an award for zero accidents in the operation of equipment or vehicles.

Incentive programs have a long history, and they can take many different forms, as the following examples demonstrate. DPR Construction pays cash bonuses of up to 20 percent of base salary to individuals and teams upon completion of a project if they meet five critical success factors that involve efficiency and reliability (estimating accuracy, scheduling, safety, zero defects, and project completion).[28] At an air freight company, container utilization increased from 45 percent to 95 percent after a program of feedback and recognition was implemented for employees who load the containers. A beverage company in New York significantly reduced accidents by its delivery truck drivers by implementing a reward program for accident-free deliveries. The rewards included free lottery tickets and the opportunity to win prizes or vacations.

The feasibility of an incentive program for improving productivity or process reliability depends on accurate measures of performance and the absence of obstacles that would prevent employees from improving their performance, such as inadequate supplies, faulty equipment, or insufficient work to be performed. The feasibility of an incentive program also depends on characteristics of the employees, such as their desire for the rewards offered and their belief that rewards are allocated fairly. Feasibility and effectiveness also depend on the magnitude of the rewards and the cost of the program. Tangible rewards must be large enough to motivate improved performance by employees, but the program should not be so costly that it exceeds the economic benefits.

There are many examples of successful incentive programs, and research confirms that tangible reward programs can improve productivity.[29] However, incentive programs can also result in spectacular failures when used in inappropriate ways. Failure is likely if rewards are based on one aspect of performance without regard for other essential aspects that may be less obvious or more difficult to measure.[30] Employees are likely to focus their efforts on the aspect of performance that is rewarded (for example, quantity) and neglect the unrewarded aspects (for example, quality, equipment maintenance, efficient use of resources). In an effort to obtain the reward, some employees may try to use detrimental shortcuts and unethical practices unless this type of behavior is expressly prohibited and monitored closely. The cost of the unintended consequences may exceed any benefits from the program. An example is provided by a large bank that offered bonuses for originating new loans without any provision for assessing the quality of the loans. The program increased the number of loans, but they included many risky loans that should not have been made, and eventual losses from them far exceeded any benefits from the program.

## Conclusions

Leaders can indirectly influence efficiency and process reliability through the use of improvement programs, management systems, and formal aspects of structure, such as formal operating procedures, specialized subunits, and standardization of facilities. Quality and process improvement programs include business process improvement, re-engineering, total quality management, and Six Sigma. Cost reduction programs include downsizing and out-sourcing. Management systems include performance management and work rules and standard operating procedures. Structural forms include functional specialization and standardization of facilities and equipment. Reward and recognition programs are also widely used to improve efficiency. Although each of these approaches can potentially add value and help an organization enhance its performance, the success depends on whether an approach is appropriate for the situation, whether it is imple-mented effectively, and whether it is supported by leaders at all levels in the organization.

# Section II

# *Innovation and Adaptation*

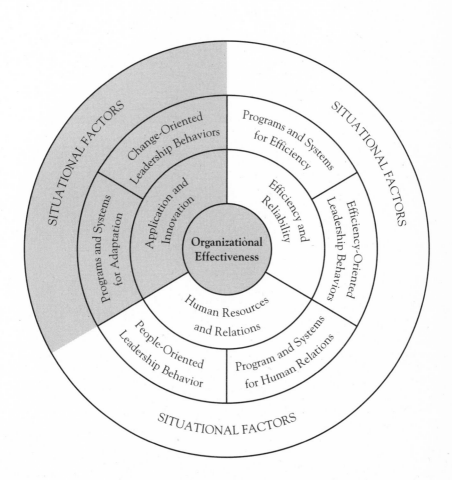

## Chapter 5

# The Challenge of Adapting to the External Environment

Adaptation to the external environment is essential if an organization is to grow and remain competitive. In a world where change is the only constant, being able to respond in a timely way to emerging threats and opportunities is crucial to any organization's ability to thrive. Adaptation involves changes made to cope with external threats and exploit opportunities created by new technology, changing markets, and the shifting needs and expectations of customers. All organizations are faced with periods during which they must adapt or perish. For some organizations these periods of crisis only occur infrequently, but for many others, there is a need for continuous change and adaptation.

The idea that organizations must be innovative to adapt to changing circumstances has become almost a truism in the recent literature on leadership, and business executives also acknowledge the importance of innovation. In a survey based on annual reports and speeches by top management, 90 percent of the large organizations surveyed indicated that they were committed to innovation.[1] Yet employees of these companies overwhelmingly indicated that innovation was more rhetoric than reality. The gap between word and action may reflect the lack of a clear and accurate model of innovation as an organizational capability.

There is a tendency to view innovation primarily in terms of improvements in an organization's products and services, but leader efforts to encourage and facilitate innovation may also be an attempt to improve another performance determinant, such as efficiency or human relations. For example, operational procedures can be made more efficient and reliable by importing best practices from other organizations, experimenting with new procedures, and reviewing work processes to identify potential improvements. These same learning practices can also be used to improve human resources and relations in the organization. Better efficiency or more talented, committed employees may, in turn, enable the organization to compete more effectively in external markets. Thus, in our view of organizational effectiveness, adaptation is the key performance determinant rather than innovation. Like collective learning and understanding of the environment, innovation is an essential process for enhancing adaptation, but it is a means to an end, not the end itself.

## Conditions Affecting the Importance of Adaptation

Adaptation is more important when the external environment is turbulent and uncertain than when it is relatively stable and benign. Uncertainty is greater when there is rapid technological change, political and economic turmoil, or new threats from competitors. In these situations, innovation is usually necessary to develop an appropriate response to emerging threats and opportunities. Examples of organizations that face uncertain environments include telecommunications companies, computer products companies, research laboratories, military combat units, and recently deregulated industries such as financial services and energy utilities.

Another condition that makes adaptation more important for the organization is a competitive strategy that emphasizes unique, leading-edge products or services designed to satisfy the changing needs of customers and clients. For this strategy to be effective there must be frequent innovation and rapid response to threats and opportunities. Examples of organizations that need to be very responsive to changing customer preferences, new technology, and new initiatives by competitors include fashion clothing, pharmaceutical companies, medical equipment companies, computer companies, advertising agencies, and the entertainment industry.

Skechers, a maker of fashion footwear, depends on innovation and constant design evolution to stay ahead of competitors. The company has a team of forty designers who are responsible for eleven distinct categories for men, women, and children. Whenever an idea for a shoe comes up, they do not wait for a particular season, but put it in the line immediately.[2]

Another example is provided by Samsung, the South Korean manufacturer of consumer electronics, which has become the third largest producer of wireless telephones. In order to maintain rapid growth in this highly competitive market they must continually add innovative features. Samsung has developed cell phones with colored screens, global positioning systems, multiple ring tones, instant messaging capabilities, and voice-activated dialing.[3]

Adaptation is relatively less important when there is little or no competition for a product or service that has strong demand. This situation occurs when a company has a patent on a unique product (e.g., miracle drug), or is the only source of a service or product in a protected domestic market. Examples include federal, state, and local government agencies and government operated or regulated industries, such as subway and bus systems, public schools, and public utilities (in some countries). There is less pressure to improve customer service or adapt to changes in customer needs and preferences when there is little or no competition, or in some cases large subsidies. Adaptation is also less important when marginally adequate service or a very slow pace of innovation will not seriously jeopardize the survival and prosperity of the organization, as in the case of monopolies and most government agencies. However, the trend in most developed, democratic countries toward privatization, deregulation, and reduced government subsidies for organizations means that few leaders today can enjoy guaranteed markets. Likewise, the increasing pace of technological change and political trends such as increased terrorism have made even protected organizations more dependent on detecting new threats and opportunities in the external environment.

## Examples of Failure in Adaptation

Although the importance of innovation and adaptation to environmental change seems clear to a majority of leaders, many organizations are not doing it successfully. In this section we will describe some unsuccessful efforts to respond to external threats and opportunities. Some companies provide examples of the difficulties in adapting to changes in the external environment are AT&T, Lucent, McDonald's, and Philips.

### AT&T

In 1996, AT&T was faced with major challenges, including changes in government legislation that would allow regional Bell operating companies to enter the long distance market, the commoditization of the long distance voice market, and the dramatic increase of data traffic. In response then-CEO Michael Armstrong tried to take the initiative by creating a new network that would bring direct broadband access into every home. Unfortunately, AT&T had to abandon the plan before it could be fully implemented due to a number of interrelated factors. AT&T paid top dollar for cable networks, which involved high financial risk for the company. The aggressive expansion of bandwidth created a bandwidth glut and price erosion, which in turn caused a decline in AT&T's revenues, profits, and stock price. Investors became concerned and pressured management to rethink the new strategy. The company eventually backed off the riskier strategy, but not before its service quality was tarnished by the purchase of inferior cable networks and by cost cutting in traditional services. In addition, as AT&T was struggling during the transition, competitors grabbed market share in the new broadband, optical, and Internet markets.[4]

## Lucent

When Lucent was spun off from AT&T in 1996, the new company also faced significant change in the external environment. At the outset it seemed that the Telecommunications Act of 1996 would be a boon for Lucent as customers decided to modernize their networks while they still had access to their monopoly revenues. These companies turned to Lucent for new equipment because Lucent had provided their existing telecom equipment (when it was still part of AT&T), and much of it would work only with upgrades from the original manufacturer. Despite this apparent advantage, Lucent ran into problems. The company failed to adapt to significant changes in the industry, including the shift from electrical to optical switching, the shift from voice to data networks, and the shift from specialty to commodity markets. Lucent was aware of these changes but was not able to respond as quickly as new competitors.[5]

## McDonald's

McDonald's entered the new millennium with declining profits in seven out of eight straight quarters, culminating in the first operating loss of its forty-seven-year history. In 1996, same-store sales had declined for four straight quarters and McDonald's had lost market share to Burger King and Wendy's. Both competitors scored higher than McDonald's in customer satisfaction surveys. Jack Greenberg, then head of McDonald's USA, decided to make an innovative change to recapture a larger share of the fast-food market. Believing that customers wanted more customized products, he overhauled the company's entire food preparation system by introducing a project called "Made for You." Instead of serving pre-cooked meals, as they had always done in the past, McDonald's began cooking burgers to order—complete with freshly toasted buns. Kitchens were outfitted with expensive new equipment: Pentium III computers to coordinate the orders, "rapid toasters," and temperature-controlled "launching zones" to replace the old heat lamps and holding bins.

However, the reality was that people eat fast food because it is fast, not because it is personalized to individual tastes. The "Made for You" process, not surprisingly, slowed down service and increased customer waiting time to double or triple what it had been previously. In the words of one McDonald's franchisee: "When the factory across the street blows the whistle and one hundred people walk in, you've got to have some food ready. 'Made for You' doesn't allow that." Unfortunately, Greenberg and his leadership team failed to recognize that fact, even after many people both inside and outside the company tried to bring it to his attention. When two mutual fund managers informed Greenberg that the new system was slowing service, he arranged for them to work behind the counter of a McDonald's in their area to witness for themselves the benefits of "Made for You." Instead, their feelings about the service problems were confirmed. Along with many other fund managers, they decided against investing in the stock.[6] The failure of the new strategy at McDonald's shows the dangers of implementing a change based on an inaccurate assessment of customer preferences.

### Phillips

One of the biggest product failures in business history can be attributed, in large part, to not paying enough attention to customers. When Philips, the giant Dutch electronics group, decided to develop a combination video machine, music system, game player, and teaching tool, it was confident that it could conquer the U.S. market. It dedicated its world-class research staff and billions of dollars to the project, only to wind up with a spectacular flop. What happened? For one thing, Philips priced itself out of the market. Although American marketing people warned that pricing would be important, the Dutch executives adamantly refused to accept the idea that they would have to sell the players at a loss and make their money on the software instead. The new game (called the CD-I) provided many more functions than games sold by Sega or Nintendo, but it cost more than twice as much and consumers were generally reluctant to spend that kind of money. Perhaps an even worse obstacle was that the system was so complicated it required a thirty-minute demonstration before people could use it. It is not clear how much Philips wound up losing on the CD-I, but estimates start at $1 billion.[7]

## Examples of Successful Adaptation

Four organizations that provide examples of successful adaptation include Southwest Airlines, Dell Computers, Maxygen, and IBM.

### Southwest Airlines

Southwest Airlines continually demonstrates its flexibility and ability to respond as industry conditions warrant. The company does not hesitate to make tactical changes without losing sight of its core competencies or disrupting its image. For the first time since its founding, Southwest is facing basic changes to its operational style. The airline's route map, for instance, is not just growing, but is evolving. Long known for its basic short-run flights, Southwest now offers nonstop transcontinental service, from Los Angeles to Baltimore. The push into longer flights was initiated in reaction to increased federal travel taxes (which represent a bigger share of short-haul fares) and delays resulting from changes in airport security procedures.[8]

Another change caused by increased airport security was the switch from reusable plastic boarding cards to printed boarding passes. Although this change may not seem significant, the plastic boarding cards gave the ground staff more time for complex station service. In response, check-in-only kiosks are being introduced.[9] Even Southwest's famously cheerful employee culture is able to roll with the punches. The terrorist attacks on September 11, 2001, put President Colleen Barrett in the position of telling her jocular employees to cool it. "For the first time ever since our inception, I believe, I actually put out a request that we needed to basically squash our humor for a while. My feeling was that emotions were very raw and not receptive to Southwest's style," Barrett said.[10]

### Dell Computers

Dell Computers has been able to modify its business model in response to changes in the external environment while continuing to leverage its core competency. Although focusing on process improvement may keep Dell ahead of its rivals, it is unlikely to drive the kind of revenue growth the stock market has come to expect from the company. Faced with a mature PC market, the computer maker has extended its products to include networking switches, handheld computers, and printers. Dell has even expanded its definition of semi-custom "commodities" to encompass enterprise computing and professional services. Dell believes the attention to processes that has worked so well in manufacturing can be extended to these services. "We are in effect commoditizing services," he says. "There is no reason why this can't occur."[11] Dell has also demonstrated a willingness to adopt best practices that deviate from its basic strategy of selling its wares through its website or over the phone. In 2002 the company supplemented this marketing strategy by opening sales kiosks at malls, supermarkets, airports, and retail chains. The kiosk idea was successfully used by Dell in Japan, then adopted for use in the United States.[12]

### Maxygen

Maxygen, a biotech company that was spun off from a Glaxo Wellcome subsidiary, provides another example of successful adaptation. Maxygen is part of an industry where the frequency and the speed of change make adaptation a critical capability for survival. Researchers have a result in mind, but rather than trying to engineer an outcome, they let the results emerge. In its search for molecules that might be suitable for commercial applications, Maxygen breeds a whole population of biological molecules, and using their state-of-the-art technology, the molecules are screened to select the ones that perform the best according to the criteria that were set. Maxygen's business model is similar to its evolutionary research model, and top management has remained opportunistic and adaptive in terms of its business strategy. Rather than setting out to capture a specific market, they let the market determine where their scientific capabilities and core technology should be applied. Their highly adaptive approach (called "planned opportunism") describes an organization that is always alert to change and ready to respond.[13]

## IBM

As the external environment changes in significant ways, a company may find that it is necessary to emphasize a different core competency or develop new ones. IBM appears to be succeeding in its attempt to transform itself from a producer of computer and software to a one-stop provider of all the information technology needs of its clients. The new CEO, Sam Palmisano, feels confident that there is a unique opportunity to help clients integrate the IT processes of their divisions and link them to suppliers, partners, and customers. Instead of just selling computers to customers, IBM now provides IT services as needed, on a variable, pay-as-you-go basis, sometimes from remote locations. Such Fortune 500 firms as American Express and JPMorgan Chase have already signed on for the service.[14]

## Reasons for Success and Failure

Adaptation usually requires implementing a large-scale organizational change. Implementing major change is difficult, and there are several reasons why an organization may be unable to do it successfully.

### Lack of Innovative Ideas

One reason for poor adaptation by an organization is an inability to develop innovative ideas. Responding to external threats and opportunities often requires the organization to come up with a creative approach. Identifying creative ideas is essential, and many organizations have difficulty getting their members to "think outside the box." Creative ideas, however, are not enough. They must also be relevant for the challenge facing the organization. Without a clear vision of desired outcomes and a good strategy to attain them, it is unlikely that an organization will be able to adapt successfully to a turbulent environment full of external threats.

While most organizations at least pay lip service to the importance and benefits of innovation, their very nature often creates barriers to innovation rather than fostering and encouraging it. A global research project conducted by Accenture surveyed more than eight hundred executives in the private, public, and nonprofit sectors and found that the majority of them considered innovation the key to the overall success of their organizations, but only 40 percent of the executives thought their organizations were sufficiently innovative. The study also found that 75 percent of executives blamed the lack of innovation on internal structural problems, 71 percent of executives said aversion to risk and fear of failure stop people from acting like entrepreneurs, and over half the executives admitted that their organizations lack entrepreneurial role models and that leaders do not encourage taking risks.[15]

Innovation takes time to come to fruition, and it generally involves some form of trial and error, rather than yielding results right from the start. To determine the feasibility of a new approach, it may be necessary to support costly, time-consuming efforts without seeing any payoff for some time. With the fierce competition for scarce resources that is the norm within many corporations and the culture of hoarding rather than sharing knowledge that frequently exists, innovative ideas can wither for lack of support. "The way we do things around here" syndrome that prevails in so many organizations has probably defeated more innovators than the tech-nical problems they faced.

### Failure to Implement Innovations

After relevant creative ideas are identified, they must be implemented, and this essential second step can be a major obsta-cle for organizations. A study of 1,000 U.S. and European compa-nies found that, although many managers expressed satisfaction with their operating abilities, they were dissatisfied with their abil-ity to implement change.[16] In addition, an extensive global study by Clayton Christensen,[17] author of *The Innovator's Dilemma*, found that many important innovations that originated in established organizations were not commercialized in those organizations. A classic example is Xerox and its Palo Alto Research Center (PARC). The graphical user interface (GUI) and the Ethernet were devel-oped there, but they were not considered promising businesses for Xerox, which was focused on high-speed printers and copiers. The technologies languished inside Xerox only to be commercialized by other companies such as Apple Computer.[18]

Another example of failure to implement innovations is pro-vided by Bowmar. Although it developed the first handheld calcu-lator, Bomar was unable to improve the product or mass-produce it. The market for calculators was soon dominated by other compa-nies that could adapt more rapidly.[19]

### Poor Timing in Implementing Innovations

When a company introduces an innovative product or service helps to determine whether it is a success or a failure. There are risks in "rushing to market" with a new product, but there are also risks in waiting until competitors "test the waters." By waiting a company may lose the potential advantage of being the one to define how customers perceive the product or service. For example,

Motorola resisted going from analogue to digital cellular phones and lost its commanding lead in this market.[20]

On the other hand, if a company moves too quickly it may not be possible to incorporate necessary technical features in the design of the product. One example of the dangers of innovation is provided by Sony's dismal experience with the Beta format in videotapes.[21] Another example is Kodak's experience with digital photography. In 1996 Kodak was faced with the threat digital photography presented to its core business in film photography. George Fisher—the CEO at the time—invested more than $2 billion in R&D for digital imaging. Unfortunately, Fisher and his team were so worried about the threat posed by the new technology they spent much of the money before they knew how the market would develop. Competitors were more successful, because they developed products based on home storage and home printing capabilities that drove the development of digital photography.[22]

### Inadequate Assessment of the Market

Some innovations fail because the company did not adequately assess demand and determine the needs and preferences of potential customers. Motorola's Iridium cell phone system provides an example of the risks of entering a new market without an accurate assessment of market demand. Motorola spent $5 billion to launch sixty-six satellites that would enable users to make a call from anywhere in the world. Unfortunately, as one commentator observed, "It was solving a problem that not many of us had." In addition, the phone weighed three pounds and cost $3,000. Users also needed a clear line of sight between the phone and one of the satellites, which meant it could not be used indoors. In 1999, Iridium went bankrupt, costing Motorola nearly $45 billion. The investment group that purchased Iridium was able to reposition the satellite cell phone as a secure communication device for military use, but this market was considerable different from the one initially envisioned by Motorola.[23]

Another failed innovation was the effort by Webvan Group Inc. to sell online groceries for home delivery. The new dot-com startup spent more than $1 billion to build distribution centers and implement its strategy of quickly expanding to serve a national market, only to file for bankruptcy in July of 2001. The company greatly overestimated market demand for e-groceries. Around the time Webvan was ramping up service, a study by the research firm Greenfield Online found that nearly 80 percent of all shoppers were ruled out as potential customers. Moreover, given the distribution problems and extra costs associated with home delivery of groceries, in order to achieve an acceptable profit margin Webvan needed to find a retail partner that could buy groceries at high volume prices.[24]

## Poor Strategic Fit

A key factor that affects an organization's ability to adapt is the match between its core competencies and the external opportunities, which is sometimes called *strategic fit*.[25] The right strategic fit can take different forms, and it is not just a matter of finding a niche market for unique products or services. A good strategic fit may involve the company's ability to deliver a standard type of product or service at a price that is much lower than any competitor, without any decrease in quality or customer service. For example, the products sold at Wal-Mart are no different from ones found at other retail store chains, but the prices are usually lower.

The importance of a good strategic fit can be seen when companies attempt to develop new products for which they lack the requisite competencies or try to enter markets they do not understand. Significant financial loss is the likely result.[26,27] When Nasser was the CEO of Ford, his intense interest in the Internet seemingly made him forget that the company's historical strength was in making cars and trucks that people would want to buy. Instead of focusing on the strengths and resources at its command to adapt to customer needs and marketplace changes, he appeared determined to transform Ford into a different kind of company. After Bill Ford replaced Nasser as CEO, most of the new ventures Nasser launched were divested in order to focus the company on its core competencies. In a similar move, one of Ghosn's first actions when he took over at Nissan was to divest non-core businesses.[28]

Strategic fit has implications not only for successful adaptation to the environment, but also for human relations and resources. It is the basis for developing a compelling vision that will attract employees and keep them motivated to attain the vision. People want to feel that they belong to a company with a strong identity, and only then can they feel real commitment to its goals. So maintaining strategic focus while adapting to changes in the environment is yet another balancing act that leaders need to perform. As an article in the *Harvard Business Review* phrased it, "It may sound paradoxical, but rapid change requires that companies have a stable center."[29]

### Resistance to Change

Attempts to implement an innovative strategy or process within an organization often fail because there is strong resistance to change by some members of the organization, which may include some of the leaders. When a major change is proposed, it will elicit strong emotions, including enthusiasm from some people and resentment or anxiety by others. Although often unpleasant, resistance is a normal human reaction that gives people time to psychologically regain balance and a sense of control. People need the opportunity to express their negative feelings about the dislocation and disruptions of change. The emotions do not disappear simply because they are not expressed, and they are likely to surface later as even bigger obstacles to change. There are many reasons for resisting change, and it is easier to deal with resistance if you can determine the reasons for it.

Resistance to a proposed change is more likely when the current way of doing things has been successful and there is no clear evidence of serious problems with it. The signs of developing problems are usually ambiguous at the early stages, and it is easy for people to ignore or discount them. Even when a problem is finally recognized, the usual response is to make incremental adjustments in the present strategy and do more of the same things, rather than doing something different. Another basic source of resistance is distrust of the leaders who proposed the change. A change may be resisted if people imagine there are hidden, ominous implications that will come to light at a later time. Mutual mistrust may encourage a leader to be secretive about the reasons for change, which will further increase suspicion and resistance.

A proposed change may also be resisted not because it is seen as unnecessary but because it seems unlikely to succeed. Radical change to the way things are done is often seen as not just difficult but impossible. If earlier change programs have failed, people are even more likely to feel cynical about the new one. Even a change with obvious benefits entails some costs. Regardless of how a change is likely to benefit the organization, there may be resistance from people who might suffer personal loss of income, benefits, or job security. Resources necessary to implement the change may be diverted from other uses, including support for traditional activities. Concerns about costs in relation to benefits may foster resistance, especially when it is not possible to estimate costs and benefits with any accuracy.

On the personal level, change makes some expertise obsolete and requires learning new ways of doing the work. People who lack self-confidence will be reluctant to trade procedures they have mastered for new ones that may prove too difficult to master. In addition, major changes in organizations invariably result in some shift in relative power and status for individuals and groups. New strategies often require expertise not possessed by some of the people currently enjoying high status as problem solvers. People responsible for activities that will be cut back or eliminated will lose status and power, making them more likely to oppose the change. Any change that appears to be inconsistent with strong values and ideals is also likely to be resisted. Threats to a person's values arouse strong emotions that fuel resistance to change. Some people resist change because they do not want to be controlled by others, and attempts to manipulate them or force them to change will elicit resentment and even hostility.

### Inadequate Support by Top Management

Some change initiatives fail because top management has unrealistic expectations about the cost and time needed to implement major change. Leaders frequently underestimate how long a major change will take and how difficult it is for people to endure the stress of the change. When unexpected delays and difficulties are encountered, many change initiatives get derailed. According to Schneider and Goldwasser,[30] studies of major change efforts found that 70 percent of the initiatives were judged not to have met initial expectations. In many cases, senior management underestimated how difficult it would be to implement a successful change. While they spent a lot of time and money on planning change, not enough was spent on successful implementation of change.

## Ways to Enhance Adaptation

The many difficulties involved in fostering adaptation in large organizations make it essential to have a culture with firmly embedded values and beliefs that support innovation and change. Relevant values include flexibility, continuous improvement, initiative, and a quest for excellence. Instead of viewing adaptation as an infrequent reaction to dramatic, one-time events, it is better for people to view it as a continuous process of adjustment that involves a combination of many, frequent incremental improvements and occasional major changes. In organizations with this type of culture, new ideas are nurtured and promoted, information is widely and freely shared, and people and systems are flexible and ready to respond to changes when they occur.

Collective learning should also be a key value in the organization culture. In "learning organizations" there is a high level of activity to develop and refine shared conceptual tools and mental models for understanding how things work, how to adapt to the environment, and how to achieve the organization's objectives. In addition, resources are invested to promote individual learning and skill development at all levels. The importance of innovation and learning is reflected in the reward and appraisal systems. People at all levels are empowered to deal with problems and find better ways of doing the work. Top management creates and sustains processes to nurture ideas and support changes initiated by people at lower levels in the organization. Knowledge is diffused and made available to anyone who needs it, and people are encouraged to apply it to their work.

Leaders can influence the organization culture over time by the values they espouse and by their actions, including what they pay attention to, what they recognize and reward, and how they react to problems and mistakes. To create a culture in which innovation and learning are genuinely respected and rewarded, leaders at all levels need to demonstrate in their own behavior an openness to new ideas, a willingness to take risks, and a total commitment to continuous learning.

In addition to their influence on organizational culture, leaders can use specific behaviors to facilitate innovation and adaptation. These behaviors include monitoring the environment and analyzing events and trends, strategic planning, envisioning change, building support for change, implementing change, encouraging innovative thinking, and facilitating collective learning. As with the other leadership behaviors discussed in this book, they may take different forms, depending on whether a senior executive, a middle manager, or a lower-level leader is using them, but their essential nature remains the same.

Leaders also use programs, management systems, and structural features to determine what types of changes are desirable and to facilitate innovation and collective learning. Examples of widely used approaches include intrapreneurship programs, external bench-marking, programs to assess customer preferences, rewards and recognition for innovation, programs to facilitate collective learn-ing, and knowledge management systems. Structural arrangements include facilities designed to encourage innovative thinking and the use of cross-functional teams for product development. Exter-nal initiatives to facilitate growth and diversification include acqui-sitions and strategic alliances.

## Conclusions

The challenge of adapting to changes in the external environment is a complex, multi-faceted one. There are many pitfalls, and fail-ure to adapt in a timely way is usually fatal for the organization. Leaders at all levels have an important responsibility to encourage and facilitate processes essential for adaptation, such as recognition of threats and opportunities, collective learning, and innovation. As leaders help an organization adapt to the environment, they must also determine how to adapt their own behavior to the ever-changing demands of the situation. Direct and indirect forms of leadership that can be used to improve adaptation will be described in the next two chapters.

*Chapter 6*

# Leader Behaviors to Enhance Adaptation

Some types of leader behaviors are especially relevant for facilitating an organization's adaptation to the external environment. These behaviors include monitoring the environment, strategic planning, envisioning change, building support for change, implementing change, encouraging innovative thinking, and facilitating collective learning. In this chapter we provide guidelines for using these behaviors more effectively.

## Monitoring the Environment

Monitoring the environment involves collecting and analyzing information about opportunities and threats in the external environment and identifying trends and opportunities to enhance business performance. The focus of external monitoring should be on the sectors of the environment on which the work unit is highly dependent (e.g., clients and customers, suppliers, competitors, and government agencies). A summary of guidelines for effective external monitoring is shown in Table 6.1.

The appropriate amount of external monitoring depends on the amount of change and turbulence in the external environment. More external monitoring is appropriate if the work unit is highly dependent on the actions of clients, customers, suppliers, subcontractors, or joint venture partners. Likewise, more external monitoring is needed when conditions are rapidly changing and hard to predict, and when the organization faces severe competition or other external threats. Monitoring the environment is especially

**Table 6.1. Guidelines for Monitoring the External Environment**

- Identify relevant types of information about the environment
- Monitor events in diverse sectors of the environment
- Identify independent sources of information about the environment
- Learn what clients and customers need and want
- Learn about the products, services, and activities of competitors

relevant when the business climate is changing rapidly and strategies and tactics need to be continually reassessed and adjusted to fit newly evolving conditions. External monitoring is also important when the organization is entering a new market or developing a new product or service for a highly competitive market.

Monitoring of the environment is often assumed to be the province of top executives, the people who are in direct contact with customers, such as sales representatives and customer service representatives, often learn earlier about changes in customer needs or competitor actions. Thus, environmental scanning and interpretation of events should not be left entirely to the CEO and other top executives. When leaders at all levels are helping to monitor the environment, the organization will be better able to identify threats and opportunities.[1]

George Devlin's experience at Compaq illustrates this point. Before the company was acquired by Hewlett-Packard, Devlin was managing director and vice president for Compaq's operations in Scotland. At that time competition from Dell was increasing, and Devlin realized that customers would not continue to pay a premium for Compaq's quality, reliability, and service. Increased sales volume was masking an increase in costs, and Devlin was not successful in convincing top management at Compaq headquarters in Houston that the company must take steps to reduce costs and improve quality. He decided he had to take action anyway and replaced the traditional assembly line system with cell manufacturing, which has teams of people respon-

sible for a product from start to finish. This change was very successful in raising productivity.[2]

Many important environmental events must be monitored,
and the abundance of available information about the environment presents a dilemma. Collecting too much information can
be costly, and the amount of information that is available can be
overwhelming to people who are trying to make sense of it. On
the other hand, a narrow focus is likely to overlook important
trends and developments. One approach is to start each scanning
cycle with a broad perspective that examines all sectors to detect
relevant trends, identify the issues in each sector that will have
an impact on the organization, then monitor and analyze these
issues more closely during the year. Involving others in the process
of gathering and interpreting the information can reduce the burden and difficulty of monitoring the external environment and
sorting through the data, while also increasing the likelihood of
accurate interpretation. Members of the organization who have
contact with clients, customers, suppliers, and other important
outsiders should participate in collecting and analyzing data and
identifying appropriate actions to respond to trends and developments. This participation will help develop an orientation to con-
tinuously evaluate and improve the organization's products, services,
and processes.

As in the case of monitoring operations, it is best not to rely on
a single source of information about an important aspect of the
external environment. To avoid personal bias in the selection and
interpretation of information and the distortion of information by
others to influence decision making, it is helpful to use independent sources of information and remain alert for new sources.
External monitoring is facilitated by a network of people who can
provide timely and relevant information about events that may
affect the organization.

It is essential to learn about the specific needs of customers and
clients and how these needs are likely to change in coming years.
The reaction of customers and clients to the company's products

and services should be assessed on a regular basis. This information can be collected in several ways, including the use of customer surveys, focus groups, customer panels, and the use of cross-functional teams that meet with customers and clients to get ideas for product or service improvements. Sometimes it is also useful to invite representatives from major customers and clients to visit your facilities and participate in problem-solving meetings with design and production personnel.

It is not unusual for people in an organization to focus on the positive features of their own products or services and assume they are better than those of competitors. External monitoring can be used to obtain comparative information about the products and services of competitors, and this information can be used to identify the strengths and weaknesses of your own products and services. Some ways to get this information include using a competitor's products and services yourself to identify strengths and weaknesses; talking to salespeople, researchers, and product managers who are likely sources for this type of information; conducting comparative testing of products or services from different companies; visiting the store or facilities of competitors to identify strengths and weaknesses; and subscribing to online data services, newspapers, and industry publications to learn about changes in competitor products or services.

## Strategic Planning

Strategy is a plan or blueprint for carrying out the organization's mission and attaining long-term objectives. It involves decisions about the type of products and services to offer, the markets in which to compete, ways to influence customers and clients, and ways to obtain financial resources for the organization (e.g., stocks, bonds, loans, donations, sales of assets). A relevant strategy takes into account changes in the external environment, and it is realistic in terms of the organization's strengths and weaknesses.

Some examples of competitive strategies for business corporations include: (1) selling products and services at the lowest price;

(2) having superior quality at a moderate price; (3) providing a unique product or service in a segment of the market ignored by competing organizations (niche strategy); (4) providing exceptional customer service; (5) having the most innovative products or services; and (6) being the most flexible in customizing products or services to meet each client's needs. It is feasible to pursue a mix of strategies at the same time, such as providing the least expensive standard product or service as well as the best customized versions. However, mixed strategies usually create more problems in managing and coordinating operations. A competitive strategy may also involve the way the product or service is produced, delivered, marketed, financed, and guaranteed.

Strategic planning is the process of determining where you are, where you want to be in the future, and how you will get from here to there. The process includes setting strategic objectives, identifying tactics and actions for attaining them, and determining the resources and actions needed to implement the strategies. While senior management drives the process and takes the ultimate responsibility for the final strategic decisions, the most successful leaders find ways to involve people throughout the organization in the strategic planning process. This wider participation aims to ensure that the formal plans truly reflect the realities of the marketplace and have the full understanding and support of people at all levels.

Strategic planning is one of the most difficult responsibilities of leaders. There is no simple answer on how to do it effectively, and it is beyond the scope of this book to provide a detailed description of how to do it. With that in mind, however, we have provided, in Table 6.2, a summary of guidelines for effective strategic planning based on a review of the practitioner and academic literature on the topic.

A review of the research on strategic planning found support for the idea that it improves an organization's performance.[3] The researchers also found that strategic planning was more important as the complexity and ambiguity of the environment increased.

## Table 6.2. Guidelines for Strategic Planning

- Determine long-term objectives and priorities
- Assess current strengths and weaknesses
- Identify strategies that capitalize on core competencies
- Evaluate the need for a change in strategy
- Determine the likely benefits and costs of a new strategy

However, a new or revised strategy will not improve organizational performance unless it is relevant and feasible. The likelihood an organization will be able to achieve a competitive advantage is determined, in part, by its ability to identify and leverage its core competencies—the knowledge and capability to carry out a particular type of activity. A core competency usually involves a combination of technical expertise and application skills. For example, a core competency for Gore is their expertise with a special type of material (Goretex) and their capability to discover and exploit new uses for this material. Core competencies provide a potential source of continuing competitive advantage if they are used to provide innovative, high-quality products and services that cannot be easily copied or duplicated by competitors.

The competitive advantage to be gained from current strengths depends on how long they will last and how difficult they are for competitors to overcome or duplicate. For example, a pharmaceutical company that has a new, patented drug that is better and cheaper than any alternative has a strong competitive advantage that will likely continue for several years. In contrast, a service company that devises a new promotion such as special discounts may only enjoy its competitive advantage for as long as it takes competitors to imitate it. An organization that is first into a market has an advantage, but only if it is difficult for competitors to follow quickly. A product or service that is very costly to develop but easy and cheap to duplicate offers little advantage if competitors can set a lower price and quickly dominate the market. Capabilities should be evaluated together, not in isolation. A unique resource, such as an improved product or process, may offer no competitive advantage if organizational weaknesses or external constraints prevent it from being used effectively.

Core competencies can be the key to the future success of an organization that is already prosperous; they help it remain competitive in its current business and enable it to diversify into new businesses. Canon's core competency in optics, acquired as a producer of quality cameras, enabled the company to become a successful producer of copiers, fax machines, semiconductor lithographic equipment, and specialized video systems, while continuing to be a successful producer of cameras and the first to develop a microprocessor-controlled camera. Honda's competence in engineering and production of engines enabled the company to be a successful producer of automobiles, motorcycles, lawnmowers, and offroad vehicles. Competence in display systems, which involves knowledge of microprocessor design, ultra-thin precision casing, material science, and miniaturization, has enabled Casio to be successful in such diverse businesses as calculators, miniature television sets, digital watches, monitors for laptop computers, and automotive dashboards.[4]

Identification of core competencies is especially important for the revitalization of an organization with declining performance. When Michael Eisner took over as the CEO of Walt Disney, the company was faltering and in danger of a takeover. Under his leadership, Disney identified the core competency of its unique combination of creative, engineering, and marketing skills involved in bringing to life the fantasies of people in different forms of entertainment, such as film, music, toys, and theme parks, and built a new strategy around them to become an international entertainment powerhouse.[5]

Sometimes it is necessary to redefine the mission of the organization to include new activities that are relevant for the environment and the organization's core competencies. For example, the DeVilbiss Company began at the turn of the century as a maker of perfume atomizers. Had they continued to define their business as such, they would have been out of business by now. However, they were able to broaden their definition of their product to encompass several uses of the basic spray technology. DeVilbiss now produces equipment used in automobile factories to paint cars, as well as components for compressors and respirators.[6] Even when a major change in strategy is not necessary to deal with a crisis, flexible leaders should continue to look for opportunities to improve the organization. Effective organizations exploit opportunities to enhance core competencies and use them to enter new businesses.

Even the most carefully formulated strategic plans change and evolve as they are tested for their strategic fit with customers and markets. A strategic plan is based on hypotheses about what will happen in the future. These hypotheses are tested and revised based on feedback from customers and new information about developments in the market environment. The actions and reactions of competitors also affect the feasibility of strategic plans. Out of this testing process, new strategies evolve. As front-line employees interact with customers and find new ways of responding to their needs, these discoveries can then evolve into more formal strategies. In this sense, strategy involves action as well as planning, and sometimes the doing comes before the planning.[7] Effective leaders avoid the trap of developing strategies that are merely reactive, and they are able to uncover new possibilities that may ultimately transform their companies and even their industries.

## Envisioning Change

Painting a vivid, appealing picture of what you want to accomplish or become helps to communicate the desired outcomes of a change initiative in a way that is understandable, meaningful, and inspiring. Having a clear, appealing picture of a potential future outcome increases the likelihood it will be achieved. Envisioning change is about putting opportunities and threats to the organization in context and clarifying how the organization needs to be different and why. A variety of elements may be included in the vision, such as strategic objectives, key values for the company, general approaches for attaining the vision, slogans and symbols, and a description of what it will mean to people when attained. Table 6.3 outlines the actions leaders can take to envision and communicate change.

It is extremely difficult to develop a compelling vision of change, and it cannot be generated by a mechanical formula. Envisioning change is the joint product of experience, personal interests, intuition, and circumstances that create a window of opportunity.[8] To develop a compelling vision, it is essential to have a solid understanding of the dynamics of the business and the factors that determine its performance (its operations, products, services, markets, competitors, and social-political environment), its culture (shared beliefs and assumptions about the world and the organization's place in it), and the underlying needs and values of employees and other stakeholders. In order to prepare a clear and concise message that will help people understand why change is necessary and beneficial, it is helpful to consider the following questions: What will change? What events and trends are driving the need for change? Why is this change important to make? What are the anticipated benefits of this change? How is it consistent with the organization's strategy? What impact will it have on day-to-day activities?

To engage people with a vision, it is essential to link it to their ideals, values, and aspirations. However, gaining this insight can be difficult because people may be unwilling or unable to explain what is really important to them. Leaders can become more aware of

### Table 6.3. Guidelines for Envisioning Change

- Develop a clear picture of what the organization can accomplish or become
- Link proposed changes to ideals, values, and aspirations
- Articulate the vision with enthusiasm and vivid language
- Express optimism and confidence that the vision can be achieved

employee needs by being accessible to people at all levels of the organization, observing employee behavior, participating in discussions with employees, and attending to more subtle clues (e.g., "water cooler" conversation, body language, and facial reactions). Even better is to involve people at all levels in developing the themes that will be the core of the vision. When people participate in formulating the vision, they are much more likely to embrace it and strive to make it happen.

The work Gary Hamel did with Nokia in 1997 demonstrates how a leader can involve people in envisioning change. He involved hundreds of people at all levels of the organization in imagining "what could be." Hamel asked them to respond to questions about how to serve new customer needs, how to change the economics of the industry and how to use Nokia's competencies in a different way. Senior management then reviewed all the ideas and tried to find broad themes that could be used to give overall direction to the company. Three main themes came out of this exercise. One theme was how to humanize technology and make it more user friendly. Another theme was how to create seamless solutions, such as offering telephone companies an integrated package of mobile phones, the software, and network hardware necessary to provide desired services. A third theme was how to think about the phone as a virtual presence that would enable it to serve many purposes, such as a credit card or security device. Over the next six years Nokia focused on these three themes, and its people were able to develop very innovative ways to use the phone.[9]

In times of great change, people look to the leader for direction and signs that the organization has selected the right course of action. Therefore, it is essential to communicate personal confidence that the vision can be achieved and the benefits will be worth the short-term sacrifices. Leaders can convey a message of confidence and optimism through the type of language they use and by consistent actions to demonstrate their conviction and support of the vision.

## Building Support for Change

Although most people would agree that change is essential if an organization is to adapt, grow, and remain competitive, change often produces anxiety and resistance. For people to support change, they must see it as necessary and feasible. Leaders build support for change by explaining the urgent need for change, building a broad coalition of supporters, identifying likely opponents and reasons for their resistance, and taking action to deal with resistance.

The complex task of persuading people to support major change in an organization is too big a job for a single leader. It is essential to build a coalition of supporters inside and outside the organization. The external members could include labor union leaders, important clients, officials of government agencies, or executives of financial institutions. To succeed in gaining approval and support for a proposed change, a leader needs to understand how people perceive it and feel about it and whether they are likely to be supporters or opponents. Guidelines for building support for change are provided in Table 6.4.

To build support for proposed changes and overcome resistance, it is essential to explain why they are necessary and to create a sense of urgency about them. For example, it is sometimes useful to explain why not changing will eventually be more costly than changing now. The head of one of Pfizer's U.S. Global Research and Development sites was faced with the need to gain support for change quickly. Not only was Pfizer acquiring Pharmacia, but Hank

Table 6.4. Guidelines for Building Support for Change

- Explain the urgent need for change
- Identify the necessary approvals for a proposed change
- Identify likely supporters and build a broad coalition of supporters
- Identify likely opponents, the reasons for resistance, and ways to deal with resistance

McKinnell, Pfizer's CEO, was asking the global R&D group to double productivity. In order to help people understand the urgent need for this change, the site head shared the business case with her team during a planning meeting. She started by describing how the economics of the pharmaceutical industry were changing and would affect the development of new compounds and the organization's expectations for R&D productivity. She then extended the scenario and described how both success and failure would affect each of them personally in terms of job security and compensation. This information made it unmistakably clear why Pfizer needed to approach the business differently and what the benefit would be to them personally.

At Intel, in order to help people understand the urgency of the need to decrease the heat generated by a computer chip as it got smaller, Pat Gelsinger, vice president and chief technology officer, used metaphors and symbolic language to help make his point. He informed people that the amount of heat generated by a chip now was as much as a hot plate. As he extrapolated trends in size reduction, he compared the amount of heat that would be generated to familiar objects (nuclear reactor, rocket nozzle, the sun's surface). The message was clear. If Intel could not figure out a radically different way to build chips, progress would come to a stop.[10]

People who like the traditional way of doing something and are skeptical about a controversial new approach may be willing to participate in an experiment on a small scale to evaluate it. For example, a new process can be implemented on a small scale in one division or facility on an experimental basis. If successful, a change that is carried out in one part of the organization can help stimulate similar changes throughout the organization, even when it is necessary to adapt the changes to the unique needs of each subunit.

Andersen Corporation, a U.S. window manufacturer, wanted to change from a functional structure to a product structure to shorten material flow and move to continuous flow manufacturing. Because this was such a dramatic change from the way people were used to doing things, rather than implementing the idea across the plant they experimented in two areas: fabrication and assembly. The hope was that a limited initiative would provide an understanding of the benefits as well as the extent of change the whole company would have to make. The experiment achieved its objective, and it also provided people experience in implementing the concept.[11]

To help overcome resistance and build support for change, it must be introduced through candid and continuous communication. Many leaders find that a key factor in building support is holding formal and informal meetings throughout the change process to ensure that two-way communication is constant and ongoing. Charles Bennett, a Mobil production foreman on a drilling platform off the Gulf Coast, is an example of a front-line manager who saw the need for change and helped his team prepare for it through continual communication. In the face of layoffs due to Mobil's poor cost position, Bennett repeatedly shared information with his crew about how management saw the business, its actual cost position compared to the competition, and what they could do to affect those indicators. Using hard data and showing how cost savings equaled jobs, he was able to motivate his team to focus on becoming the lowest cost producer in order to take business away from competitors.[12]

## Implementing Change

Implementing large-scale change involves a process of experimentation and learning, because it is impossible to anticipate all the problems or prepare detailed plans for how to carry out all the aspects of the change. A change program is less likely to be successful if a top-level leader tries to dictate in detail how it will be implemented in each part of the organization. Authority to make decisions and deal with problems should be delegated to the leaders who are responsible for implementing change in their subunits. After the process of change is underway, the primary leadership role for top management is to provide encouragement, support, and necessary resources to other leaders who are serving as change agents and to guide and coordinate change efforts across different subunits of the organization. Direct leadership behaviors that facilitate implementation of change include filling key positions with competent change agents, preparing people to adjust to change and cope with the pain of making a transition, providing opportunities to celebrate early successes, keeping people informed about the progress of the change, and ensuring that leaders at all levels demonstrate continued commitment to the change. Guidelines for implementing change are summarized in Table 6.5.

The objectives of a change are more likely to be achieved if the people who will be affected and who have relevant knowledge are involved in developing a plan for implementing the change. For example when a large Eastern U.S.-based pharmaceutical company needed to improve overall operating efficiencies and reduce costs, top management decided to sell or close some of their manufacturing facilities. It was uncertain whether they would be able to find a buyer for one plant in New York, which placed them in a quandary. They had to keep production levels up to fulfill their commitments to internal clients, but it was only fair to let employees know that their jobs might be in jeopardy. In the pharmaceutical industry, production quality is obviously critical. People have to follow strict protocols and maintain high standards. The challenge facing the company was to let people know they might need to look for new jobs soon, yet retain key employees and maintain high levels of morale and productivity during the transition. To address this issue,

#### Table 6.5. Guidelines for Implementing Change

- Fill key positions with competent change agents
- Prepare people to adjust to change and cope with the pain
- Provide opportunities to celebrate early successes
- Keep people informed about the progress of change
- Demonstrate continued commitment to change

the top management developed a plan that allowed for the possibility of either selling the plant or closing it, while still maintaining production levels. Once this plan was formulated, a series of meeting were held. The first meetings were with the next level of managers to get their commitment to the plan and clarify what they needed to do to ensure its success. The next set of meetings was to communicate the plan to the rest of the plant's employees, clarify the likely implications for them, and make clear their role in maintaining quality and making the plant look desirable for sale.

The "change agents" who are responsible for implementing change must support it with their actions as well as their words. They should be people who are committed to the vision for the change and have the ability to communicate it clearly. Whenever people in key positions are unwilling to implement a change after it has been approved, they should be replaced. If left in place, these opponents may go beyond passive resistance and use political tactics in an effort to block additional change. Pockets of resistance can acquire sufficient strength to prevent the new strategy from being implemented successfully. Acting quickly to remove opponents who symbolize the old order also signals that you are serious about the change.

Making sure people experience successful progress in the early stages of the new project or change initiative can increase their confidence and optimism. Also, skeptics are likely to become supporters after they see evidence of progress in initial efforts to do things a new way. To help ensure there will be evidence of early success, a complex and challenging activity can be broken into small steps with short-term goals that do not appear too difficult. People are more willing to undertake an activity if they perceive that their efforts are likely to be successful and that the cost of failure would not be great. As the initial steps or goals are accomplished, people experience success and gain self-confidence. Then they are more willing to try for larger wins and to invest more resources in the effort.[13]

When a new strategy does not require many visible changes in the early stages of implementation, people will begin to wonder whether the effort has died and if things are going back to the way they were. People will be more enthusiastic and optimistic if they know that the change initiative is progressing successfully. One way to convey a sense of progress is to communicate what steps have been initiated, what changes have been completed, and what improvements have occurred in performance indicators. Hold ceremonies to announce the inauguration of major activities, to celebrate significant progress or success, and to give people recognition for their contributions and achievements. These celebrations provide an opportunity to increase optimism, build commitment, and strengthen identification with the organizational unit. When obstacles are encountered, explain what they are and what is being done about them. If the implementation plan must be revised, explain why it is necessary. Otherwise, people may interpret any revisions to the plan or schedule as a sign of faltering commitment.

Even enthusiastic change agents are not immune from the difficulties experienced in a long-term change effort. Alternating successes and setbacks may leave people feeling as if they are on an emotional rollercoaster ride. Ambiguity about progress and the recurring discovery of new obstacles increase fatigue and frustration. These negative aspects of change are easier to deal with if people expect them and know how to cope with them. Rather than presenting change as a panacea without any costs or problems, it is better to help people understand what adjustments will be necessary. One approach is to provide a realistic preview of some typical types of problems and difficulties people can expect. For example, ask people who have experienced a similar change to speak about their experiences and what they did to get through the change successfully.

Although responsibility for guiding various aspects of the change can be delegated to other change agents, the leader who is identified as the primary proponent or sponsor of the change must continue to provide the attention and endorsement that signal a commitment to see it through to the end. People look to their leaders for signs of continued commitment to the change objectives and vision. Any indication that the change is no longer viewed as important or feasible may have ripple effects that undermine the change effort. Supporters will be lost and opponents will be encouraged to increase overt resistance. Continued attention and endorsement signal a leader's commitment to see the change initiative through to a successful conclusion.

The leader should persistently promote the vision guiding the change and display optimism that the inevitable setbacks and difficulties will be overcome. The leader must reject easy solutions for dealing with immediate problems when these solutions are inconsistent with the underlying objectives of the change effort. Demonstrating commitment is more than talking about the importance of change. The leader must invest time, effort, and resources in resolving problems and overcoming obstacles. When appropriate, the leader should participate in activities related to the change. For example, attending a special meeting or ceremony relevant to the change sends a clear signal to other people in the organization that the change must be important.

## Encouraging Innovative Thinking

Identifying innovative ways to improve strategies, processes, products, or services is one requirement for successful adaptation, and there are many ways a leader can influence more innovative thinking by employees. The leader can encourage people to look at problems from multiple perspectives, to question implicit assumptions about the work, and to brainstorm better ways to do things. Another approach for encouraging innovative thinking is to set innovation goals for units or individuals. When there is a specific innovation goal for which people will be held accountable, this type of activity is more likely to get the attention and effort it deserves. Guidelines to encourage innovative thinking are provided in Table 6.6.

It is common for people to have many implicit assumptions of which they may not be fully aware, and these assumptions bias how

| Table 6.6. Guidelines for Encouraging Innovative Thinking |
| --- |
| • Encourage people to question assumptions about the work |
| • Encourage people to look at problems from different perspectives |
| • Encourage people to spend time on developing innovative ideas |
| • Provide rewards and recognition for innovative ideas |

they interpret events and approach their work. Such assumptions are usually part of a person's "mental model" about how things work. Mental models provide the context that enables us to make sense of events and of information we receive. However, mental models can also limit our perspective and restrict the possibilities that are considered when we attempt to solve a problem. Special activities such as contests can be very helpful in encouraging employees to question their assumptions and consider whether established procedures are really necessary.

The Portland, Maine-based Banknorth Group runs a "Stupid Rules" contest, inviting employees to identify corporate rules that just do not make sense. Any employee who "nominates" a rule that the company decides to abandon gets a small cash reward. A good example was the rule that forced customers to wait outside in the cold if they arrived before the bank opened in the morning. Banknorth checked FDIC requirements and found that it was okay to let people in before the official opening time. Now, early arrivals are invited inside and offered a cup of coffee.[14]

Another way to encourage innovative thinking is to have people look at problems from a different perspective. For example, engineers have been trying for years to improve the battery life of computers by focusing on longer-lasting batteries and software solutions that dimmed or shut off the display. The engineers at 3M's Microreplication Technology Center reframed the problem: how to make a display that used less power. With this frame of reference, they turned to a technology used in the 1950s to increase the brightness of overhead projectors and adapted it to magnify the brightness of back-lit flat panel displays. Their Brightness Enhancement Film significantly extends battery life and is being used by numerous laptop manufacturers.[15] Another example is asking people to "stand in the shoes" of the customer or client. Understanding the customer's perspective can be achieved by visiting the customer's office or facility to observe how the product or service is used and to hear what customers like and dislike about it.

Many important innovations are developed informally by employees apart from their regular job activities. A leader should encourage entrepreneurial activity and help employees find the time to pursue ideas for new or improved products, services, and processes. These activities usually require only a small investment of resources in the development stage. Yet the pressure of meeting normal deadlines tends to leave little time for reflective thinking about ways to make things better. One way to ensure people spend time working on creative ideas is to set innovation goals for individuals or teams. Goals can also be set for the application of ideas. Some companies set a goal to develop a specified number of new or improved products each year, or to have new products or services (those introduced within the last three years) account for a specified percentage of sales each year. For example 3M, which develops over five hundred new products a year, uses "stretch objectives" as a way to push employees toward innovation and away from business as usual.[16]

Leaders also have an opportunity to promote more innovative behavior through rewards and recognition. People tend to repeat behavior that is recognized as valuable and rewarded. Recognizing can take the form of positive reinforcement, awards, or recognition ceremonies. In addition, because there can be little innovation without risk taking, it is helpful to recognize attempted innovations that were unsuccessful, thereby sending the message that it is safe to take risks. Recognizing and rewarding efforts to be innovative, whether they are successful or not, encourages people to take risks and try new things.

## Facilitating Collective Learning

More collective learning is likely to occur when an organization has leaders who are flexible, open to new ideas, curious about many things and dedicated to creating a learning environment. An example of such leadership is provided by Cisco's CEO, John Chambers, who actually stepped up support and funding for organization-wide learning when the company was experiencing its first major slump. While some leaders might have decided to cut back on such "discretionary" programs at a time when profits were plunging, Chambers actually saw learning as a path to recovery.[17] Actions leaders can take to facilitate collective learning are summarized in Table 6.7.

To facilitate collective learning, a leader must create an appreciation for flexibility and learning among people at all levels of the organization. Major change will be more acceptable and less disruptive if people develop pride and confidence in their capacity to adapt and learn. Confident people are more likely to view change as an exciting challenge rather than an unpleasant burden. To encourage an appreciation for learning, all practices should be considered temporary and examined regularly to see whether they can be improved or eliminated. Leaders should also encourage people to use learning practices such as after activity reviews, experiments, and benchmarking of performance at other organizations.

Leaders should also encourage the active sharing of ideas and new knowledge in the organization. Secrecy is the enemy of learn-

---

**Table 6.7.  Guidelines for Facilitating Collective Learning**

- Encourage people to experiment systematically with new approaches
- Encourage people to find ways to adapt best practices used elsewhere
- Encourage the active sharing of ideas and new knowledge in the organization
- Encourage the use of after-action reviews to identify lessons learned
- Implement systems to facilitate the diffusion of ideas and new knowledge

---

ing, whereas easy access to information about the organization's operations, including problems and failures, facilitates learning. Leaders should encourage employees with a difficult problem to reach out to other people in the organization and discover how they handled a similar task in the past. The potential benefits of internal knowledge sharing are demonstrated in an incident that occurred at AMP Inc. After John Davis, an AMP manager, conducted an external study of best practices in customer service, he was surprised to discover that some divisions within his own company had already developed effective customer service practices that were exactly what he needed to solve his problem.[18]

Leaders can do several things to encourage the active discussion and sharing of ideas in the organization. One approach is to hold meetings to share ideas and talk about mutual good ways to solve common problems. At Toyota, Takeshi Yoshida, the chief engineer for the 2003 Toyota Corolla, implemented a new approach to planning and engineering in order to cut costs and boost quality. He did not try to tear down silos or put people on special teams. Rather, every month for two years before the car went into production, he brought people together from all parts of the organization to share information. He called it "Oobeya," which means "big, open office," and it is focused on creating more communication among the design, engineering, manufacturing, logistics, and sales groups. Between meetings people kept the discussion going using email and phone calls or set up their own smaller conversations to deal with specific problems.[19]

When innovations are developed in one part of the organization, there are a number of ways to facilitate diffusion of this knowledge to other parts of the organization. After an innovative change has been implemented successfully in one unit, some members of this unit can be transferred to other units to help them implement the same type of change. Seminars and workshops can be conducted by internal experts or outside consultants to teach people how to perform new activities or use new technology. When it is not feasible for people to attend formal training, a team of experts can be dispatched to different sites to demonstrate how to use new procedures. Video and Internet-based conferencing capabilities can also be used to facilitate broad sharing of ideas. Finally, it is important for leaders at all levels to support the effective use of knowledge management systems like the ones described in the next chapter.

## Relationships Among Change-Oriented Behaviors

The leadership behaviors that facilitate adaptation have a synergistic effect and are seldom used on their own. For example, monitoring the environment, envisioning change, and strategic planning are frequently used as a set of interrelated leadership behaviors. The discovery of emerging problems or opportunities as a result of external monitoring is of little consequence unless a leader plans how to deal with them. This information provides the basis for determining how the organization must change to remain competitive. Using the envisioned change and applying the information gathered from external monitoring, strategic plans can be developed or altered to help make the envisioned change a reality. Likewise, monitoring the environment and strategic planning provide much of the context that drives innovation. An understanding of the environment, including markets, customers, competitors, and suppliers, is necessary to recognize and respond to opportunities and threats.

Although the relationship between encouraging innovative thinking and facilitating collective learning seems obvious enough, there is not an automatic synergistic effect. It is possible to encourage innovative thinking but not have new ideas widely shared and implemented in the organization. Thus, it is essential for leaders to encourage and facilitate both the discovery of new knowledge and its diffusion and application in the organization.

Also closely linked are behaviors such as envisioning change, building support for change, and implementing change. It is not enough to explain the need for change or to articulate an appealing vision. To be successful, leaders must build broad support for a proposed change, then guide the processes required to implement the change, which often takes several years of concerted effort.

## Conclusions

Rapid adaptation is relatively more important when the external environment is turbulent and uncertain, and when the organization's strategy emphasizes unique, leading-edge products and services. Adaptation may require small incremental improvements or major changes in products, services, operational processes, and the competitive strategy. Effective leaders assess the external environment to identify threats and opportunities, and they help people interpret events and determine the implications for the organization. These leaders are able to recognize when there is a need for major change, and they know how to develop support from the people who can make change happen. Envisioning a better future and developing a relevant strategy are two ways leaders guide and promote major change in organizations. Since most innovations result from a bottom-up process in large organizations, effective leaders understand how important it is to inspire and empower all members of the organization to learn from experience, develop creative ideas, and share new knowledge across subunit boundaries. Finally, effective leaders understand that implementation of major change is a slow and difficult process that requires their consistent attention to succeed.

*Chapter 7*

# Programs, Systems, and Strategies for Enhancing Adaptation

Most leaders at the senior level can initiate formal programs, management systems, or other approaches to encourage and facilitate collective learning, knowledge management, innovation, and adaptation. In this chapter we briefly describe several widely used approaches to enhance the organization's ability to adapt to the environment, including intrapreneurship programs, benchmarking programs, programs to assess customer preferences, reward and recognition programs, collective learning practices, knowledge management systems, structural arrangements such as the design of subunits and facilities, and the use of acquisitions and strategic alliances.

## Intrepreneurship Programs

Intrepreneurship is the development and commercialization of new and innovative ideas by an individual or team within an established organization. Most successful new product ideas come from individuals who had an obsession about something, or stumbled on new discoveries by accident, or found a use for a product that was intended for a different market.[1] Scotchgard®, for example, was "invented" when a lab assistant at 3M accidentally dropped a bottle that contained a batch of synthetic latex, spilling some on his canvas tennis shoes. He kept trying to wipe it off, only to find that everything he used kept running off the shoe "like water off a duck's back."

New ideas are fragile, and do not have a long life expectancy if they have prolonged exposure to a hostile environment.

Intrapreneurship programs provide an infrastructure and specific guidelines to help ensure people are supported and motivated to develop new ideas that will reach the appropriate target market. Formal programs usually include some or all of the following components: (1) strong commitment from top management to encourage and support new ideas; (2) specific parameters for providing resources at each stage of development; (3) a review process with clear criteria for getting to the next level of approval; (4) recognition and fair rewards for developing innovative ideas, even if not successful; (5) training in skills required to develop innovative ideas; and (6) formation of intrapreneural teams that meet in a location where creativity will not be inhibited.[2]

Establishing a successful intrepreneurship program can be a challenging undertaking, but there are many examples of organizations that have been successful. Johnson Controls, a manufacturer of industrial controls and maker of aircraft cockpits, is a good example of a company that set up a program to nurture and develop promising new ideas. The company encourages people to spend time pursuing new ideas, and it also has a process to facilitate the selection and evaluation of high-potential ideas. At the front end is a series of hurdles that each idea must get past. Early in the process Johnson will have many ideas that get moderate funding to allow them to develop. A cross-functional team within the business unit periodically reviews the ideas as they take shape. When they get to a go-or-no-go decision point, these teams determine whether the idea should continue to receive funding. A lot of ideas are filtered out at this point, and the funding for the remaining ideas is increased. The screening process is repeated several months later, and ideas that survive are selected for serious development by the company. The final stage requires a credible business case in order for the idea to be accepted.[3]

Royal Dutch/Shell used another approach to nurturing and promoting new ideas. In 1996 they implemented the GameChanger initiative to help institutionalize innovation. The GameChanger team was composed of a group of Shell employees who set up a five-day experience aimed at dramatically accelerating the development of new ideas into practical plans for a new business. Over the five days each team presented its idea to a "venture board," whose job was to identify high-potential ideas and allocate funds for the next round of development. Today any employee can give a ten-minute presentation to the GameChanger panel followed by a ten-minute question-and-answer session. Ideas that are approved receive funding. Those that are not are entered into a database to create a repository of innovative ideas to help others shape their ideas or bring new insight to existing ones. GameChanger has produced measurable results; four of Shell's five largest growth initiatives for 1999 had their start in GameChanger.[4]

British Telecom (BT) developed a program called BT Ideas to encourage innovation. As part of the process, BT uses clear criteria for accepting ideas, and there is an initial screening process to help manage information overload. There is also a sympathetic champion or impartial third party to ensure that new ideas receive serious attention. An idea contributor has a chance to develop the idea online with the help of other interested parties. There is also an opportunity to get a share of the financial benefits that result from successful ideas. For ideas that may not be well-articulated, do not have an obvious home, or may be too radical for immediate application, BT uses an Idea Incubator.[5]

## External Benchmarking

Benchmarking is a process used by many companies to enhance adaptation. Benchmarking involves measuring products, services, and practices against the toughest competitors or those companies recognized as industry leaders.[6] By establishing systematic processes of searching for and importing best practices and innovative ideas, a firm can identify new and promising areas for improvement and gaps in critical areas for success. Of course, to facilitate change, the new knowledge has to be applied. Therefore, benchmarking should be used, not as an end, but as a means to an end. As one expert writes, "Gaining knowledge and learning lessons from other companies is not the deliverable. The deliverable is the implementation of real, meaningful change back at the workplace."[7]

Benchmarking is often carried out by special teams of employees with the skills to make systematic comparisons and assessments of processes used in different organizations. As noted by one enthusiast, "Benchmarking teams can sound the alarm when the first signs appear on the horizon that the organization has fallen behind the competition or has failed to take advantage of important operating improvements developed elsewhere. Best practices benchmarking provides executives with the tool, the rationale, and the process to accept change as constant, inevitable, and good."[8]

As it happens, many companies are not especially eager to provide specific information that might threaten their competitive advantage. Thus, companies often conduct benchmarking beyond their immediate group of competitors—and beyond even their own industry. In the early 1990s, for example, Xerox benchmarked American Express for accounts payment, L.L. Bean for order processing, and Florida Power and Light for quality management. In another example, Southwest Airlines wanted a dramatic decrease in the amount of time it took to refuel its airplanes. Since Southwest already had one of the best refueling times in the airline industry, management looked outside the industry for the most efficient refuelers in the world. Adopting the turnaround process used during pit stops in Formula One racing, Southwest reduced the time it takes to refuel a plane from forty minutes to twelve minutes.[9] As these examples show, it is always possible that the latest innovations in technology and business practices may not reside within a company's industry. Looking outside your industry can give you a like comparison while providing fresh ideas and "out-of-the-box" thinking.[10]

Imitating the best practices of others can be a source of innovative ideas, but the relevance of these practices should be carefully evaluated before adopting them. It is important to remember that imitation seldom provides much of a competitive advantage, and it can become a substitute for development of original ideas in the company. It is essential to improve upon the best practices of others and to adapt imported ideas to fit the unique needs of the company. It is also essential to invent new approaches not yet discovered by competitors. Studying what other organizations do is not the only way to acquire knowledge. Other ways include purchasing the right to use specific knowledge or technology, hiring outsiders with special knowledge to fill key positions, using external consultants to provide training in new processes, entering joint ventures that will provide learning opportunities, and acquiring companies with relevant expertise and technology.

## Programs for Understanding Customers

As we discussed in Chapter 5, understanding customer needs and expectations is essential for successful adaptation. Knowledge about the attitudes, values, needs, and perceptions of current and potential customers can be used to determine how the company's products or services can be made more appealing. Many companies use market survey techniques, customer panels, and focus groups to assess the reactions of current customers or the preferences of potential customers. However, it is not just a matter of tracking environmental trends and sales patterns or conducting market surveys. Different types of customers have different needs, preferences can change abruptly, and many customers are not sure themselves what is most important to them. Even an innovative product that is clearly the best one available may fail to elicit adequate sales if potential customers do not understand the benefits or are not willing to pay significantly more for better quality. Thus, descriptive accounts of successful companies have a recurrent theme that involves intensive efforts to get close to customers and understand their needs and desires.[11,12,13]

Some organizations use formal programs to encourage employees to learn about customer perspectives and act on this knowledge.

At Hewlett-Packard, teams of technical and marketing people visit current and former customers to get their suggestions for new products and advice on how existing ones could be improved. The "scanning units" then get together and, based on customer input, identify innovation targets. The program is designed to improve both innovation and efficiency at the same time. The innovation targets are then screened against ten factors the company has found critical to success, and only the most promising innovations are funded.[14]

Some organizations do not have formal programs for assessing customer needs, but efforts to understand customers are encouraged and employees are empowered to pursue promising opportunities. At Autodesk, the world's leading provider of PC computer-aided design software, a highly profitable spinoff, Buzzsaw.com, was born from conversations with customers in the construction business about how they used the company's products. Anne Bonaparte, the Autodesk sales representative, was surprised to hear her customers saying that they did not need any more CAD functionality. Instead, they wanted help getting their construction projects completed. One specific need was a better way for the dozens of participants in a construction project to share their drawings electronically and jointly resolve any problems with them. It seemed obvious from what she had been hearing that a well-designed Internet workspace to facilitate project management would be a huge success in the marketplace. A development team was formed, and it began by researching exactly how the different participants in construction projects worked. An advisory board of six professionals from various aspects of the construction process was formed to make sure that every aspect of the product would be developed with customers' needs in mind. Just one year after Buzzsaw.com was officially introduced in 1999, 20,000 construction projects were already underway through the website. New clients include large corporations such as DuPont and Walt Disney; leading architecture and engineering firms such as Ellerbe

Becket and Skidmore, Owings & Merrill; and many small architectural firms.[15]

## Reward and Recognition Programs

Recognition and reward programs can be used to influence innovative adaptation as well as efficiency and human resources. Many companies use internal reward and recognition programs to identify and recognize centers of excellence and innovation around the organization. These internal award winners are often showcased in internal conferences or "share fairs."

AMP, an electronics company that was acquired by Tyco, brought 1,700 people together at its annual meeting to communicate innovative initiatives and integrated a share fair into the meeting. Units with outstanding practices that might be broadly applicable across the organization set up exhibit booths staffed by people who know the practice well. The people staffing the booths received a great deal of recognition and were able to network with people who wanted to learn more about them.[16]

Another company with an incentive program to reward innovative ideas is Cleco Power. Their "Ideas for Excellence" program offers employees a 5 percent cash reward (up to a maximum of $5,000) for new ideas that lead to quantifiable savings. When Clark Bordelon, a senior engineering project coordinator, proposed that the company use an empty fuel tank already onsite to meet its need for additional storage space, rather than building additional facilities, Cleco saved $350,000.[17]

Union Pacific's "Idea Works," a formal employee feedback program established in 1997, feeds all employee suggestions into the organization's systems for strategy evaluation. Any employee or team whose idea is implemented is awarded points that they can choose to redeem for either travel or merchandise. At the railroad's Salt Lake City office, one team that included employees involved in daily track repairs came up with a suggestion that saved the company $470,000 by making the process of replacing broken bolts much more efficient and less damaging to track parts.[18]

At Amazon.com Jeff Bezos, the CEO, has taken his passion for innovation and empowerment and backed it up with concrete action. One of Amazon's most prestigious in-house awards is called the "Just Do It." To win, an employee has to take the initiative to implement a well-thought-out idea he or she thinks will add value to Amazon without getting a supervisor's permission; it doesn't even have to be successful. The idea is to reinforce and reward risk taking and initiative.[19]

## Collective Learning Practices

Several types of "learning practices" can be used to facilitate collective learning in organizations. Two examples of learning practices include after-activity reviews and controlled experiments. These practices can be introduced either as organization-wide programs or on a smaller scale for specific individuals or teams.

The after-activity review (also called after-action review or postmortem) is an especially effective way to learn from experience with important, recurring initiatives and projects. Members of the organization who participate in the project meet to review what was done correctly, what mistakes were made, and what can be done better next time. The focus is on identifying lessons learned about how to conduct the activity more effectively in the future, not on blaming people for mistakes and failures. A brief report is prepared so that the lessons learned will become part of the organizational memory and the same mistakes will not be repeated.

Controlled experiments make it possible to evaluate innovative processes or procedures to assess their consequences and determine how well they work. In recent years there has been an increase in the use of small experiments by organizations to facilitate learning. Capital One, an issuer of credit cards, has focused its efforts on creating a company whose staff can learn from tests. Capital One's "test and learn" approach has helped it create mass customized offers that suit the lifestyles, demographics, and credit risk profiles of each credit card applicant. Rich Fairbank, co-founder of Capital One, believes that "the key thing is that they (employees) are learning. I think that, in many ways, failure is a better teacher than success. Our organization tries to institutionalize learning so that we don't make the same mistakes. Failure is not great, but learning is, and allowing people to take risks is a big part of that."[20] A somewhat better known example of an organization with an experimental orientation is Wal-Mart, which regularly conducts hundreds of tests in its stores on sales promotions, displays, and improving customer service.

The amount of learning that results from an experiment depends on how well it is designed and executed. Even a simple experiment can provide useful information. However, experiments do not always produce useful knowledge, and the results may be misleading. Careful planning is needed to ensure that a controlled test yields clear, meaningful results. A clear set of criteria that will be used to measure success should be identified before the test begins. If possible, the experiment should be conducted under the same conditions that will be faced during implementation. When appropriate, a representative sample of potential users or clients should be involved in the experiment to accurately assess the potential of the approach being tested.

## Knowledge Management Systems

New knowledge is of little value unless it is used. Some organizations are very successful at discovering knowledge, but fail to use it effectively. A well-known example is General Motors, which entered into a joint venture with Toyota to learn its manufacturing and assembly practices in order to transfer them to other locations in GM. Despite GM's best efforts, practices did not transfer to any great extent and GM had to create a completely new division, Saturn, to begin using the new forms of work and labor relations they learned from the Toyota joint venture and elsewhere.[21]

Knowledge management systems are used to ensure that new knowledge and learning are retained and disseminated to people who need it in different parts of the organization. Knowledge management is the process of taking information and putting it into a format that can be reused for future work, as well as reviewing the information later to determine how it needs to be changed so that it can continue to be useful. These systems also serve as places to store ideas that are a bit ahead of their time but can be useful at a later time or for another purpose than initially intended.

What does it take to implement a knowledge management system that actually works? Some organizations have been more successful than others. Pillsbury is a good example of a well-intended attempt that did not meet expectations. An R&D scientist who was having trouble with the consistency of waffles was convinced there was a tremendous amount of knowledge about batter in the organization that was not being used. The scientist worked with the IT department to set up a virtual space on the company's network to share knowledge about batter. An invitation to share information was sent by email to all potential users, but after six months nobody showed any interest in it. An analysis of reasons for the lack of interest determined that there was a lot of relevant information within the R&D group but no incentive to help other people solve their problems. The culture did not reward or recognize this type of behavior.[22]

At IBM's Global Services Group, they had the opposite problem. They recognized the importance of conserving knowledge early in the group's history, and consultants made an effort to contribute their expertise to the database. But as the business grew and the database became unwieldy, they realized that they had neglected to put a process in place to manage the content. To address the problem, they tied the quality of the contribution to the performance evaluation system but found that people were making their submissions near the end of the performance cycle to ensure compliance. They eventually moved to a more effective submission process that involved a network of experts who reviewed submissions and requested contributions.[23]

In 1997, Bradbury H. Anderson, then the COO of Best Buy, wanted to accelerate the conversion of knowledge and insights into actual practice. Anderson realized that the organization had to shorten the learning curve for all 60,000 employees so that new knowledge from around the company could be communicated to everyone quickly. This objective was accomplished in two ways. The first way was to use monthly training sessions about products, services, and operations to help people stay current with new technology. The second was to create a knowledge management database. For example, before beginning work to install a custom car stereo in a Porsche, an employee checks the database to identify potential problems to avoid and remedies for problems that may occur. With this information the employee can avoid making the same mistake over and over, enabling the company to save hundreds of thousands of dollars in unnecessary expenses.[24]

Knowledge sharing is less likely to occur when the system encourages internal competition among individuals or subunits. In Hewlett-Packard, the 150 divisions were measured against one another, and few of them had been willing to share information about successes or failures with any of the others. In response to this situation, the company's senior management established a new unit (called SpaM) to save its clients money through the use of powerful modeling techniques. This unit disseminated information about its activities to all the divisions and enabled them to help their clients reduce costs.[25]

## Structural Forms to Facilitate Innovation

Aspects of the formal structure of an organization and the design of facilities can facilitate development of innovative products, services, or processes. How the work is structured and the physical proximity of team members can dramatically increase the opportunities people have to discuss ideas and exchange information.

Reflective North America, a maker of reflective materials, rearranged its plant into work centers in which small teams of employees work on one product from customer order to final inspection. They also moved the customer service department to the shop floor and created ten-minute overlaps from shift to shift. This change facilitated conversations about work-related matters among people from different shifts and departments.[26]

At Ideo, an organization in Palo Alto, California, innovative thinking is increased by programs that encourage and stimulate creativity and facilities that make it easy to informally interact to share ideas and information. For example, six Ideo offices in scattered locations have cabinets known as Tech Boxes in which designers have placed over four hundred objects that intrigue them. It began with one designer's collection of interesting items, but it has now become a pooled fund of inspiration, with each Tech Box managed by a "curator" and each piece documented on the company's intranet. Ideo's designers visit the boxes, play with the objects, and pride themselves on finding new ways to use them in their projects. Ideo's design studios are also laid out in such a way that designers can interact informally, or even overhear other meetings and drop in to share ideas.[27]

Innovative activities such as new product development can be facilitated by use of temporary structural arrangements such as a cross-functional team. These types of teams usually include representatives from each of the functional subunits involved in the project, and in some cases there are also representatives from outside organizations such as suppliers, clients, and joint-venture partners. The membership may be stable over the life of the team, or it may change as some functions become more important and others decline in importance. Cross-functional teams allow flexible, rapid deployment of personnel and resources to solve problems as they are discovered.[28] Coordination is improved and many problems are avoided when people from different functions come together to work on a project at the same time, rather than working on it sequentially. The diversity of member backgrounds fosters creativity in the generation of ideas and problem solutions.

Working on a cross-functional team also helps members learn to view a problem or challenge from different perspectives, rather than from only a narrow functional viewpoint. Many organizations have reported great success in the use of cross-functional teams to facilitate rapid innovation. For example, at Hallmark Cards, a company with a 44 percent share of the market for the 7.3 billion holiday and greetings cards sold in the United States each year, the use of teams drastically reduced the time needed to bring new cards to market from more than three years to less than one year, while also improving quality and responsiveness to changing customer preferences.[29]

## Mergers, Acquisitions, and Strategic Alliances

External approaches used by corporate leaders for promoting innovation, growth, diversification, or increased market power include mergers, acquisitions, and strategic alliances.

### Mergers and Acquisitions

An acquisition occurs when one company buys a controlling interest or total ownership in another company with the intention of making it a subsidiary business. The acquisition of another company to facilitate growth, diversification, or market power has been a popular strategy among U.S. firms for many years. There are several potential benefits for the acquiring firm.

Horizontal acquisitions of competitors in the same industry may enable a company to gain more market power in relation to customers and suppliers. Acquisitions of firms in related industries make it possible to rapidly increase the customer base when the products or services of each firm will be purchased by the customers of the other firm. Acquisitions in a related industry also enable a company to leverage existing core competencies by applying them to broader diversity of products and services and to acquire new capabilities that will enhance existing products and services. Acquiring a company that has desirable products or capabilities is often faster and less risky than trying to develop them internally, especially when development is expensive and takes a long time (for example, pharmaceuticals).

Vertical acquisitions of suppliers or distributors may enable a company to gain more control over essential inputs or more control over the distribution of products to consumers. Unrelated acquisitions may enable entry into another industry with less risk and better opportunities for growth and profitability. Such acquisitions also provide a way to gain entry into markets with formidable barriers (e.g., high capital requirements, foreign markets). [30,31]

Studies on the outcomes of acquisitions find that they seldom provide positive returns to the acquiring firm.[32,33,34] There are many obstacles to achieving the benefits expected from acquisitions. One major reason for failure is the difficulty in integrating companies with different cultures, operating processes, and financial systems. Leaders often underestimate the difficulty and time required to combine dissimilar organizations and achieve the desired synergies. Problems with the merger may become so time-consuming that they distract attention for other important issues and reduce the leadership effectiveness of top management. The high price paid for many acquisitions makes it difficult to obtain sufficient benefits to justify the investment. Additional risks are entailed if the company takes on significantly more debt to make the acquisition; the risks include a lower credit rating and less capability to respond effectively to future threats. Unrelated acquisitions are especially risky, and they are more difficult to manage successfully. If the new owner has little appreciation for the leaders who made the acquired company successful, they will be replaced or their power severely limited, which can reduce the performance of the acquisition.

Some acquisitions result in a financial disaster for the acquiring company. The acquisition of Snapple in 1994 by the Quaker Oats Company provides an example of what can go wrong. Quaker paid a premium price of $1.7 billion for Snapple, and the acquisition involved a substantial increase in debt. Quaker executives hoped that Snapple would provide the same type of benefits as their highly successful Gatorade brand had done in previous years. They expected to achieve these benefits by applying the marketing expertise used for Gatorade, but they failed to understand some important differences in the markets, distribution channels, and customer attitudes for the two types of beverages. The Quaker executives planned to market Snapple in the same way as they had done previously for Gatorade. The expertise of former Snapple executives was disregarded. Two of the top Snapple executives left after the acquisition (along with many key employees), and the only remaining executive had little power over strategic decisions. Competition was increasing in the tea and fruit drink markets, and there were many problems and delays in implementing the new strategy. As a result, sales for Snapple products declined, and the delays made it impossible for Quaker to regain lost market share. In 1997 Quaker sold Snapple to Triarc for $300 million ($1.4 billion less than it paid for the company).[35]

Research comparing successful and unsuccessful acquisitions has identified some of the conditions associated with success.[36,37] The merger will be more successful if the two firms have complementary capabilities. For example, when SmithKline acquired Beckman Instruments, the strategic intent was to advance their biomedical research by combining SmithKline's strengths in health care and pharmaceuticals with Beckman's capabilities in diagnostic technology. In addition, excess cash at SmithKline could be put to good use financing more research and development at Beckman. Friendly acquisitions are more likely to be successful than are hostile takeovers, and it is also beneficial if the acquisition was preceded by a strategic alliance or other cooperative experience. Hostile takeovers create resentment and can undermine future cooperation, delay integration, and cause talented members of the acquired organization to leave. Top management can facilitate success by emphasizing improvements in innovation and competitive advantage more than cost reduction from economies of scale. Finally, success is more likely when the leaders have the skills and resolve to rapidly integrate the two companies and focus on innovation and leveraging of expanded capabilities.

Similar results were found in research conducted by Right Management Consultants.[38,39] The research found that integration efforts are usually focused on achieving tangible financial benefits and that it is essential for leaders to balance this concern with an equivalent concern for the "softer side" human resources and cultural issues. The results confirmed that success is very dependent on competent leadership before, during, and after the acquisition. For a merger or acquisition to be successful, competent leadership is needed not just in top management positions, but at all levels and divisions throughout the organization.

## Strategic Alliances

Strategic alliances involve cooperation between two or more firms that combine their capabilities and resources. One form of strategic alliance is a joint venture in which the participating organizations create an independent company to pursue a collaborative activity that requires a long-term commitment of resources. The participating firms may be equal partners or may have unequal amounts of equity in the joint venture company. In a non-equity strategic alliance, the participants share resources and conduct joint activities without forming a separate company. The alliance may involve licensing agreements, distribution agreements, contracts to supply materials or services, or agreements to jointly conduct research that can be used by all of the alliance partners. This type of strategic alliance requires less commitment of resources for the partners, and it is easier to arrange in response to a new opportunity or threat. Strategic alliances may also involve attempts to influence political decisions, public attitudes, or market prices. However, in the United States and most developed countries, explicit collusion to fix prices or limit competition is illegal.[40]

Strategic alliances have become increasingly popular in recent years as a way for firms to facilitate adaptation to intense and rapid change in competitive markets. The alliances make it easier to develop competitive advantage when there is rapid technological change and strong competition in a global economy. An alliance may allow member firms to leverage their existing capabilities while simultaneously acquiring or developing new capabilities.[41] Large firms now often have different types of alliances with many different partners. For example, in 2001 Procter & Gamble had more than 120 strategic alliances with a diverse set of partners.[42]

As with mergers, strategic alliances often involve dissimilar companies that have complementary capabilities. FedEx formed a strategic alliance with KPMG, the global consulting and professional services firm, to develop supply-chain solutions for large and medium-sized companies. The capabilities and expertise of FedEx in transportation and logistics and in related information management systems will be combined with the expertise of KPMG in supply-chain consulting and e-integration services to help companies achieve total supply-chain solutions for clients.

There has also been an increase in strategic alliances between competing firms. Federal Express has formed an alliance with the U.S. Postal Service. FedEx is allowed to place drop boxes in post offices, and FedEx transports Postal Service packages on its planes. The deal generates more than $7 billion in additional revenue for FexEx, and it reduces shipping costs for the Postal Service.[43]

The potential benefits from strategic alliances are significant. It is estimated 35 percent of the total revenue for the largest one thousand U.S. companies may be from activities involving strategic alliances.[44] However, strategic alliances often fail to provide the expected benefits. There are many reasons for the high rate of failure, including cultural differences, disagreements about the mission or strategies, misrepresentation of capabilities, different interpretations of agreements, failure to honor commitments to provide resources or expertise, and power struggles involving influence over decisions. The structures and processes established for making decisions and the interpersonal skills of the leaders involved in the joint venture are important determinants of success.[45]

Global One, a joint venture in 1996 among Deutsche Telekom, Sprint, and France Telecom, illustrates many of the problems. There was disagreement about many issues, including the target customers, the location of the headquarters office, and who would manage the various divisions. The centralization of decision making in a high-level board of chief executives, in combination with the bureaucratic procedures for dealing with customer requests, prevented a rapid, flexible response to the changing needs of customers. The partnership was ended after only three years, and the venture is now managed by France Telecom.[46]

## Conclusions

Whether there is a need for small, incremental improvements or major, revolutionary changes will depend on the type of organization and its environment. However, neither type of process will occur without leaders who are willing and able to encourage, guide, and facilitate it. Various structural arrangements and features provide one way to improve innovation and collective learning. Effective leaders also use programs, systems, and structural arrangements designed to encourage and facilitate innovation and collective learning. Finally, external strategies such as acquisitions and strategic alliances can be used to facilitate growth, to increase diversification, to acquire new knowledge and expertise, or to obtain more resources and relevant capabilities for risky new ventures.

Some of the same indirect forms of leadership can also be used to improve other performance determinants such as efficiency and human resources. Operational procedures can be made more efficient and reliable by importing best practices from other organizations, experimenting with new procedures, and reviewing work processes to identify potential improvements. Knowledge management systems can be used to ensure that creative ideas for improving efficiency and reliability are widely shared and applied anywhere they are relevant in the organization. Learning practices such as external benchmarking and after-activity reviews can be used to improve skill training, talent management, and succession planning.

# Section III

# Human Resources
# and Relations

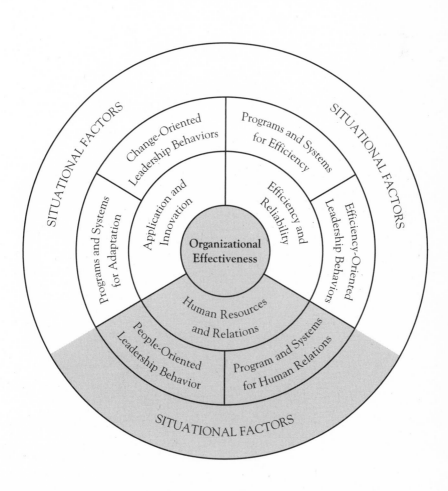

SITUATIONAL FACTORS

Change-Oriented
Leadership Behaviors

Programs and Systems
for Efficiency

SITUATIONAL FACTORS

Application and
Innovation

Efficiency and
Reliability

Programs and Systems
for Adaptation

Efficiency-Oriented
Leadership Behaviors

Organizational
Effectiveness

Human Resources
and Relations

People-Oriented
Leadership Behavior

Program and Systems
for Human Relations

SITUATIONAL FACTORS

## Chapter 8

# The Challenge of Managing Human Resources

There is a growing realization that, in the final analysis, people are the organization's most valuable asset. To describe this asset, the term "human capital" is becoming popular. The unique capabilities of the organization's members are an important source of core competencies. Human resources and relations include people's knowledge, technical expertise, and creativity; people's commitment to the organization and its mission (it is not "just a job" for them); the mutual trust and respect that enables people to achieve synergy and do collective work effectively; the capacity of people to learn and evolve over time; and their willingness to undertake risky new ventures with enthusiasm and confidence.

There is also a growing body of hard evidence that the development and motivation of an organization's "human capital" has a tangible impact on business results. A study of three thousand companies conducted by the University of Pennsylvania found that spending 10 percent of revenue on capital improvements boosted productivity by 3.9 percent; a similar investment in human capital increased productivity by 8.5 percent—more than twice as much.[1] Research at Sears found that a five-point improvement in employee attitudes about their job and about the company at a given store led to a 1.3 unit increase in customer impressions, which yielded a 0.5 percent increase in revenue growth.[2]

## Conditions That Affect the
## Importance of Human Resources

Managing human resources and relations is especially important when the work is complex and difficult to learn, new members require extensive training, and successful performance requires a high level of skill and motivation. These conditions can be found in hospitals, consulting firms, legal firms, advertising agencies, and research universities. In addition, human relations are more important when there is high role interdependence among members of the work unit and successful unit performance requires a high level of cooperation and teamwork. Finally, human relations are more important when it is difficult to recruit and train competent replacements for people who leave. Recruiting and retraining key members is especially important when the organization's competitive strategy relies on services delivered by unique experts who, if dissatisfied, can find jobs in competing companies or start their own competing company. Examples of organizations with extreme levels of dependence on uniquely talented, loyal members include professional sports teams, advertising agencies, research universities, talent agencies, and some types of entertainment companies.

Professional baseball is a sports business in which success depends on recruiting, developing, and retaining talented people. The professional teams have sophisticated systems to manage human resources and relations. Most teams prefer to bring players into the system when they are young and just starting their professional careers. Retention of young players, particularly at the minor league level, is critical because many players become discouraged and quit due to the pressures and difficult travel schedule. Each athlete gets a thorough athletic, psychological, and physical analysis. Scouts, who are responsible for finding and recruiting young talent, get to know each prospect personally in order to learn more about the person's background and commitment to baseball. In addition, the scout who initially recruited a player often remains involved in his development and serves as a mentor while he is in the minor leagues. To ensure that players reach their full potential, the coaching staff attempts to enhance key skills such as fielding, pitching, and hitting. To help retain players the teams attempt to create a family atmosphere in which everyone collaborates in working toward the same common goals.[3]

Investment banking is another industry that relies very much on the talents of specific individuals who broker the important deals. Over the previous ten years, senior bankers have been able to make enough money to make different life choices—and many are considering leaving the business to pursue personal interests or other professions. This trend presents a problem because, although it may be possible to eliminate thousands of mediocre employees, there are some important ones the banks do not want to lose. To help retain high-quality investment bankers, the organizations are offering sabbaticals or allowing some individuals to work on a project or part-time basis.[4]

Human resources and relations are never unimportant, but this performance determinant is relatively less important when only a small number of people are needed to get the work done. One example is an organization with highly automated processes and little chance of human error or equipment failure. Another example is a "virtual organization" for which nearly all functions are outsourced to contractors and there is only a small headquarters staff consisting mainly of top managers who oversee operations. Human relations and resources may also be perceived as less important by leaders in a company that has an ample supply of unskilled labor available, as in the case of manufacturers that make low-technology consumer products for large retailing chains. These manufacturing companies are commonly located in developing countries, where people with little education are willing to do simple repetitive work without much pay and there are few labor laws or other limitations on how employees are treated. The "sweat shop" clothing factories in countries such as China, Thailand, and Malaysia provide a good example of this situation.

Many of the conditions that increase the importance of process reliability and adaptation can also increase the importance of human resources and relations. When successful performance requires high reliability and mistakes can have serious consequences, there is a need for high commitment and vigilance, even if the work is repetitive and easy to learn (e.g., security guards, screeners at airports, medical laboratory technicians). In the same way, human relations and resources are also more important when adaptation is required and the organization depends on members to help develop and implement necessary innovations.

## Implications of Strategy for Human Resources

The appropriate level and mix of human resources in an organization depends in part on its strategy. How changes in competitive strategy can affect human resources is evident in events at Charles Schwab. During the first half of 2002, Schwab announced a global change in the company's strategy to adapt to changing client needs and to decreasing investment activity among its core middle class clients. Previously, Schwab had successfully applied a strategy of offering no frills execution of trades to middle class Americans. The need for change came when Schwab realized that its discount-brokerage service was in dire straits after the technology stock crash in 2000. Daily trades were down 34 percent, revenue was down 25 percent, and net income was down 72 percent.

The growing market of affluent clients with at least a half-million dollars to invest suggested that it may be more profitable to offer high-end clients personal financial advice instead of merely trading their stocks. Many of these potential customers wanted to manage their own portfolios rather than investing in mutual funds. The company's hope was that these clients, disillusioned with traditional brokers and investment bankers, would be attracted by the opportunities for one-on-one conversations with a personal financial advisor who would provide investment ideas on matters ranging from asset allocation to stock selection. Thus was born Schwab Private Client, which began on May 16, 2002. The new strategy required a change in workforce capabilities. The order takers who were the backbone of Schwab's brokerage were now under-qualified to offer the kind of advice the new private clients wanted. To help close this skill gap Schwab began hiring more expensive "investment consultants" from other financial companies. The success of the new initiative will depend on the ability of Schwab to assimilate and retain the new employees while also maintaining the commitment of the older employees. As it moves away from its roots as a discount brokerage firm, Schwab's corporate culture must change to support this new strategy.[5,6]

Another example of a change in strategy that affected human resources could also be found at airports around the United States soon after two hijacked airplanes were intentionally flown into New York City's World Trade Towers on September 11, 2001. The incident raised serious questions about airport security and the capability of airport baggage screeners and security personnel. Prior to 9/11, publicly held companies provided airport security and paid employees slightly more than minimum wage. It was also discovered that the background checks made on new hires was lax and people with criminal records were sometimes hired. After 9/11, the airport security system was revamped and new standards and equipment were put in place for baggage and passenger screening. Training procedures and standards were also upgraded and made more rigorous. These changes required a parallel improvement in employee capability and performance. As a result, selection and training systems also had to be adjusted and salaries were raised to reflect the increased level of employee skill.

## Examples of Good Human Relations

As Vince Lombardi said, "The challenge for every organization is to build a feeling of oneness, of dependence on one another because the question is usually not how well each person works, but how well they work together." Several organizations have made managing human resources and relations a priority and have put in place effective programs and processes that are coordinated across the organization to ensure employees are highly motivated, capable of doing their current job, and prepared to take on the next assignment. General Electric, Southwest Airlines, and Pitney Bowes are three examples of companies that have been successful in managing human relations.

### General Electric

GE has long been recognized as an industry leader for the training and development of its employees. Providing their employees with top-quality training has allowed GE to become one of the most successful companies in America. GE has also been called "one of the best at grooming top talent internally."[7] When Jack Welch was about to retire, the candidates to be his successor were all GE managers. In 2001, Jeffrey Immelt, the head of GE Medical Systems, was selected as the new CEO. GE executives also have a reputation for becoming CEOs at other companies. Soon after Welch's retirement, James McNerney, head of the GE aircraft engine division, was named CEO and chairman of 3M, and Robert Nardelli, head of the GE power systems division, became president and CEO of Home Depot, Inc.

Under former CEO Jack Welch, GE implemented various training programs for their employees to boost productivity and worker education. Welch is credited with introducing "reverse mentoring" to his company, a process through which employees with certain strengths and knowledge bases mentor other employees, including some bosses. In 1999 Welch implemented the program at GE and ordered five hundred of his top managers to find workers who were well-versed in the Internet and tap into their expertise. His goal was to use the knowledge that resides within an organization to its full advantage.[8]

## Southwest Airlines

The top management at Southwest Airlines has focused on building and maintaining high levels of employee motivation. Former CEO Herb Kelleher, who has been called the most effective airline chief in the industry, created a corporate culture in which workers are loyal and committed to achieving maximum productivity.[9] The basics, according to Kelleher, are to hire motivated people, give your employees creative space to plug their ideas into their jobs, and involve them in the decision-making processes.[10] If employees feel that their ideas are valued and they really make a difference, they will work harder for the organization. After the 9/11 attacks by terrorists, other airlines scrambled to cut costs by laying off employees, but Southwest did not lay off a single employee. The current CEO—James Parker—provided the following explanation: "We try to treat other people the way we would like to be treated. I believe we followed the Golden Rule with respect to our employees, our customers, and our shareholders in the aftermath of Sept. 11."[11]

## Pitney Bowes

Another company that manages human resources well is Pitney Bowes. At Pitney Bowes the HR professionals provide the resources needed to support leadership development, such as 360-degree feedback, traditional training programs, and leadership simulations, as well as a talent management system to help build the leadership bench for the future. The work of managing human resources at Pitney Bowes started with a revision and validation of their existing leadership competency model to ensure it reflected the "One Pitney Bowes" philosophy. The competency model was then used in a survey of the top 185 leaders to identify strengths and skill gaps. The team created a simple visual format that graphically described the performance, potential, and competency assessment of each top leader and provided relevant background information about the person. This information was used to create succession plans, to support the performance management process, and to facilitate other development initiatives. Using a consistent approach across the organization streamlined and simplified the process and enabled Pitney Bowes to identify leadership gaps. By using a common format and language, they are better able to support cross-functional mobility and develop managerial talent consistent with their competitive strategy. The visual model is used to track progress in developing skills and competencies for each of the leaders assessed, and it provides a tool to monitor changes and the development of organizational capability over time.

## Examples of Human Relations Problems

Indicators of poor human relations include employee distrust, low commitment to the organization, high turnover, and grievances or lawsuits filed against the company by groups of employees. Some organizations that have provided examples of poor human relations include Denny's, the U.S. Postal Service, and Radio Shack.

### Denny's

Many organizations have periods when, due to poor employee policies or poor implementation of acceptable policies, human relations reach a low point. Denny's, the nation's largest family restaurant chain, is one such example. In the early 1990s Denny's found itself faced with series of racial bias lawsuits. The company settled those cases and took immediate action to address the problem. They found that their recruiting practices were partly to blame, and they hired recruitment firms owned by minorities and women to take advantage of their more diverse networks. Denny's also found that its performance appraisal system placed no value on diversity and had no incentive to hire diverse candidates. To address this situation, the company changed the process so that it was focused on ten core competencies, including valuing diversity. They also based

25 percent of senior management's bonuses on the number of women and minorities in their divisions.[12]

Although Denny's made improvements in the area of diversity, their human relations problems were not completely behind them. In June of 2000, ninety managers of Denny's operations in Washington State sued the company, claiming Denny's routinely forced managers to work as much as twenty-five hours per week overtime without pay. The lawsuit also claimed that Denny's misclassified salaried employees as managers, thus exempting them from overtime, even though 50 percent of their time was spent on tasks typically performed by hourly workers.[13]

### United States Postal Service

"Going postal" is a phrase that has entered America's vocabulary due to the U.S. Postal Service's unenviable reputation as a place where work tensions are apt to boil over into violence. The Postal Service has been trying to improve its human relations for years, with mixed success. Over the years relationships have deteriorated to the point where even the smallest disagreements between workers and supervisors are difficult to settle. In 1995, according to the Government Accounting Office, unresolved grievances within the Postal Service had soared to 73,300. Much of the breakdown in human relations has been attributed to the Postal Service's authoritarian, command and control culture. Many supervisors appear to enforce rules and regulations to the letter. According to union officials, these supervisors use a "get tough" policy with the workers and take arbitrary disciplinary action to show them who is in charge. In addition, over the years, restructuring has led to the loss of tens of thousands of experienced workers. As a result, many inexperienced workers were suddenly put into supervisory jobs and asked to manage their former peers, who were overworked and angry about the changes.[14] Although things have improved somewhat in recent years, both unions and management indicate they still have a long way to go.

## Radio Shack

In 2002, Radio Shack settled a class action lawsuit (while deny-
ing any wrongdoing) filed on behalf of 1,300 current and former
store managers. The suit claimed that store managers spent more
than half their time selling and cleaning the stores and were not
being paid for the overtime they put in. "It gets quite stressful, very
tiring," says Omar Belazi, the lead plaintiff. "You get up and go to
Radio Shack and go home and go to sleep. They gave me all these
sales achievement awards, but it didn't do me any good. They
didn't pay me."[15]

## Ways to Improve Human Resources and Relations

Many studies show that employee motivation and commitment are
key determinants of job performance. To clarify what motivates
people on the job, Right Management Consultants surveyed three
thousand employees across several industries, including financial
services, manufacturing, hotels, and chemicals. Employees were
more satisfied, committed to the organization, and willing to stay
in their jobs when they: (1) understood how their jobs fit with the
overall strategy; (2) had a job that was a good fit with their skills;
(3) perceived that their direct manager was doing a good job;
(4) were part of a strong team; (5) were treated with respect and
courtesy; (6) perceived that everyone was held accountable for performance; (7) perceived that decisions were made in a timely manner; (8) received regular feedback and recognition; (9) had an
opportunity to improve skills; (10) perceived that the organization
was committed to employee success; and (11) had a good pay and
benefits program.[16] Two additional findings emerged from the study.
The first was that, contrary to what many people may believe,
money is not the key factor in motivating and retaining good
employees. The best employees desire learning opportunities,
meaningful feedback, and healthy relationships with their bosses
and co-workers.[17] The second finding was that the behavior of an

employee's immediate boss is an important determinant of job satisfaction and commitment.

It is obvious from extensive prior research conducted during the past half-century that an important component of leadership effectiveness involves ensuring that people are highly motivated and have the skills and knowledge they need to do the job. Leaders can use relations-oriented behaviors to influence mutual trust and cooperation, the skills and confidence of people, job satisfaction, and commitment to the organization. Evidence for these effects comes from more than a half-century of research on many thousands of managers. The direct behaviors most relevant for influencing human resources and relations include developing, recognizing, supporting, consulting, empowering, and team building. Although used most often with direct reports, there are also situations where the behaviors can be used with peers, bosses, or people outside the organization (e.g., clients, suppliers, joint venture partners). Managers can also influence human resources and relations through indirect forms of leadership, such as programs, management systems, and structural features.

## Conclusions

Human resources and relations are always important, but especially when the work is complex and difficult to master, when the task requires a high level of cooperation and teamwork, or when it is difficult to attract and retain competent people. The importance of this performance determinant is also increased in situations where necessary improvements in efficiency and adaptation can only be achieved by the collective efforts of talented, highly motivated members of the organization. The challenge for leaders is to mobilize people, focus them on high-priority outcomes, and ensure they have the capability to do the work. Direct and indirect forms of leadership that are relevant for improving human resources and relations are described in the next two chapters.

*Chapter 9*

# Leader Behaviors for Enhancing Human Resources

Some leader behaviors are especially relevant for enhancing human resources and relations. These people-oriented behaviors include supporting, recognizing, developing, consulting, empowering, and team building. In this chapter we examine these behaviors in more detail and provide guidelines for using them effectively.

## Supporting

Supporting includes a variety of behaviors by which a leader shows consideration, acceptance, respect, and concern for the needs and feelings of others. Examples of supporting include backing people up in a difficult situation, giving encouragement when a person has a difficult or stressful task or responsibility, offering to provide advice or assistance when someone needs help with a difficult task or problem, and being patient and helpful when giving complicated explanations or instructions.

More supporting is necessary when deadlines are tight and people are working long hours to meet them, when people are frustrated and discouraged by temporary setbacks and lack of progress on major projects, when the work is repetitive and tedious, when it is necessary to interact with demanding or dissatisfied customers, when people are going through major changes in their personal lives (new baby, relocation, divorce, death or serious illness of family member), when people have serious illness or injury, and when people are worried about their safety or the safety of their families. Guidelines for demonstrating supportive leadership are shown in Table 9.1.

## Table 9.1: Guidelines for Supportive Leadership

- Show positive regard and concern for people
- Provide empathy and support when someone is upset or worried
- Enhance and maintain the self-esteem and confidence of others
- Provide assistance with work-related or personal problems when it is needed
- Remember names and important details about people

Supportive leadership conveys positive regard for others and shows that the leader views them as worthy of respect and consideration. The use of supporting behaviors helps build and maintain effective interpersonal relationships with others and is strongly related to satisfaction with the leader.[1,2] Effective leaders try to spend some time with direct reports and important colleagues to get to know them better and relate to them as individuals. In the process, there are opportunities to build mutual respect and trust that will provide the basis for a cooperative working relationship. The emotional ties created by supporting make it easier to gain cooperation and support from people on whom the leader must rely to get the work done. It is more satisfying to work for or with someone who is friendly, cooperative, and supportive than with someone who is cold and impersonal, or worse, who is hostile and uncooperative.

People need to feel that they are held in high regard as human beings as well as being valued for what they contribute to the organization's success. One way to demonstrate interest in someone as an individual is to show that you remember details that are significant for the person, including interests and activities outside of the workplace (birthdays, family trips, hobbies, names of children). Another form of supportive behavior is to say and do things that strengthen a person's self-esteem and confidence. Such behavior is especially relevant when assigning work to a direct report who is worried about being able to do it effectively. Research has shown that the person who feels competent is likely to perform better than a person who feels incompetent.[3]

A good measure of supportive leadership is how you react when a colleague or direct report is upset or worried about some aspect of the work. By listening attentively and trying to show that you understand what a person is saying and feeling, you communicate strong concern and the desire to be helpful. Effective leaders are able to suspend their biases and preconceptions, make an active effort to understand and appreciate why someone is upset, demonstrate sincere sympathy, and provide appropriate support (comforting words, adjustment of assignments or deadlines, backing the person up during a stressful or controversial situation).

Supportive leadership is also relevant when a personal problem is adversely affecting job performance. Roy Pelaez works for Aramark and leads a workforce of 426 mostly low-paid immigrant employees who clean airplanes for Delta and Southwest. Morale was very low, turnover was 100 percent, and passenger valuables found during clean-up were sometimes kept by the crews. To turn the operation around, Palaez believed he had to help his employees deal with aspects of their personal lives that were affecting their work. "Any problem that affects the employee will eventually affect your account," he says. "If you take care of the employees they will take care of you and your customer." It was in this spirit that he brought in English-language teachers to tutor employees on their own time, he added Friday citizenship classes to help employees become citizens, he arranged for certified baby sitters subsidized by government programs, he invited representatives from the IRS to come and give free tax advice to help low-income earners take advantage of an earned income tax credit, and he brought in another government representative to tell employees how they could get free health insurance for their children. The result was just as dramatic as his actions; turnover dropped to 12 percent per year, and 250 wallets with more than $50,000 in cash were returned to passengers who left them on airplanes.[4]

In another example, although not evident when he began the conversation, a managing director at a large investment bank found himself faced with a situation involving a direct report with a personal problem. The managing director had anticipated a straightforward discussion about performance, but the employee became angry and upset by what he characterized as unjust accusations. They both agreed to take a few minutes to cool off before continuing the conversation. When the employee walked back into the office, he admitted that he had a substance abuse problem. The managing director took time to listen and communicate how important it was to deal with the problem, for personal as well as career reasons. Both agreed that a referral to the employee assistance program was in order. At the end of the conversation, the employee thanked his boss for being sympathetic and nonjudgmental and indicated that having a chance to talk about his problem had been an enormous relief.

Supportive leadership is often demonstrated as part of a broader interaction, and it can take many forms. Consider the following examples. When a sales representative was concerned he might not receive credit for a sale made outside his region, even though he had played a significant role in closing the deal, the boss helped to persuade the other regional manager that the sales representative should get partial credit for the sale. In another example, when an employee at an investment bank was concerned about not spending enough time with her young children, the managing director she reported to arranged for her to work from home two days a week.

## Recognizing

Recognizing is giving praise and showing appreciation to others for effective performance, significant achievements, and special contributions. This type of leadership behavior has several potential benefits, including improved relationships, higher job satisfaction, and stronger commitment to the organization. Although we typically think of recognition as something that is given to direct reports, it can also be used with colleagues, with people outside the organization, and even with bosses. Recognizing can take many forms, and it includes providing praise, giving awards, and holding recognition ceremonies.

Everyone from the clerk in the shipping department to the vice president of operations wants to be recognized for effective performance, significant achievements, and important contributions. We all want to be winners or heroes. Recognizing can be one of the most effective behaviors for improving working relationships. Guidelines for effective recognition are summarized in Table 9.2.

Surprisingly, despite its general relevance and potential effectiveness, recognizing is also one of the most underutilized leadership behaviors. Many leaders fail to notice and reward positive behavior by their direct reports. It is much more common to notice and criticize ineffective behavior under the mistaken impression that criticism will prevent it from happening again. Although critical feedback can be an important part of performance management, positive reinforcement is usually more effective,

To determine what sorts of contributions and accomplishments merit recognition, it is first necessary to determine what things are important for the success of the work unit and consistent with the values of the organization. With a little effort, it is possible to find examples of effective behaviors and indicators of successful performance in any type of job. Examples of things that may merit recognition include: demonstrating initiative and extra effort in carrying out an assignment; achieving challenging performance goals and

### Table 9.2  Guidelines for Recognizing

- Recognize a variety of contributions and achievements
- Actively search for contributions to recognize
- Use a variety of appropriate ways to provide recognition
- Be sincere, timely, and specific when providing recognition
- Recognize commendable efforts that were not successful

standards; making personal sacrifices to accomplish a task or objective; offering helpful suggestions and innovative ideas for improving efficiency, productivity, or the quality of the unit's products and services; making special efforts to help a co-worker or a customer deal with a problem; and contributing to the success of other individuals or teams.

In the words of Ken Blanchard, it is important to "catch people doing something right." Ralph Gonzalez, a store manager with Best Buy in Florida, took this idea very literally and with great results. Ralph was charged with turning around one of the stores with declining performance. He began providing recognition to employees for any small achievement. In addition, he gave employees whistles to blow every time they caught someone doing something that supported the turnaround. In short order Ralph's store became one of Best Buy's best stores as measured by almost any metric: sales growth, profit growth, customer satisfaction, or employee retention.[5] As Ralph Gonzalez demonstrated, recognition does not take much time and costs little or nothing, yet provides powerful benefits.

Many people think of recognition as appropriate only for major achievements, thereby limiting the opportunity to gain the benefits of this potent leader behavior. It is not uncommon to provide recognition for highly visible achievements, while largely ignoring people whose contributions are less visible and more difficult to measure. However, the people who get no recognition may be the ones who need it the most. Recognition should be given to people in support functions as well as to people in line functions (such as production or sales) where it is easier to measure performance.

Another fallacy is that recognition must be limited to successful efforts. Recognizing honorable failures communicates that the organization values risk taking and initiative. For example, celebrating when a research scientist terminates a project that is failing rather than prolonging it at great cost to the company reinforces the search for innovative approaches, but also communicates the value of limiting exposure and risk.

Some managers believe that recognition should be limited to a few best performers in each type of job, thereby creating strong competition among people. However, extreme forms of competition can create undesirable side-effects, such as unwillingness to help coworkers and resentment by people who perform well but receive no recognition because someone else had slightly better performance. If limited to persons with exceptional performance, most people would receive little recognition. It is better to recognize many winners rather than only a few. For example, the leader can give an award to everyone who exceeds a challenging performance standard rather than giving an award only to the person with the best performance.

Even for people with only average performance, some form of recognition for significant improvements in performance can encourage and strengthen efforts toward additional improvements. Recognition of improvement is especially relevant for new employees or employees who do not have much self-confidence. The leader should clearly communicate an expectation of continuing progress toward excellence, not acceptance of average performance as adequate. Even when recognition is provided to many people, it is still possible to have different amounts of recognition for different levels of performance. Unless the people with the best performance receive greater recognition, their accomplishment will be unnecessarily diminished and the desired benefit from recognition may not be realized.

Leaders generally use three types of recognition: praise, awards, and recognition ceremonies. Awards and recognition ceremonies are often established as formal programs, and they are described in the next chapter. In contrast, praise is usually an informal activity that is directly provided by a leader, and it can be used for peers and bosses as well as for direct reports. Praise is more likely to be successful if it is specific, relevant, and timely. Instead of merely commending someone for carrying out an assignment or completing an initiative well, it is better to explain what the person did well and why it is important to the team or organization. Describing the person's behavior and the beneficial impact it had will clarify why the behavior was deserving of recognition. Specific praise is more believable than general praise because it shows that you actually know what the person has done and have a sound basis for a positive evaluation. In addition, citing specific examples of effective behaviors communicates what behaviors you value and guides the person toward repeating those behaviors in the future. Finally, research shows that praise is more effective when provided soon after desirable behavior occurs, rather than waiting until a future time, such as saving it for the annual performance appraisal.

There is no simple, mechanical formula for determining what type of recognition to use. The appropriate form of recognition will depend on the type and importance of the accomplishment to be recognized, the norms and culture of the organization, and the characteristics of the leader and recipient. Whatever form of recognition is used, it must be sincere. Most people are able to detect efforts to manipulate them with praise or rewards. Finally, leaders should avoid overusing a particular form of recognition, because its effect can be diminished if it becomes too commonplace.

## Developing

Developing includes several managerial practices that can increase relevant skills, aid adjustment to the current job, and facilitate career advancement. Examples of developing behavior include providing coaching and feedback, encouraging people to participate in relevant training programs, setting developmental goals for direct reports, making developmental assignments, promoting a person's reputation in the organization, and providing opportunities for people to demonstrate their skills and potential for advancement. Developing is usually done with a direct report, but it may also be done with a peer, a colleague, or even with a new, inexperienced boss. Responsibility for developing direct reports can be shared with other members of the work unit who are competent and experienced. For example, some leaders assign an experienced employee to provide coaching and advice to a new employee in the unit. Guidelines for developing others are provided in Table 9.3.

Developing offers a variety of potential benefits for the organization, the leader, and the recipient. Potential benefits for the organization include higher employee commitment, higher performance, and better preparation of people to fill positions of greater responsibility in the organization as openings occur. Potential benefits for the leader include better working relationships and a sense of satisfaction from helping others grow and develop. Potential benefits for recipients include better job adjustment, more skill learning, greater self-confidence, and faster career advancement.

Coaching is one of the most effective ways for leaders to enhance human resources, and it includes efforts to improve skills relevant for performing future jobs, not just skills necessary to perform a current job. Even a highly motivated person may not be able to improve performance or learn new skills without assistance, and coaching is one way to provide this assistance. Sometimes it is appropriate to offer specific advice about how to do a difficult task, but in many cases it is more helpful to assist the person in discovering how to solve a problem or improve performance.

Effective coaches help people assess their strengths and weaknesses, identify reasons for mistakes or problems, and evaluate whether improvement plans are feasible and appropriate. Asking probing questions is a good way to help a person identify key issues and explore options that were not obvious. Sometimes it is helpful

#### Table 9.3.  Guidelines for Developing

- Provide help in assessing skills and identifying strengths and weaknesses
- Be patient and helpful when providing advice or instructions
- Provide opportunities to learn new skills and demonstrate competence
- Encourage and facilitate attendance at relevant training activities
- Provide helpful advice about career advancement and job success

to suggest specific things the person may want to consider when confronted with a difficult problem.

An essential quality for effective coaching is patience. You cannot expect people to change overnight or learn everything immediately. It takes time to learn complex skills, and learning is inhibited when someone is frustrated and anxious. It is important to be helpful and supportive when a person is frustrated and discouraged by slow progress or repeated mistakes.

Like coaching, career counseling can be used to increase the skills and self-confidence of direct reports and help them achieve their potential. In order for it to be done effectively, career counseling requires an understanding of the other person's background, interests, and career aspirations. Spending some time with each direct report is the best way to gather this information. To avoid becoming overbearing, it is advisable to ask a direct report to indicate how you can be helpful in his or her career planning process. Some potential forms of assistance that can be provided to a direct report include: encouraging the person to set ambitious career goals that are consistent with the person's ability and interests, helping to identify career paths and promotion opportunities in the organization, and explaining the advantages and pitfalls of various assignments or potential job changes. Often it is useful to share insights learned from experience with problems or choices similar to those now faced by the person. Another way to help is to suggest someone else in the organization or profession who can be trusted to provide good career advice.

One way to facilitate career advancement is to help a direct report identify and acquire the skills needed to prepare for a promotion, new assignment, or a career change. To help direct reports acquire relevant skills, a leader can inform them about opportunities for skill acquisition (training programs, courses, workshops), encourage them to take advantage of these opportunities, and facilitate attendance by providing financial compensation and rearranging the work schedule to allow time away from work.

Another way to facilitate skill acquisition is to make developmental assignments that provide an opportunity to assume new responsibilities. It is important to provide opportunities to learn from experience in dealing with challenging assignments, but it is also essential for the person to experience progress and success in learning new skills rather than a series of repeated failures. Thus, developmental assignments must be made carefully, and the leader should provide adequate support, encouragement, and coaching. For example, in many investment-banking firms the development of junior bankers is seen as an important responsibility of the senior bankers. Frequently the development process starts with doing the research related to a particular deal and working on the team that is preparing the proposal. The senior banker provides coaching, and suggestions are made to help enhance performance. As junior bankers gain more knowledge and expertise, they are invited to attend client meetings as observers. When there is evidence of sufficient learning, the junior banker may be asked to participate in the sales call and the presentations to the client. As the person's confidence and competence increase, the senior banker will delegate more responsibility until, eventually, the junior banker becomes a primary interface with members of the client organization.

Leaders can also facilitate the career advancement of direct reports by promoting their reputation, increasing their visibility in the organization, and helping them develop networks of contacts with important people. For example, you can introduce a direct report to important people at meetings or social events, tell superiors and peers about the person's achievements and expertise, and assign the person to a high-profile project or committee that provides an opportunity to gain more visibility in the organization and demonstrate relevant skills.

An example of developing by a first-line supervisor is provided by Dan Greaves, a shift supervisor at Dyno Nobel, a maker of explosives and explosive devises. An employee with a Machine Operator I classification may move up to a Machine Operator II classification after one year if certain production criteria are met. Cindy, a Machine Operator I, approached Dan and asked if she could be moved up to the next category before completing her year. When Dan checked her performance he found she had the lowest numbers on the shift. He explained that her performance had to be exceptional for her to be moved up sooner and told her that he would re-evaluate her in one month. During the next few weeks Dan spent time with Cindy at her machine pointing out shortcuts that the top producers used to raise their efficiency levels. He regularly monitored her performance and made a point to provide recognition when it was good. As a result, Cindy became the top producer in the department and received her upgrade at the end of the month.[6]

## Consulting

Consulting means involving people in decisions that will affect them. This type of behavior, which is sometimes called "participative leadership," can take different forms that involve different amounts of influence over the final decision. The options include asking for suggestions before making a decision, revising a tentative decision after listening to the concerns expressed by others, and asking an individual or group to make a decision jointly with you. You can invite people to participate in any stage of the decision process, and the stages include diagnosing a problem to determine the cause, selecting decision criteria, identifying alternatives, evaluating alternatives against decision criteria, and developing action plans for implementing the decision.

Examples of consulting behaviors include asking people to help plan a task or activity that will require their support and assistance, describing an objective or strategy in general terms and inviting others to suggest ways they could help to attain it, and modifying a tentative proposal or plan to deal with their concerns and incorporate their suggestions. Consulting should be used with direct reports and colleagues when they have relevant knowledge and information needed to develop strategies and plans, and when the success of a decision or plan depends on their commitment to implement it successfully

Potential benefits from participative leadership include better decisions, more understanding of the reason for decisions, more commitment to implement decisions successfully, and higher job satisfaction. When people are invited to participate in making a decision or planning an activity or change, they are more likely to understand the issues relevant for a decision and the reasons why a particular alternative was accepted or rejected. Participating in the process also gives people the opportunity to voice concerns about a proposal and to influence the development of a solution that deals with these concerns. People feel valued when they are involved, and they are more motivated to work toward accomplishing goals that are important to the organization and to the work unit. These potential benefits are not automatic, however, and if consulting is not used skillfully for appropriate situations it can have negative consequences. Table 9.4 outlines actions relevant to participative leadership.

An example of participative leadership is provided by a senior HR executive at UBS. She was already the head of payroll and compensation, and restructuring within the company also gave her responsibility for managing the Benefits Group, which added forty-five people to her headcount and four additional direct reports. She realized that the structure of her expanded unit needed to change to create more efficiencies and enable her to

**Table 9.4. Guidelines for Consulting**

- Encourage people to express concerns and make suggestions
- Look for ways to build on a suggestion rather than dismissing it
- Show appreciation for suggestions and constructive criticism
- Listen to dissenting views without becoming defensive
- Explain how a suggestion was used or why it could not be used

manage the unit effectively. Although she had the authority to make structural changes on her own, she realized that consulting with the managers who reported to her would help gain their commitment to any changes and decisions that were made. Participation in the decision making would also provide an opportunity for the managers to develop their skills, and it would improve morale during a tough economic time when raises and bonuses were sparse and layoffs were rampant. With these objectives in mind, she began a series of meetings to assess the current organizational design and determine the best options for restructuring. At first, the managers were reluctant to share information because they had not been consulted on such decisions previously. However, once she explained that she was looking for their input and demonstrated that their ideas truly mattered by incorporating their suggestions into the solution, they felt empowered and the exchange of ideas became more fruitful.

To elicit more candid reactions and helpful suggestions during consultation, it is better to present a tentative proposal and encourage people to improve it, rather than asking people to react to an elaborate plan that already appears complete. In the latter case, people will be more inhibited about expressing concerns that appear to be criticisms of the plan. Another way to encourage candid expression of concerns is to listen carefully without becoming defensive or angry. Use restatement of a person's concerns in your own words to verify that you understand and to show that you are paying attention.

How suggestions are treated during consultation is also important, especially novel ideas that may not be fully appreciated when initially proposed. Many people tend to focus on the weaknesses of a new idea, without giving enough consideration to its strengths. It is helpful to make a conscious effort to find positive aspects of an idea before mentioning negative aspects. An initial idea that is incomplete can often be turned into a much better idea with a little conscious effort. Even an idea with obvious weaknesses should not be automatically rejected. By discussing how the weaknesses could be overcome, it may be possible to develop better ideas that build on the original one.

It is important to make a serious effort to use suggestions and deal with concerns expressed by the people who are consulted. People will stop making suggestions if they are dismissed without serious consideration or simply ignored

Whatever the outcome, it is important to get back to people and explain how their ideas or suggestions were used, or how a proposal or plan was modified to respond to their concerns. Appropriate recognition and appreciation should be provided for helpful ideas and suggestions. If an idea or suggestion was not used, thank the contributor and explain the reasons why it was not feasible or appropriate.

## Empowering

Empowering is allowing substantial responsibility and discretion for meaningful tasks that are important, giving people the information and resources needed to make decisions and implement them, and trusting people to solve problems and make decisions without receiving prior approval. An important component of empowering is delegation, which involves assigning new projects and responsibilities to individuals or a team and providing the authority, resources, direction, and support needed to achieve the expected results. Guidelines for empowering are outlined in Table 9.5.

In today's organizations, leaders are neither able nor expected to do everything themselves. Substantial delegation is essential in

#### Table 9.5. Guidelines for Empowering

- Allow people appropriate discretion in how to carry out an assignment
- Encourage initiative in solving work-related problems
- Delegate relevant decisions to competent individuals and teams
- Provide adequate formal authority for an assigned task
- Treat mistakes and failures as a learning experience

fast-changing environments that require high initiative and a quick response by front-line employees. Delegation is also important in organizations that have flattened their hierarchies and increased the number of people reporting to each manager.

Delegation has several potential benefits, including better and faster decisions, more commitment to implement decisions, more development of direct reports' skills, more meaningful and interesting jobs for direct reports, and less decision overload for the leader. Delegation can result in better decisions when individuals or teams have more expertise or are closer to the problem and can obtain more timely information. There is likely to be more commitment to implement a decision when people feel that they have ownership of the decision and are accountable for the consequences. Delegation can provide more opportunity for people to learn new skills as they struggle with a challenging task that requires them to exercise initiative and problem solving. When a leader is overloaded with responsibilities, delegation is a good way to free time to focus on key responsibilities.

The potential benefits of delegation will not be realized unless it is used in situations where it is appropriate, and it is carried out in a skillful way. People are unlikely to be successful in carrying out a delegated task unless they are provided adequate resources, clear objectives, and appropriate authority and discretion. Failure may result if responsibility for tasks is delegated to people who lack sufficient expertise and essential skills or to people who are already overloaded with other tasks and cannot get any relief or assistance in doing them.

Delegation involves giving people the discretion to determine how to do a task without interference, but it is only natural for the leader to be concerned about the quality of the output or the ability of the person or team to handle problems along the way. To achieve the potential benefits of delegation, the leader must find a good balance between autonomy and control. Monitoring too closely will send a message of lack of trust in a person's ability, but abdicating all responsibility may contribute to failure and frustration for the person or team assigned to the task. The leader should clearly explain the amount of discretion to be allowed, and it should reflect the skills and experience of the people who are empowered.

Use of progress review meetings provides a way to monitor progress without having to be involved too closely on a day-to-day basis. Mistakes and failures should be treated seriously, but the response should not be one of criticism or blame. Instead, the episode should become a learning experience for both parties as they discuss the reason for the mistake and identify ways to avoid similar problems in the future. If it becomes obvious that the person does not know how to do some essential aspect of the work, the leader should provide additional coaching and guidance.

Examples of effective empowerment can be found in many successful companies, and they often involve front-line employees who have direct contact with customers. For example, at Dell Computers, a technician rushed to the airport to fix a customer's notebook computer while his customer was changing planes. When British Airways allowed their customer service representatives to deal with each case individually, rather than following rigid protocols for handling customer complaints, their customer retention rate doubled to about 80 percent.[7] At Jetway Systems, Dan Brown designed a console pre-tester on his own initiative, saving delays that were costing the company up to forty-eight hours for re-manufacturing of consoles that were discovered to be defective further down the assembly line. The device resulted in a savings of $20,000 over the first six months.[8]

## Team Building

The purpose of team building is to increase mutual trust, cooperation, and identification with the team or organization. Even a talented, well-organized team may fail to carry out its mission unless there is a high level of cooperation, cohesiveness, and mutual trust among team members. Cooperation is especially important when the group has tasks that require members to share information, equipment, and other resources, help each other, and work in close proximity for long periods of time under stressful conditions. Lack of trust and acceptance is more likely to be a problem in newly formed teams or in teams with members who disagree sharply about work-related issues. A major challenge for leaders in this type of situation is to use team-building practices and related behaviors to build mutual trust and cooperation. Table 9.6 outlines guidelines relevant for team building.

Ceremonies and rituals can be used to increase identification with the group and make membership appear to be very special. Initiation rituals are used to induct new members into a group, and retirement rituals are used to celebrate the departure of old members. Ceremonies that are used to celebrate special achievements or mark an anniversary of special events in the history of the group are most useful when they emphasize the group's values and traditions. Symbols of group identity such as a team name, slogan, logo, or insignia can be very effective for creating strong group identification, especially when group members agree to wear or display the symbols of membership.

Rick Burch, a senior vice president at Pfizer, recognized the power of symbols and ceremonies when he created the Master's Group for senior sales reps to reenergize a group of people who were experiencing low motivation and burnout. He created self-reinforcing teams of four to seven senior reps throughout the

#### Table 9.6. Guidelines for Team Building

- Emphasize common interests and values
- Talk about the importance of cooperation and mutual trust
- Use ceremonies, rituals, and symbols to develop team identity
- Use stories to communicate shared values and beliefs
- Encourage and facilitate positive social interactions
- Celebrate work unit achievements and successes

company and had the teams compete with each other and the rest of the sales force. Each member of the team was given a green jacket that resembled the famous jackets awarded at the master's golf tournament. The teams meet once or twice a year, and all the masters meet once a year in San Diego to socialize and recognize team and individual achievements. The impact has been dramatic—Burch's group has exceeded sales quotas and beaten sales force averages in seven out of the last nine years.[9]

The development of a cohesive group is more likely if members get to know each other on a personal level and find it satisfying to interact socially. Periodic social activities such as dinners, lunches, parties, and outings can be used to facilitate social interactions. Various types of outings can be used to facilitate social interaction (for example, go to a sporting event or concert together or go on a camping or rafting trip). When group members work in the same facility, social interaction can be promoted by designating rooms that can be used for informal meetings, lunch, and coffee breaks. The room can be decorated with symbols of the group's accomplishments, statements of its values, and charts showing progress in accomplishing group objectives.

## Relationships Among the Behaviors

Although each of the specific behaviors can have a significant impact on human relations and resources, these behaviors are more effective when used in complementary ways. Consistent use of supporting and recognizing conveys the leader's respect and positive regard for people and improves interpersonal relations. These behaviors can be used effectively not only with direct reports, but also with peers, bosses, and people outside the organization. Consulting, empowering, and developing can be used together to improve decisions and build employee skills, self-confidence, and commitment. Developing more skills and self-confidence in people makes it more feasible to involve them in making important decisions and to delegate important tasks to them. In

turn, the performance of challenging tasks and assignments provides people with an opportunity to further refine their skills as
they learn from experience. Team building to increase mutual
trust and cooperation among people with an interdependent task
also makes it more feasible to empower the team to determine for
itself how to solve problems and accomplish shared goals. Developing the skills necessary for effective teamwork can facilitate the
more effective use of teams.

## Conclusions

Behaviors that are directly relevant for enhancing human resources
and interpersonal relations include supporting, recognizing, developing, consulting, empowering, and team building. Although the
people-oriented behaviors focus on motivating employees and
building trust and cooperation, they are not "soft" skills; they have
a direct impact on achieving business results. Leaders at all levels
need to use a mix of the people-oriented behaviors in a way that is
appropriate for the situation. The people-oriented behaviors should
also be compatible with indirect aspects of leadership that are used
to enhance human resources and relations. These programs and
management systems are described in the next chapter.

Chapter 10

# Programs and Management Systems for Enhancing Human Relations

The specific people-oriented leadership behaviors can be used by leaders at all levels of the organization to improve human relations and resources. Most of the leaders at the highest levels in an organization also have an opportunity to initiate formal programs or systems that are designed to improve human relations and resources. This type of indirect leadership may involve the use of human resource planning systems, employee development programs, empowerment programs, recognition and reward programs, quality of work life programs, and orientation and team-building programs.

## Human Resource Planning Systems

Formal systems for human resource planning are essential for ensuring that key jobs will be filled with qualified people. Common names for these systems include talent management and succession planning. The primary objective of such systems is the effective utilization of human resources, but most human resource planning systems also seek to improve developmental opportunities for individuals. Making the wrong choice to fill a key position, or not having a successor ready when a position becomes available, can be costly to an organization. Moreover, insufficient opportunities for advancement can result in the loss of competent employees who find better opportunities elsewhere.

Obviously, assessing talent, clarifying organizational needs, and building a pool of talent that is capable of filling key positions should be done before the need arises. However, despite the obvious importance of human resource planning, many companies do not appear to have an organization-wide system in place to ensure that people will be ready to fill key positions. In the April 2000 Corporate Leadership Council's study "Challenges in Managing High Potential Employees," 72 percent of companies predicted they would have an increasing number of vacancies in leadership positions over the next three to five years, and 76 percent were concerned that they would not be able to fill those positions with qualified people.[1] Only 1 percent of companies polled by Development Dimensions International rate their succession management plans as "excellent," and about two-thirds describe them as "fair" or worse.[2] Among the top two hundred firms, 50 percent of new CEOs are outside recruits, compared to 7 percent in 1980.[3]

The impact of poor human resource planning can be seen in the business press almost every day. For example, Mount Sinai Hospital was unable to name a replacement when Judith Waterston left her post as president and CEO, even though they knew of her plans months in advance.[4] McDonald's had to bring James Cantalupo out of retirement after the struggling company posted its first quarterly loss in January of 2003.[5]

Human resource planning involves assessing the capabilities of the organization's current workforce, anticipating what skills and knowledge will be required for success in the future, and determining how to recruit, develop, and retain people with relevant skills and experience. This analysis will make it possible to identify any gaps between the talent currently in place and the talent that will be needed in future years. The assessment should be done in a systematic and consistent way, not in a superficial and sporadic way. In most organizations with formal human resource planning, division managers review the strengths and weaknesses of key employees and the readiness of these individuals to take on more responsibility. These division-level assessments are then combined into a company-wide review of talent. The focus is on the progress each employee has made since the last review and on the job assignment that would be most appropriate for the employee's continued development.

It is impossible to write about an effective talent management system and not mention General Electric. The company uses succession planning to help ensure that there are talented executives ready when needed to fill key leadership positions. The GE process captures the rigor and commitment required to make a talent management system work. At the beginning of each year, the company's top five hundred executives meet to set business priorities. Then, at quarterly meetings of the corporate executive council, leaders review talent requirements and discuss what to do with the top 20 percent and the bottom 10 percent of employees. The council identifies the two or three most qualified candidates to fill any high-level position that might become vacant. If no qualified candidates are available for a position, a priority is set to develop candidates with methods such as making stretch assignments to expand a manager's skill and experience.[6]

Another company that has built succession planning into the core of its culture is Wellpoint Health Network, a Fortune 500 health insurance company. All managers are required to oversee the career development of their direct reports, and how well this career planning is done is part of each manager's performance appraisal. Wellpoint's Board annually evaluates the top five hundred people to identify future leaders. A custom development plan is created that includes training, job rotation, and coaching. Progress is reviewed quarterly to ensure employees are on track to achieve their development goals and that the goals are still relevant. After this human resource planning system was implemented, turnover decreased, and Wellpoint is now confident that it can fill any top leadership position from a list of internal candidates.[7]

At Dana Corp., an auto parts maker, Southwood "Woody" Morcott understood that developing organizational talent was a process and not an event. When he became CEO, Morcott implemented a formal succession planning process. Each business division creates a "depth chart" for key employees that highlight their strengths, weaknesses, and corporate experience. People on the depth chart are assisted by their supervisors in developing their capabilities. Dana's five-member policy committee has its own depth chart to track a few dozen division managers and other senior employees. Just as at the division level, training and developmental challenges are used to produce several qualified candidates for the top leadership positions.[8]

An organization must ensure it is developing people at all levels so that it has a continuous stream of potential candidates to feed the system. To achieve this objective it is important that everyone in the organization has a personal development plan. Such plans should not be limited to a small number of high-potential employees. Development plans should be an output of the performance review process and should be created collaboratively with the person's boss. The development plan for a person should be based on an assessment of the individual's strengths, weaknesses, and career objectives. The plan should include specific actions and developmental opportunities (job assignments, training programs) that will provide the experience, skill, and knowledge needed to assume additional managerial responsibilities.

## Employee Development Programs

Most organizations have formal programs designed to develop employee skills. Major types of developmental programs include skill assessment and feedback programs, employee training programs, education assistance programs, and formal mentoring programs. These programs are not mutually exclusive, and an organization may use all of them together to develop the skills needed by employees to perform their current and future jobs.

### Skill Assessment and Feedback Programs

The use of behavioral feedback has become a popular method for leadership development. It is called by various names, including 360-degree feedback, multi-rater feedback, and multi-source feedback. In a feedback program, leaders receive information about their skills and behavior from a standardized questionnaire filled out by other people such as direct reports, colleagues, and bosses. In some programs the feedback includes narrative comments and suggestions for improvement in addition to numerical ratings of skills and behavior. Each participating leader receives a report that summarizes the feedback. In most cases the leader will attend a workshop conducted by an experienced facilitator who provides assistance in interpreting the feedback and identifying strengths and weaknesses. This information can be used to create development plans and select appropriate developmental activities.

Compared to feedback workshops, assessment centers use more intensive measurement procedures and multiple methods for assessing managerial skills. The methods may include interviews, aptitude tests, personality tests, situational tests, an exercise to assess oral presentation skills, and an exercise to assess writing skills. Information from these diverse sources is integrated and used to develop an overall evaluation of the person's strengths, weaknesses, and potential. Although assessment centers are most often used to evaluate an employee's skills and potential for advancement, they can also be used to identify developmental needs for employees.

### Training and Education Assistance Programs

Formal training programs are designed to increase employee knowledge and skills, and there is usually more emphasis on skills needed by people in their current positions than on skills needed to prepare for promotion to a higher position. Most formal training occurs during a defined period of time, and it is usually conducted away from the person's immediate work site by training professionals. Formal training is especially appropriate for learning complex skills that may not be easily acquired through informal coaching. The leader should help employees find relevant training courses that are available for employees. The courses may be offered by the organization, by local colleges and universities, by professional associations, or by consulting companies. When reviewing training opportunities, it is important to probe beneath the superficial description presented in a college catalogue or training brochure to determine whether the needed skills are actually taught in a particular course or workshop.

Many organizations offer education assistance programs to encourage learning and development by employees. The company usually reimburses all or part of the tuition expenses for college or university courses (or an advanced degree) that will enhance the skills needed for an employee's current job or for a more demanding assignment in the company.

### Mentoring Programs

Mentoring is a relationship in which a more experienced manager helps a less experienced protégé. The mentor is usually at a higher managerial level, but is not the protégé's immediate boss. The most basic principle of mentoring is to have a genuine concern about an individual's development and career progress. A mentor should encourage a person to set ambitious career goals that are realistic in terms of the person's ability and consistent with the person's interests. Effective mentors encourage people to set specific goals for self-development, respond enthusiastically to requests for advice or assistance, and provide social and emotional support as well as career-related support.

There is ample evidence that mentoring programs improve recruitment, development, and retention of employees. In a study by the Center for Creative Leadership, 77 percent of companies reported that mentoring programs were effective in increasing retention. In an Emerging Workforce study conducted by Spherion, more than 60 percent of college grads listed mentoring as a criterion for selecting an employer. In a study by ASTD, 75 percent of executives said mentoring played a critical role in their career development. Mentoring can also promote better career opportunities for women. According to Catalyst, 81 percent of female executives said a mentor was critical or important to their career advancement.[9]

In an attempt to bring the benefits of a mentoring relationship to a wider audience or to people who would not normally have access to a mentor, many organizations began to implement formal mentoring programs. These attempts at structuring a mentoring relationship have had a mixed record of success because, according to Chip Bell, senior partner with Performance Research Associates, they are often "overly structured and crumble under their own weight."[10] The success of a mentoring program depends on how it is implemented, including the selection and training of the mentors. Success is more likely when participation of mentors and protégés is voluntary, mentors have some choice of a protégé, both parties understand the potential benefits and pitfalls, and both parties understand their expected roles and responsibilities in the mentoring process. Mentoring is not a one-way street in which the mentor has all the answers, but rather a partnership for which both people share responsibility. The core of a successful mentoring relationship is mutual trust and respect, which requires an investment of time and effort from both parties.

One company with a good balance between formality and informality in its mentoring program is Intel. The mentoring program at Intel matches people not by job title or by years of service but by specific skills that are in demand. The mentoring is not limited to one-on-one counseling. Email and the company intranet are used to facilitate the matchmaking, and mentoring relationships stretch across division boundaries. To ensure that the mentoring program gets results, Intel also uses written contracts between mentors and protégés.[11]

## Empowerment Programs

Several types of programs have been used to increase employee empowerment, influence over decisions, and feelings of ownership. The programs can take different forms, and variations can be found in different countries and for different types of organizations. American universities often have a faculty senate with elected representatives who share authority for some types of decisions. In addition, the academic departments often have a chairperson with a defined term of office who is elected (or nominated) by department faculty. Voluntary organizations and local governments often have elected officers who are required to hold open hearings on major decisions, to disclose budgets and financial transactions, and to obtain member approval for increased assessments. In some European countries, the board of directors for a company is required by law to include members representing employees, and some organizations have an employee council with elected representatives from different subunits. In the United States, formal empowerment programs found in many corporations include employee stock ownership programs, open-book management, and self-managed teams. These corporate programs will be described in more detail.

### Employee Ownership Programs

An employee stock-ownership plan (ESOP) is a type of tax-qualified employee benefit plan in which all of the assets are invested in the stock of the employer. Employees do not actually buy shares in an ESOP. Instead, the company establishes an ESOP by creating a trust and contributing money or stock to it. These contributions are tax-deductible, and stock is allocated to individual employees based on seniority and compensation. Over eight million employees in over eleven thousand companies participate in such plans. ESOPs should not be confused with stock option plans that grant employees the right to buy company shares at a specified price once the option has vested. Stock options can be given to as few or as many employees as the company desires, but ESOPs must include all full-time employees.[12]

For ESOPs to promote a true culture of ownership, employee shareholders must have a real voice in the way a company is being managed.[13] One company that has achieved synergy between employee ownership and participation in decision making is Reflexite Technology Corporation, which manufactures reflective materials. In his first year of employment at Reflexite, factory worker David Korncavage earned six shares of company stock, which entitles him to twice-yearly dividends and monthly bonuses based on the company's financial performance. "I felt like I owned a piece of the company right away," he says. As an "owner," he was allowed to set his own daily schedule of tasks in the manufacturing and materials-flow department, which range from tracking computerized orders, to trucking parts to another Reflexite facility, to sweeping the floor. "I've worked at traditional jobs where you bang the clock, go home, and don't think about work until the next day," says Korncavage. "Here I'm on call twenty-four hours a day, and I'm glad to come in when a problem arises."[14]

Companies with a true ownership culture empower employees by actively teaching them about the business and training them to be owners. At Reflexite, for example, employees are taught to understand financial terms so they can discern how company performance relates to bonus and dividend payments or why dividend payments fell sharply when management decided it was necessary to invest capital in new plants in Ireland and Germany. Instilling ownership awareness at Reflexite also extends beyond teaching employees to read financial statements. "Every bit of technical or quality training we do is piggy-backed onto owner-awareness training," says Lisa Casey, Reflexite's employee-development director.[15]

### Open-Book Management

Another formal program to empower employees though communication and learning is known as open-book management. As the name suggests, top management "opens the books" to employees to give them a clear understanding of financial information, such as revenues, profits, and costs.[16] For this type of program to be successful, however, it involves more than just sharing financial information with employees; it also requires training that will enable employees to understand the information and use it to improve company performance. A good example is provided by Springfield ReManufacturing Corp. The CEO—Jack Stack—who has increased sales from $16 million to $160 million, tries to ensure that all employees receive weekly financial information about the company and are able to understand it. Managers in each department provide informal training on a specific item, such as the labor-performance rate, and explain to employees how it is determined, how they affect it, and how it affects the company.[17]

### Self-Managed Teams

A large part of empowerment is involving people in decision making and encouraging people to make decisions themselves. One type of program for increasing empowerment is the use of self-managed teams. Unlike traditional work units where a formal manager usually makes all the key decisions, members of self-managed teams meet to determine how to do the work and who will do each task. Self-managed teams are most appropriate for complex, self-contained projects that require a high level of initiative, skill, and motivation. Self-managed teams are not appropriate for independent tasks that are performed individually by employees rather than by a team. As noted by Henry Sims,[18] the author of *Business Without Bosses*: "You don't use teams with insurance salesmen and long-haul truckers."[19]

Self-managed work teams offer a number of potential advantages for an organization. Greater autonomy and variety can result in more satisfied employees, with lower turnover and absenteeism. Having team members cross-trained to do different jobs increases the flexibility of the team in dealing with personnel shortages resulting from illness or turnover. Increased knowledge of work processes helps team members solve problems and suggest improvements. Employees who can make decisions and initiate changes are more likely to take responsibility for their work and may be more motivated to produce a high-quality product or service. Finally, the changeover to self-managed groups typically reduces the number of managers and staff specialists in an organization, which lowers costs.[20]

How many of these potential advantages are realized depends greatly on how the teams are implemented in an organization. When used in an appropriate way, self-managed teams can increase member commitment and improve quality and productivity. However, self-managed teams are difficult to implement, and they can be a dismal failure when used in inappropriate situations or without competent leadership and adequate top management support.[21,22]

## Recognition, Award, and Benefit Programs

Recognition, award, and benefit programs are widely used in organizations to show individuals and teams that they are valued members, to keep employees satisfied and loyal, and to sustain commitment to business objectives and cultural values. There are numerous types of programs, and they work best when tailored to the company's culture and business objectives.

### Recognition Programs

Many organizations have programs to recognize continued loyal service, significant contributions, or important achievements that make an employee more valuable to the organization. As with informal praise, formal awards are more effective when the specific accomplishment or contribution is clearly cited. That way, other people know why the award was given and understand that it was based on meaningful criteria rather than favoritism or arbitrary judgments. Awards that are highly visible reinforce private praise, because others can share in the process of commending the person and showing their appreciation. Formal awards are not only a form of recognition but also serve to communicate values and priorities to people in the organization. Thus, it is important that awards be based on meaningful criteria rather than favoritism or arbitrary judgments. The basis for making the award is more important than the form it takes.

It is also common to use ceremonies and celebrations to formally recognize contributions and achievements by individual employees. Examples include recognition for continued years of service at regular intervals (ten years, twenty years), achieving a sales target, or being granted a patent for a discovery or process. A recognition ceremony ensures that an individual's contributions and achievements are acknowledged not only by the person's leader and immediate co-workers, but also by other members of the organization. Recognition ceremonies can be used to celebrate the achievements of a team or work unit. Special events to honor particular employees or teams can have strong symbolic value when attended by top management because they demonstrate the concern for the behavior or performance being recognized. Such ceremonies demonstrate greater appreciation for the behavior or performance being recognized than a simple announcement in a newsletter or on a bulletin board.

At Great Plains, employees who are nominated by their peers, managers, and customers participate in a week-long company celebration during which top managers present deserving individuals and teams with awards in categories, including innovation, customer service, learning, quality, and lifetime achievement. During the celebration, employees and their families participate in activities such as a picnic and formal dinner dance.[23]

At a major insurance company, the chief technology officer includes a recognition ceremony in the annual meeting of his extended management team of eight direct reports and their sixty subordinates. The managers work in small groups to develop a list of the accomplishments they consider most significant, and they identify who was involved and each person's contributions. Then the accomplishments are presented briefly by the group's spokesperson. This process not only informs people about what occurred in the previous year, but it also has an energizing effect on the team; sometimes they could not have imagined everything they did. Finally, the CTO summarizes the themes that have emerged from the presentations, explains how they contributed to the success of the business, and passes on favorable comments received from his own boss or peers.

AFLAC, an international insurance company based in Columbus, Georgia, has been named five years in a row as one of *Fortune* magazine's 100 Best Companies to Work for in America. In April the company sponsors an Employee Appreciation Week. Every day that week there is a series of giveaways, drawings, and rallies that demonstrate the company's appreciation for the effort its employees have made to support the business and serve customers.[24]

### Employee Benefit Programs

Benefit programs are used to attract and retain talented employees in an organization. Benefits that are used for this purpose include annual pay increases for employees, healthcare insurance, retirement pension plans, subsidized stock purchase plans, and stock option plans. How benefits are allocated to different types of employees communicates a strong statement about how they are valued by the organization. In some organizations the benefits for all professional employees and levels of management are approximately equivalent (proportional to their salary), whereas in other organizations the upper-level managers have unique benefits that are not available to other employees. Examples of special benefits for executives include retirement plans protected against bankruptcy, golden parachute severance clauses in their employment contracts, subsidized housing, liberal expense accounts, and large interest-free loans. The differential between the benefits provided to top management and regular employees conveys an important message about the extent to which regular employees are valued and appreciated.

## Quality of Work Life Programs

Many people spend at least one-third of their day at work, and the workplace enables people to fulfill their social needs as well as their economic needs. Balancing the demands of work with the demands of an active family life can be challenging. It has been known for some time that a pleasant and supportive work environment increases satisfaction, motivation, and commitment to the organization.[25] Over the years organizations have developed a wide range of programs to enhance the quality of work life and make membership in the organization more enjoyable and desirable. The specific objectives of the programs vary widely. Some programs are designed to improve employee health and fitness, which affect job performance and healthcare costs. Other programs are designed to make it easier for people to deal with responsibilities and problems outside the job that might otherwise distract from job performance. Examples include maternity leave, day care assistance, elder care assistance, flexible work schedules, telecommuting, job sharing, and on-site services such as dry cleaning and banking.

Serentec, a small firm that provides regulatory compliance systems validation for the pharmaceutical industry, has a unique paid time off program that allows employees to combine vacations, holidays, and sick days and take time off whenever they want. All employees have laptops and Internet access, which allows them the option of telecommuting.

Rex Healthcare, a company of 3,500 employees that offers comprehensive health services, offers on-site childcare for children who are ill and cannot attend school, as well as regular childcare. Rex employees and their families have free access to an employee wellness center. RexAware, an employee assistance program, offers free counseling and support for everything from substance abuse to everyday stress. Rex also offers an on-site adult day care center that provides affordable care for adults needing daytime assistance.

Analytical Sciences Inc. offers employees a flextime program that provides some choice in when they must be in the workplace. The core business hours are 9:00 a.m. to 3:00 p.m. and people can come and go outside those hours at times that best suit their needs.[26] Some organizations, such as Pfizer, allow employees to work a four-and-a-half-day week during the summer months.

## Orientation and Team-Building Programs

Orientation and team-building programs are used to help assimilate new employees faster, transmit organizational culture and values, and build a sense of community among members of the organization. The scope of these programs can vary widely from company to company. Some organizations spend an hour or two going over key policies and procedures and asking new employees to fill out paperwork. Other organizations use the orientation as an opportunity to indoctrinate new employees and immerse them in the company's culture and values.

McDonald's Hamburger University and Walt Disney's orientation and training of new "cast members" are examples that have received much publicity. Another good example is Commerce Bank, based in Cherry Hill, New Jersey. Commerce is one of the fastest growing banks in the country, and they have an almost obsessive focus on building a service culture. Inspired in part by Hamburger University at McDonald's, the bank established a training unit called Commerce University to strengthen customer service values, clarify expectations, and get new employees excited about joining the company. Vernon Hill, the president and CEO, works with new managers as part of the program. "We're asking you to forget the way you delivered your skill at other banks," he says. "In many ways you've joined a service cult."[27]

At Jo-Ann Stores, all new hires go through the same three-day orientation program. "The focus isn't on filling out paperwork," says Rosalind Thompson, Jo-Ann's executive vice president of human resources. "It's about introducing employees to our company culture and values." During the program, new hires play a Jeopardy®-style game to learn about the company and a grab-bag guessing game to introduce them to Jo-Ann's different products. The new hires spend the third day of the program at one of the company's stores cutting fabric, working the register, and unloading trucks. New hires are also assigned a mentor who tells them the rules and procedures and helps make introductions.[28]

Some organizations take a more creative route to integrating new employees into the organization. Persistence Software, in San Mateo, California, puts a tray of bagels and muffins near the desk of the new hire. An email invites everyone to meet his or her new colleague. Akili Systems Group, in Dallas, issues new employees a mock passport. New employees try to get twenty different stamps in the passport for things like attending a company event, drawing the company organization chart, or accurately recounting company folklore.[29]

Executive assimilation is a type of orientation and team-building program that is targeted to middle and senior managers. The objective of the program is to accelerate a manager's transition to a new position and increase the likelihood of success in that position. The program helps the new manager build a cognitive framework for the new position and builds shared expectations with the new team. A skilled facilitator starts the process by gathering input from the members of the team about what they already know about the new manager, what they would like to know, and what the new manager needs to know about them and the organization. The facilitator then debriefs the new manager and provides coaching on how to respond to the team. The new manager then guides an open discussion with the team and responds to questions. As a follow-up, the team develops a shared process for communication, problem solving, and decision making.

## Conclusions

Leaders can influence human resources and relations by the use of programs, management systems, and structural features. Widely used approaches include human resource planning systems, employee development programs, empowerment programs, recognition and reward programs, quality of work life programs, and orientation or team-building programs. Although these indirect approaches can improve employee skills, commitment, mutual trust, cooperation, and job satisfaction, their success depends on whether they are appropriate for the situation and on how well they are used and supported by leaders at all levels in the organization.

# Section IV

# *Finding the Right Balance*

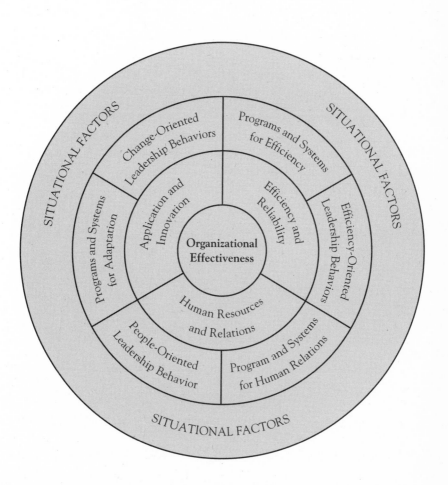

*Chapter 11*

# Multiple Challenges and Tradeoffs for Leaders

For purposes of clarity, we have been looking at each of the three performance determinants separately to see how leaders can influence them. But as we have seen in the real-life situations that leaders face on a daily basis, the performance determinants are often interrelated in complex ways and must be dealt with simultaneously. It should almost go without saying, for example, that the success of many attempts at increasing adaptation or efficiency will depend, at least in part, on how effectively leaders deal with the challenge of managing human resources. Yet if that sounds too much like simple common sense to need repeating, it is nonetheless something that many leaders forget. An essential requirement for flexible leadership is to identify the relative importance of the different performance determinants, then to find ways to enhance them with an integrated set of behaviors and programs, while simultaneously balancing the tradeoffs.

## Tradeoffs Among the Three Performance Determinants

Efforts by leaders to influence improvements in efficiency, adaptation, or human relations are complicated by potential tradeoffs among these performance determinants. Attempts to improve one of them may make another worse. Thus, it is essential for leaders to understand the complex relationships among the performance determinants and to identify how direct and indirect leadership is likely to affect each of them.

### Efficiency vs. Adaptation

When major changes are implemented in an organization to facilitate adaptation, there is likely to be a period of lower efficiency. One reason is that a substantial investment of extra resources is usually required to implement major change. In addition, there is usually a period of difficult adjustment and relearning by individuals and groups, which will cause a temporary decline in efficiency and reliability. Additional declines in efficiency or reliability may result from the diversion of effort and resources to political activity, as people try to resist the change or protect their power and status in the organization.

When adaptation requires innovative products and services, the cost of research and development can be very great. A case in point is the pharmaceutical industry. As one commentator puts it, "Drug research is quite possibly the least efficient endeavor in the world of business." A startling 96 percent of pharmaceutical research projects can be expected to fail. At Pfizer, one of the major drug companies, the R&D budget is over $100 million per week, which means roughly $96 million per week is being spent on projects that lead nowhere.[1]

Leaders who are too focused on responding to market changes may fail to pay sufficient attention to efficiency and process reliability. Jacques Nasser, the former CEO of Ford, was so determined to be "an agent of change" and so convinced that the Internet was where the action was, that he spent over a billion dollars to achieve his goal to "put the Internet on wheels" and further millions to launch a telematics unit that would enable drivers to use their cars as Net portals. Nasser took a money-is-no-object approach to innovation, even proposing to give every employee a free computer and Internet access. Suddenly, ordinary Fords contained voice-activated navigation, organic LCD video displays, and other high-tech features. In his efforts to make Ford the king of the information superhighway as well as the highway, Nasser entered into expensive joint ventures with high-tech companies such as Yahoo. Under his leadership, Ford also launched an expensive initiative to sell its cars online.[2]

Nasser's actions increased the price of the company's automobiles and led to spiraling costs. As one industry analyst summarized the problem, "Vehicle prices were way out of line with what the marketplace was willing to pay. They cost too much to build, and when the economy nose-dived, fewer people were willing to pay premium prices." The Harbour Report, a respected measure of North American automotive manufacturing productivity, noted that these problems contributed to Ford having the lowest per-car profits among the Big Three automakers.[3] The lesson to be learned from what happened at Ford is that, in competitive markets, innovative changes should be as efficient as possible.

There is also a potential tradeoff when efforts are concentrated on improving efficiency. Leaders can increase efficiency by refining work processes, establishing norms and standard procedures, investing in specialized personnel, facilities, or equipment, and organizing around the strategy. However, these practices tend to reduce flexibility and make it more difficult to change strategies and work processes at a future time in response to environmental threats and opportunities. When efficiency is the dominant concern, leaders tend to focus effort and resources on refining the existing strategy rather than on discovery of new approaches.[4] Opportunities may be overlooked until long after they are feasible to exploit. Emerging threats may be ignored or discounted until they are finally so serious that it will be more difficult and costly to deal with them. Finally, in order to minimize costs, an organization may not allocate adequate resources to research and development of new products or services.

The efforts of leaders to cut costs can also undermine product quality or customer service. When superior service or product quality is an important aspect of a company's competitive strategy, attempts to cut costs can have the unintended effect of reducing sales and profits. Events at Home Depot illustrate how attempts to improve efficiency can adversely affect both human relations and

adaptation. The company had always encouraged its store managers to view their stores as their own and to manage them as they
saw fit. While this approach motivated employees to be entrepreneurial and customer-focused, it did not always result in a low cost
of operations. When Bob Nardelli became chairman and CEO, he
decided to improve efficiency by cutting costs, centralizing purchasing, and establishing clearer performance standards. These
changes involved more centralized control over the individual
stores, and the store managers no longer had as much freedom to
make their own decisions. The policy of reducing inventory meant
that customers could no longer be sure of finding what they needed.
The policy of hiring more part-time people (up to half of the workforce) as a cost-cutting measure led to higher turnover and more
customer complaints that they could no longer get advice from
knowledgeable, experienced salespeople. Many talented managers
chose to leave rather than surrender their autonomy to headquarters. Sales slowed dramatically, and the stock fell by 51 percent in
the first few years of Nardelli's tenure. In the race to achieve greater
efficiency, the adverse impact on customers and the importance of
managing human relations and resources had been overlooked.[5]

Nardelli soon realized that the changes had created new
problems, and he acted quickly to find a better balance among
efficiency, human relations, and adaptation. To strengthen the
commitment of store managers, each manager who achieved quarterly sales goals was rewarded with a pickup truck painted orange
in the logo color of the company. Many individual employees in
high-performing stores were rewarded with Disney cruise vacations
or trips to the theme parks. In a move to improve both customer
service and human resources, the number of full-time employees
was increased significantly. To deal with customer complaints about
out-of-stock merchandise, inventory was increased by 25 percent;
to attract more women as customers, a do-it-yourself workshop was
conducted for 40,000 women nationwide. A $250 million store
remodeling program was also initiated, and it incorporated features
copied from other successful retail chains, such as Lowe's and Tar-

get, using wider isles and bigger signs to help customers find merchandise. Finally, some improvements in advertising were also made. Reflecting all these changes, sales and profits at Home Depot have turned around and are on the increase.[6]

### Efficiency vs. Human Relations

There is a potential tradeoff between efficiency and human relations, because some ways of improving human relations will reduce efficiency. Providing a high level of compensation and financial benefits may increase member satisfaction and willingness to remain in the organization, but operating costs will increase and net earnings will be lower. Likewise, employee satisfaction is increased by a policy of guaranteed employment and quality of work life benefits like the ones described in the preceding chapter. However, an organization that is overly generous about allocating resources for the personal benefit of members will have lower efficiency.

Levi Strauss & Co., the maker of blue jeans and other fashion apparel, is an example of an organization in which the emphasis on human relations adversely affected efficiency and adaptation. Levi paid attention to issues of worker loyalty and trust long before it became fashionable to do so. Robert Haas, the CEO, articulated the company's view on the importance of managing human relations in this way: "I believe that if you create an environment that your people identify with, that is responsive to their sense of values, justice, fairness, ethics, compassion, and appreciation, they will help you be successful." As a result, employees could expect generous profit-sharing initiatives, lavish quality of work life programs, high job security (through the 1990s Levi resisted closing U.S. plants and moving production offshore), and a culture of compassion and inclusion. This philosophy served the organization well and helped contribute to decades of excellent financial performance. However, in the late 1990s, increased debt due to a leveraged buyout and a drop in market share due to nimbler, more efficient competitors compelled Levi top management to focus on financial discipline. The resulting layoffs, plant closing, and cost cutting challenged the firm's ability to maintain an emphasis on human relations.[7]

On the other side of the equation, an excessive concern to improve efficiency or process reliability can degrade human relations and resources. Cutting spending on salaries, training and development, and benefits usually improves efficiency, but an unintended consequence may be lower organizational commitment and increased turnover. For example, extensive downsizing to reduce the number of employees will reduce labor costs, but it may also reduce the satisfaction and commitment of the remaining employees, especially when they are asked to do more for the same compensation. If large numbers of experienced older employees are encouraged to retire early, this form of downsizing can also result in a serious decline in employee skills, which will adversely affect process reliability and performance.

Extensive rules and procedures imposed by the organization and elaborate control mechanisms, such as quality inspectors, television cameras in the workplace, and monitoring of telephone conversations and email messages, may improve reliability or reduce theft but undermine employee commitment and job satisfaction. Dell Computers faces this very dilemma. Although the company is well-known for its dedication to efficiency and reliability, some former employees complain that the constant pressure for improving processes and the increasing rigidity of work procedures can become dehumanizing. Dell's drive to apply the same techniques to the service side of the business may run into obstacles, since employees working in services traditionally place a high value on individual skills.[8]

Boeing's infamous forty-day strike by engineers and technicians in early 2000 illustrates how efforts to implement major improvements in efficiency can undermine human relations. In the late 1990s, due to stiff competition, Boeing found it necessary to increase operating efficiency and reliability as they entered a period of competition when sales depended on a low price as well as on product quality. New management was brought in from the outside (a change from the

Boeing tradition of recruiting from within the organization), and there was increased emphasis on cost cutting and efficiency. The increased priority of financial performance in relation to engineering excellence caused the engineers to feel that their contribution was no longer valued as greatly as in the past. Because most of Boeing's internal employee communication was downward, top management failed to listen and respond to the needs and concerns of its engineering employees. As a result, many of the new efficiency and cost-cutting initiatives were resisted and the tension between management and professional employees culminated in a devastating strike.[9]

Verizon's confrontation with its labor unions is a more recent example of how the drive for efficiency can adversely affect human relations. In an effort to reduce costs and enhance the efficient use of human resources, Verizon entered into a very heated and acrimonious battle with its unions. Verizon wanted to eliminate jobs, move jobs to other regions, and reassign workers based on economic and technology factors. The expired contract limited such maneuvers to external events outside normal everyday business, such as a natural disaster. The company also asked for health and pension benefit concessions from employees, even though senior executives received a high level of compensation ($427 million over the past four years), and net income for the company in 2002 was $4.2 billion. During the angry and heated negotiations between the union and management, workers also complained of forced overtime and stressful work conditions. As one observer noted: "It's important that employees feel their employer cares about them. One of the hallmarks in collective bargaining is that despite hard fighting, there is a good-faith belief that one side isn't trying to take unfair advantage of the other."[10]

### Adaptation vs. Human Relations

There is a potential tradeoff between adaptation and human relations. When external changes threaten to seriously reduce sales and profits, successful adaptation is likely to require a substantial investment of resources diverted from other uses. In the middle of an economic crisis for the organization, fewer resources are available to satisfy the individual needs of members. Leaders must ask for sacrifices and make unpopular changes that affect members. In addition, when leaders are preoccupied with making changes, there is less time for people-oriented concerns, such as being supportive and developing member skills other than those directly relevant to the change. There will be less tolerance of people who lack the competencies or commitment necessary to implement change successfully.

Major change is likely to be very stressful for members of the organization. There will be significant effects on roles, relationships, power, and status. People may be uprooted and moved to different locations. Important aspects of the old culture may be lost. Expertise that was important may become irrelevant. If the change is not considered necessary or appropriate, there will be attempts to reverse or delay it. Efforts to resist major changes will increase conflict and reduce trust and cooperation. Even when change is not actively resisted, the disruptive effects of implementing a major change can undermine commitment to the organization and increase turnover among people who have more attractive options for employment.

The strategies leaders select in response to new threats or opportunities may require additional human resources. If the necessary people are not available, or if they cannot be obtained except at an excessive cost, then the strategy may fail. We can see this challenge in the earlier example from Charles Schwab: their new emphasis on a more complex type of customer service created the need for employees with skills not adequately represented in the company's current workforce.

Adaptive changes that emphasize cost reduction may also lower the requirements for employee skills, and the resulting layoffs may undermine employee trust and commitment among the remaining employees.

Conversely, too much emphasis on human relations may inhibit adaptation to a changing environment. When the organization uses a large proportion of its surplus funds to improve compensation and benefits for members, there will be less investment in activities that promote future adaptation, such as research and product development. When there is a high priority for protecting employee privileges, benefits, and job security, necessary steps to implement major change successfully may be avoided. For example, the organization may be unwilling to reassign or dismiss members who are not performing to acceptable standards or those who refuse to accept the changes.

A company cannot afford to neglect crucial matters relating to adaptation in order to maintain good human relations. At Levi Strauss this tradeoff also presented problems for the company. As we have mentioned, Levi has been a values-based company for decades. "The problem is some people thought the values were an end in themselves," says retired president Peter Jacobi. "You have people who say, 'Our objective is to be the most enlightened work environment in the world.' And you have others who say, 'Our objective is to make a lot of money.' The value-based people look at the commercial folks as heathens; the commercial people look at the values people as wusses getting in the way." Levi's culture of inclusion and "principled reasoning approach" made it difficult to be responsive. "Unless you could convince everyone to agree with your idea, you didn't have the authority to make a decision," says former CFO George James. A case in point was the collapse of sales when the company missed the trend toward wrinkle-free pants. That same year the company reported its first decline in profits since 1988.[11]

## Changes in Performance Determinants

The task of balancing tradeoffs among the performance determinants is complicated by changes in conditions affecting the absolute or relative importance of the performance determinants. A leader may achieve a good balance only to find that changing conditions have upset it again. As noted in earlier chapters, the importance of each performance determinant depends on the situation and the competitive strategy for the organization. An especially important situational variable is the amount of uncertainty and volatility in the external environment. It is a major determinant of the importance of innovation and adaptation, but it also affects the importance of efficiency and human resources. The amount of environmental turbulence varies for different types of organizations; and even for organizations in the same industry, it can vary over time.

In general there appears to be a trend toward increased uncertainty in the external environment for business organizations, and for most other types of organizations as well. The uncertainty is increased by globalization, mergers and acquisitions, new competition from developing countries such as China and India, rapid technological change that can make products obsolete in months rather than years, social changes that affect customer preferences, international trade agreements such as NAFTA, the effects of terrorism on the economy and on specific industries such as the airlines, and political change such as the expansion of the European Union and increased terrorism.

An abrupt change in the external environment is likely to involve more uncertainty and turbulence for years afterward, and it may require a new strategy for the organization and major changes in the direct and indirect leadership. For example, the banking industry in the United States had a relatively stable external environment from World War II until the Gramm-Leach-Bliley Act of 1999 allowed the convergence of the banking, insurance, and securities industries and eliminated most requirements for regulatory approval for overseas acquisitions. Since then, the banking industry has become increasingly turbulent and uncertain. Competition for customers, the opportunity to offer financial services that were formerly prohibited, opportunities for mergers, and new technologies such as ATMs and electronic banking have greatly increased the need for innovation and adaptation.

IBM also faced a dramatic change in the external environment that required top management to rethink their strategy and business model. IBM had positioned itself as the premier provider of proprietary information systems utilizing mainframe computers. Starting in the mid-1980s the market began to shift to smaller desktop computers, and many more choices of products and services became available to customers. Top management realized that to survive the company had to move beyond its hardware focus and pursue a strategy that included a range of services, such as system integration, operations outsourcing, and network design and management, aimed at helping clients optimize their IT investment. The new strategy involved another significant departure for IBM: now the company would have to support third-party products and recommend the best solution regardless of manufacturer.[12]

Dramatic changes and events are not limited to a particular type of business or industry, and they can affect many types of organizations, including government agencies, educational institutions, and voluntary organizations. For example, after the 9/11 terrorist attacks, the primary mission of the FBI shifted from fighting crime to preventing terrorism, and local police forces were suddenly tasked with providing security against terrorist attacks on civilian targets.[13]

## Examples of Effective Balancing

Regardless of the difficulties, it is an essential responsibility of leaders to balance competing demands and reconcile tradeoffs among different performance determinants. How well it is done will determine the continued prosperity and survival of a company. Meeting this challenge is the essence of flexible, adaptive leadership. Several studies find evidence that the best companies are ones that have been able to achieve high efficiency, timely adaptation to external change, and a high level of commitment and cooperation by talented employees at all levels. Nissan and MetLife provide two examples of effective balancing.

## Nissan

At the time Carlos Ghosn was appointed CEO of Nissan in 1999, the company was in a state of spectacular decline and had lost money in all but one of the previous eight years. Nissan's factories had the capacity to build almost a million more cars each year than the company could sell. Designers were taking orders from engineers who focused totally on performance, and managers were much more concerned about internal processes than their customers. Nobody was really asking, "What do our customers want from us?" Meanwhile, purchasing costs were 15 to 25 percent higher than at Renault, Nissan's part-owner and Ghosn's employer.

Only Renault's willingness to bail out the company by assuming $5.4 billion of its many billions in debt had saved it from going bankrupt. Still, there was widespread skepticism about Nissan's chances or about the possibility of a foreigner being able to turn the company around. It was generally regarded as impossible to get rid of the well-entrenched Japanese system of lifetime employment and a rigid seniority system that rewarded people for their age and length of service. Ghosn's own diagnosis was that "Nissan suffered from a lack of clear profit-orientation, insufficient focus on customers, and too much focus on chasing competitors, no culture of working together across functions, borders, or hierarchical lines, lack of urgency, and no shared vision."[14]

Ghosn immediately launched a sweeping set of changes to turn the company around. A week after assuming his post, he created nine cross-functional teams and gave them the responsibility for analyzing the company's manufacturing, purchasing, and engineering functions to help him decide what needed to be done to revive the company, including extensive cost-cutting efforts. Such teams had never been deployed at Nissan before. Even more radical was to include not only senior executives, but also a broad cross-section of employees from different levels of the company, as well as some managers from Renault.

To achieve innovation and efficiency simultaneously required major changes that were quite radical for a Japanese company. In Japan there is a long history of hierarchy, pay and promotion based on seniority, lifetime employment, and other features that work against the kind of transformation that happened at Nissan. Changing the attitudes and values represented by these practices was more crucial to a successful adaptation than any changes to specific business processes and systems. How could the new leadership transform these strongly embedded aspects of the culture without engendering resentment and totally demoralizing employees? That was perhaps Ghosn's greatest challenge.

One change was to establish a merit pay plan. Instead of being paid and promoted according to their length of tenure and their age, as had always been the case, employees were expected to earn their promotions and raises in salary through performance. New bonuses provided employees an opportunity to earn up to a third of their annual salaries based on performance. Stock options were offered for the first time in Nissan's history. Areas of accountability were sharply defined so that performance could be measured in relation to goals.

Even more shocking, Ghosn closed five factories, and more than 21,000 jobs (14 percent of the global workforce) were eliminated. Many suppliers were eliminated, and supplier costs were cut by 10 percent. This was an unheard-of measure in a country where supplier relationships were considered sacrosanct and concessions seldom demanded. Non-core assets were sold, and the dealership system was pared down to get rid of unprofitable dealerships.

To address the problem of lackluster design, Ghosn hired the innovative designer Shiro Nakamura, who became another key leader in the turnaround effort. He insisted that the designers had to have authority over the engineers, rather than vice versa, and he and the designers came up with a whole new design approach, including a new logo to signal the rebirth of the company. For the first time in over a decade, Nissan began coming up with cars that excited customers both in Japan and abroad—ranging from a new version of the Z sports car that had once been a symbol of Nissan's design superiority to a revamped model of its once popular Altima sedan and a new subcompact. Just two years later, in 2001, Nissan earnings were at a record high for the company: $3.8 billion on sales of $47.7 billion. The new Altima alone outsold previous versions by 40 percent and became three times as profitable as in the past. Nissan's stock soared, and the company introduced eight new vehicles in 2003.

### Metropolitan Life Insurance Company (MetLife)

A similar example is the story of what happened at MetLife, until a few years ago a company with some oddly Japanese features. When Robert Benmosche took over as chairman of the company in 1998, he and his senior team had to contend with a long history of virtually guaranteed lifetime employment, which, together with the free lunches offered to employees for decades, had earned the company the half-contemptuous nickname "Mother Met." The business had been showing poor returns relative to the rest of the industry for years—return on equity was just 7 percent in 1997—and was planning to go public. Obviously, dramatic change was needed.

Some of that change took the form of massive cost-cutting efforts (including unprecedented firings), the restructuring of the business, and the launch of new products and services. But Benmosche and his senior team were just as concerned with developing a culture that, unlike the old MetLife, would encourage and reward excellent performance. Formerly, performance reviews had tended to be, in the words of one commentator, frequently just "meetings of mutual admiration societies," while bonuses were predictably awarded to virtually everyone each year, with little differentiation between strong and average performers.[15]

Lisa Weber, senior VP and chief administrative officer, oversaw the change to a system that developed, promoted, and encouraged high performers. The new system called for employees to be measured on a five-point scale against their peers and given an annual grade. Bonuses are awarded according to performance ratings. Those who exceed expectations (people rated four or five on the scale) can expect to receive bonuses 46 percent higher than Grade Three employees, who in turn can expect to see bonuses 68 percent higher than their colleagues in Grades One or Two. "When you treat your top performers like the stars they are, you will get their loyalty forever, and that's what it's all about," Weber says. "When you have the loyalty, you get the production, and that is how the company can win from within." While overall turnover for the company is 17 percent, the turnover among the highest grade of employees is only 7 percent.[16]

In addition, the message about improving productivity was reinforced by week-long training programs for managers at all levels, and Benmosche himself spent a full day working with program attendees to address the management dilemmas they faced. Such a commitment on the part of the chairman of the organization served to send a clear message that this was an important initiative, just as the revisions to the performance management system and the new kind of training managers received were an unmistakable signal that the old culture was no more.

## Other Tradeoffs for Leaders

Several types of challenges are involved in the balancing act performed by leaders. The need to balance the performance determinants in a way that is appropriate to the situation has already been discussed. This challenge is not limited to chief executives; middle and lower-level leaders are also confronted by competing demands that involve performance determinants such as efficiency, adaptation, and human relations. In addition to the primary challenge of balancing the performance determinants and adjusting to changes in conditions that affect them, leaders at all levels must also deal with some other difficult tradeoffs that are related to the ones already examined.

## Stakeholders' Demands and Expectations

Another challenge for leaders is to deal with competing demands from different parties or "stakeholders" whose support and cooperation are needed by leaders. The three primary types of stakeholders identified by most business writers are employees, customers, and owners (or shareholders). Each of these stakeholder groups tends to have somewhat different priorities in relation to efficiency, human resources, and adaptation. For example, employees are especially concerned about human resources issues, compensation, and job security; customers are especially concerned about product quality, price, and customer service; and shareholders are especially concerned about short-term profits, which depend heavily on efficiency and cost reduction.

Nevertheless, it is important not to oversimplify or exaggerate these associations between stakeholder groups and performance determinants. While the three types of stakeholders cannot be said to have identical interests or priorities, they may have a strong, shared interest in the capacity of the organization to survive and prosper. It is this shared interest that provides the possibility for leaders to find integrative solutions to competing demands from stakeholders, to build support for drastic actions needed to deal with crises, and to inspire collective enthusiasm for risky initiatives needed to pursue opportunities.

How leaders balance competing demands from different stakeholders is of primary concern for scholars interested in ethical leadership and the appropriate role of leaders in organization.[17,18,19] In contrast to the traditional conception of chief executives as agents who must represent business owners, some of these scholars prefer to view the leader as a "servant" or "steward" who should seek to represent all relevant stakeholders and seek ways to integrate their primary concerns. In the eyes of these scholars, it is unethical to favor stakeholders who will provide the highest personal gain for the leader, or to play stakeholders off against each other for personal benefit (for example, by encouraging negative stereotyping and mutual distrust). Instead, these scholars argue that leaders who are both ethical and effective must recognize conflicts of interest among stakeholders, openly acknowledge them (rather than pretending they do not exist), and find integrative ways of resolving them.

The following incident described by Nielsen[20] provides an example of a leader who took an integrative approach for resolving competing demands from different internal and external stakeholders. The division manager for a paper products company was confronted with a difficult problem. Top management decided to close some paper mills unless operational costs for them could be reduced. The manager was concerned that cutting costs would prevent the mills from meeting government pollution control requirements. However, unless costs were reduced, the mills would close, seriously hurting employees and the economy of the local community. The manager decided to look for an integrative win-win solution. He asked the research and engineering people in his division to look for ways to make the mills more efficient and also reduce pollution. He asked the operations and financial people in his division to estimate how much it would cost to build better mills and when the operations would achieve a breakeven payback. When a good solution was finally found, he negotiated an agreement with top management to implement the plan.

The challenge of dealing with competing demands from different stakeholders is not limited to chief executives or elected political leaders. Middle and lower-level managers have similar challenges, and they are often confronted with competing demands from parties within the same organization who have different priorities for the performance determinants. One type of conflict involves competing demands from bosses and direct reports. For example, deans or department heads in a university may find it necessary to balance the desire of higher administrators for larger classes and fewer electives (more efficiency) against the desire of professors for smaller courses and more specialized electives (more satisfaction and commitment). Likewise, the desire of administrators to have classes scheduled in a way that will utilize rooms efficiently must be balanced against the desire of professors to have their classes scheduled at times convenient for them.

Competing demands are also found when functionally specialized subunits become advocates of a particular performance dimension. For example, in a company that makes and sells products for customers with diverse tastes, the marketing and production subunits may have different priorities. Marketing may prefer to offer a large variety of different models to facilitate adaptation, and production may prefer to make a small variety of models to increase efficiency and reduce the difficulty of production scheduling. The general manager responsible for reconciling the different priorities will need to find a good balance, and this balance can shift if customer preferences are changing or new competitors enter the marketplace with cheaper or better products and services.

### Short-Term vs. Long-Term Objectives

Another challenge for leaders is to balance tradeoffs involving short-term and long-term objectives. Leader decisions are more difficult when there are delayed effects on some types of outcomes. In this situation, the immediate effect of a change is too often to make things worse instead of better. Efforts to improve efficiency, innovation, or human resources may have a delayed effect before any improvements are actually realized, and it may be necessary to increase short-term costs in order to attain long-term benefits. For example, when new technology is acquired to improve efficiency, there will be additional costs to purchase the technology and train employees to use it. These costs and a temporary decline in productivity as people learn how to use the technology may reduce efficiency and profits in the short term. The eventual results may be higher efficiency and profits, but they will occur only after the changes are fully implemented.

The converse is also true. Profits may be increased in the short run by eliminating costly activities that have a delayed effect on profits, such as equipment maintenance, research and development, investments in new technology, and employee skill training. In the long run, the effect of cutting these essential activities will be lower profits, as the negative consequences slowly increase and eventually outweigh any benefits. The delayed effects may encourage leaders whose primary concern is looking good in the short term to make decisions that will endanger the longer-term prosperity and survival of the organization. Unfortunately, many business leaders emphasize short-term profits more than the long-term prosperity and survival of the company. In the same way, many elected leaders pander to the short-term desires of constituents, regardless of the negative consequences that will occur long after the leader has left office.

The appropriate balance between short-term and long-term objectives depends in part on the situation. There is growing evidence from research on companies that are successful over a long period of time that effective leaders emphasize long-term objectives more than short-term ones.[21,22] Nevertheless, when there is a financial crisis, short-term objectives become relatively more important than they are in times of prosperity, and it may be necessary to cut costs drastically to ensure that the company survives. However, even in this situation, the challenge for leaders is to determine what type of cuts and changes will ensure not only that the company survives, but also that it will be effective after the crisis has passed.

### Stability vs. Change

Another challenge for leaders is to balance competing values regarding stability and continuity versus change and innovation. Stability can provide potential benefits for an organization. It is easier to achieve efficiency and process reliability if there is at least a moderate amount of continuity in work processes, and stability creates less turmoil and stress for members of the organization. To increase stability, the leader institutionalizes new knowledge and best practices into standard procedures and traditional practices and builds commitment to implement them. Respect for tradition is strengthened by rituals, ceremonies, and stories that celebrate past accomplishments, company heroes, and proven best practices.

However, strong respect for tradition and established practices can obscure the need for new approaches to deal with changing conditions. Successful adaptation in a turbulent environment usually requires flexibility and innovation. In this situation, leaders are expected to be visionary reformers and agents of change, not defenders of tradition. To foster innovative thinking, the leader can encourage people to challenge traditional assumptions and examine established practices to find any weaknesses. The leader can empower people to experiment with new approaches and work around restrictive rules and procedures to get results.

The tradeoff between stability and innovation is related to (but not the same as) the tradeoff between efficiency and adaptation. It is often easier to achieve a high degree of efficiency and reliability if there is at least a moderate degree of continuity in work processes and practices. The costs involved in making frequent major change may exceed any benefits. On the other hand, a major innovation may result in a significant improvement in efficiency or reliability that could not be achieved with small, incremental improvements.

Given the current high level of uncertainty and change for most organizations, it is appropriate to have a higher priority for innovation and change than for stability and tradition. It is an essential role of leaders to ensure that respect for tradition and past achievements not be allowed to obscure the fact that times are changing and what works well now may not be appropriate in the future. Research on companies that failed to make necessary changes found that a major reason was a belief that the company already knew what was best and had nothing more to learn about being successful. This arrogant attitude was more likely to be found in companies with a prior record of great success, a strong culture reflecting established practices, and reverence for the heroic lead-ers who were credited with the success.[23]

Wang Laboratories is a classic example. The company was founded in 1951 by An Wang, and by 1988 it had gross sales of $2.9 billion. The company's rapid increase in sales resulted from the design, manufacture, and distribution of its VS minicomputer. But Wang's equipment was mostly proprietary, meaning that it did not communicate with machines made by other companies. While this strategy initially locked in business, customers eventu-ally began asking for open systems. However, An Wang failed to recognize the need for change and refused to adapt his proprietary word-processing system to the open-standards world of networked PCs.[24] Sales faltered, then plummeted, and the company filed for bankruptcy in 1992. It was eventually acquired (in 1999) by Getronics NV of the Netherlands.[25]

Despite the importance of innovation and adaptation for orga-nizations, there is also a risk in becoming too change-oriented. A strong bias for change may encourage bold ventures based on wish-ful thinking rather than careful analysis of risks and feasibility. It can result in more change than is necessary, and the costs of major change can exceed the benefits.

Efforts to implement major change quickly may involve polit-ical risks for leaders if strong resistance occurs. In 1999, Durk Jager, the former CEO of Procter & Gamble, was brought in to shake up the bureaucratic culture and grow the company. Before Jager took over, P&G's last innovative new product was Pampers in 1961. "The core of the business is innovation," he said. "If we inno-vate well, we will ultimately win."[26] Seventeen months later, he was out of a job. The general consensus in the industry was that he pushed change too fast for the organization to absorb. By abruptly changing longstanding management practices, Jager alienated the people whose support he needed.[27]

A strong bias for change can also encourage the elimination of established traditions or practices with roots in the distant past and a purpose that is no longer evident without a careful examination of past events. While it is easy to find absurd examples of old practices that are no longer relevant, it is also easy to find cases where established practices were abandoned only to find that the problems they prevented have re-emerged. Such examples caution leaders to remember the old maxim that those who forget the lessons of history are destined to repeat them.

### Control vs. Empowerment

Another type of tradeoff that has important implications for effective leadership involves the way responsibility and authority are distributed among the leaders at different levels in an organization. A major challenge is to find an appropriate balance between centralized control and local autonomy. Too much centralization stifles local initiative and creativity, and it may result in a loss of employees who desire more meaningful and challenging jobs. On the other hand, too much decentralization can result in inefficiency and failure to achieve coordination and potential synergy among subunits. The appropriate balance will depend on the type of organization, its competitive strategy, and the relative importance of the different determinants of organization performance.

Most leadership scholars emphasize the benefits of empowerment, but there has been little explicit discussion of the risks from too much decentralization or of the difficulties it creates for leaders at all levels. What is best for the department or division may not be best for the organization, and empowered unit leaders can become so preoccupied with their local problems that they fail to adequately consider the needs of the larger organization. Local autonomy also creates the possibility of reduced coordination among subunits of an organization, and the result can be reduced efficiency and reliability. The failure of the CIA, FBI, and other government agencies to share important information and coordinate their watch lists for terrorists was a major reason they were unable to discover the 9/11 plot in time to prevent it. The chief executive has the ultimate responsibility for ensuring that the needs of leaders at different levels are reconciled and that there is close coordination and cooperation among different subunits.

## Conclusions

Leadership is a balancing act, and it often feels like it must be done on a tightrope in front of a critical audience. The appropriate balance depends on the situation, which may be different tomorrow than it is today. Effective leaders seek to integrate different objectives and reconcile the competing demands and priorities of different parties. However, it is not always possible to find "win-win" solutions to conflicts, and difficult choices cannot be avoided. The balancing act is made more difficult by tradeoffs between short-term and long-term objectives, between stability and change, and between control and empowerment. Effective leaders find an appropriate balance that takes into account all of these tradeoffs, but reflects a primary concern for the long-term effectiveness and survival of the organization.

The fates of leaders at all levels are closely intertwined in complex ways, and it is important for each leader to understand how his or her decisions and actions will affect other leaders and the overall organization. The performance of the organization depends not only on the decisions and actions of the chief executive, but on commitment, cooperation, and coordination among leaders at all levels and in different subunits. The following chapter will examine what leaders can do to be more flexible and effective in dealing with the difficult responsibilities placed on them.

*Chapter 12*

# The Path to Flexible Leadership

The real art of leadership is to perform a balancing act. The most effective leaders are those who can diagnose the situation, evaluate the challenges, balance competing demands, and integrate diverse behaviors in a way that is relevant for meeting the challenges. Effective leaders are careful not to focus so much on one type of challenge that the others are neglected, and they look for ways to deal with multiple challenges at the same time.

No magic formula will guarantee success in determining what needs to be done by leaders or the best way to do it. However, useful insights are provided by leadership research conducted over more than half a century by hundreds of scholars, by our own research, by the reflections of successful leaders, and by descriptive research on successful and unsuccessful organizations. In this chapter we examine six processes and five competencies that can facilitate development of flexible, shared leadership in organizations.

## Guidelines for Effective Leadership

Many of the direct and indirect forms of leadership described in earlier chapters are useful for dealing with the challenges that confront leaders in all types of organizations, but success requires more than just a good mix of those behaviors and programs. In this section we will suggest what else leaders can do to make their direct and indirect leadership behavior more effective. The guidelines, which are summarized in Table 12.1, build on ideas in earlier chapters but involve broad issues rather than specific behaviors.

## Table 12.1.  Guidelines for Effective Leadership

- Build commitment to a core ideology
- Build capable leadership at all levels
- Involve and empower people at all levels
- Keep lines of communication open
- Use reward systems to support multiple objectives
- Encourage and exemplify leadership by example

Although the emphasis is on strategic leadership, multiple challenges, and the "big picture," the guidelines are relevant for improving the effectiveness of leaders at all levels. An underlying theme of the guidelines is that it takes flexible leadership to enhance organizational processes and facilitate collective efforts to achieve shared objectives.

### Build Commitment to a Core Ideology

In an earlier chapter we talked about the importance of a vision or strategic objective that will sustain the effort and excitement of members for the long haul. It is difficult to find an appealing vision unless there is widespread agreement about the primary mission and purpose of the organization. It is difficult to achieve consistent and coordinated action among many leaders in different parts of the organization unless there are shared ideals and values to guide each individual. It is difficult to balance competing demands from different stakeholders and tradeoffs among performance determinants unless there is a core ideology to anchor judgments and remind leaders that short-term profits are not the only important criterion.

Core ideology refers to shared agreement about the primary purpose for the organization. It may be captured in a mission statement, values statement, strategic objective, or an articulated vision, and it may be embedded implicitly in the culture in the form of stories, myths, and shared values that people can describe if asked.

The core ideology is likely to involve not only the purpose of the organization, but also how members fit into that purpose and will be treated individually and collectively. In successful companies, the individual rights and responsibilities of members are clearly reflected in policies, programs, and criteria used to select members, assess their contributions, and recognize and reward them.

A primary responsibility of leadership at the top is to help members come together in support of a shared purpose or mission for the organization. A primary responsibility for the leadership at middle and lower levels is to build support for the core ideology by ensuring that it is clear and by explicitly using it to guide decisions and actions. When decisions are made, the ideals and values should be emphasized more than the policies, rules, and procedures that supposedly reflect them. In other words, the "spirit of the law" should be emphasized more than the "letter of the law" when the two are not consistent. Otherwise, rules and procedures are too easily twisted to support actions or objectives that are not consistent with ideals and values.

The core ideology provides a compass to help leaders identify appropriate ways to adapt to environmental change. Successful adaptation requires a good understanding of markets and customers, but it is not appropriate to do anything customers want just to increase sales. The primary reason for listening closely to customers is to maintain a good strategic fit, and the response to customer preferences should be consistent with the core values and ideals of the organization.[1] For example, clients of auditing firms, consulting firms, and financial firms may prefer to get a rosy report or recommendation that overlooks or minimizes serious problems. However, covering up weaknesses to ensure future business from a client is inconsistent with the ideal of providing accurate, objective, appraisals and recommendations. Dealing with a conflict of interest that involves values and ethics requires courageous leadership, and it is essential for leaders at any level to provide strong support for someone at a lower level who is trying to uphold the core values and ideals.

Research by James Collins and Jerry Porras[2] found that companies with a strong, consistent core ideology were more likely to survive and be successful over a long period of time. Examples of such companies include Hewlett-Packard, Sony, Merck, and 3M. These companies "understood that it is far more important to know who you are than where you are going, for where you are going will certainly change as the world about you changes. Leaders die, products become obsolete, markets change, and new technologies emerge, management fads come and go; but core ideology in a great company endures as a source of guidance and inspiration."[3] Unfortunately, there are also many examples of companies that do not appear to be guided by a core ideology. Companies like Enron, WorldCom, Adelphia, and Tyco have virtually been destroyed by the actions of a few senior executives who appear to have been guided by self-interest rather than an enduring ideology, purpose, and set of values that put the interests of employees, stockholders, and customers first.

### Build Capable Leadership at All Levels

Effective leaders understand that, in the final analysis, people are the organization's most valuable asset and an essential aspect of the "dynamic capabilities." A key responsibility of leaders at all levels is to ensure that the organization has competent, dedicated leaders. In earlier chapters we described direct and indirect forms of leadership used to enhance human resources, but the unique challenges of attracting, developing, and retaining leadership talent in the organization deserves special attention.

Types of formal programs and direct leadership behaviors that help to build capable leadership at all levels and ensure adequate succession for top leadership positions were identified in Chapters 9 and 10. Studies show that a significant amount of leadership development occurs as a result of experiences on the job and that there is more learning when a person has challenging assignments that require adapting to new situations and dealing with a variety of different types of problems. Leadership development is also enhanced when there is a strong learning culture and developmental activities are integrated with other human resource activities such as career counseling, staffing decisions, performance appraisal, and succession planning.[4,5,6]

An essential role for top management is to integrate these elements and keep them consistent with an organization's strategic objectives. Developmental activities and programs are more likely to be successful when there is strong support for them from top management. Studies of successful organizations find that the chief executives are deeply involved in planning and implementing leadership development activities. One effective behavior is to make an appearance at key programs, or even to serve as a workshop facilitator; these symbolic acts clearly communicate the importance of leadership development in the organization.[7,8]

In successful organizations, primary responsibility for leadership development is not limited to top management or the human resources department. It is a key responsibility of leaders at all levels and in all subunits to help create favorable conditions for leadership development.[9] These leaders must support developmental programs and enhance leadership development with relevant direct behaviors such as coaching, mentoring, supporting, recognizing, and empowering. However, it is not always as easy as it may sound. Facilitating development of direct reports can involve difficult tradeoffs for a leader. For example, it may be more efficient to assign a difficult task to the most experienced person, but more development will occur if another direct report is assigned the task and provided appropriate coaching by the leader or by a mentor. To find an appropriate balance will require careful consideration of the immediate situation and the relative priorities of different objectives.

### Involve and Empower People at All Levels

A cooperative effort is needed to meet the leadership challenges effectively and to balance them properly. Successful leadership in organizations requires the skills, expertise, and knowledge of many people throughout the company, and it cannot be provided by a single, heroic leader. Leaders at different levels of the organization and within different subunits must act in ways that are mutually compatible. The cooperation and commitment of people who are not in formal leadership positions is also needed, and leaders must find ways to involve and empower them as well. Studies show that the most successful organizations have a strong culture in which members with shared values are empowered to find ways to accomplish the mission or achieve the vision.[10,11,12,13]

At Southwest Airlines, which as an organization has shown a remarkable ability to meet and balance all the leadership challenges throughout its history, employees are not only encouraged but are expected to take initiative and solve problems. Southwest has demonstrated the ability to achieve efficiency and reliability through innovation and to respond to customer needs while still cutting costs. It was the first major airline to offer ticket-less travel, the first major airline to offer online booking (which saved them hundreds of thousands of dollars in travel agent costs, while allowing customers to book at any time), and the first to eliminate seat assignments, thereby making twenty-minute turnaround at the gate possible. Southwest's ability to keep costs low while still keeping employees satisfied is even more remarkable. Despite the carrier's relatively low pay scale, the employees are loyal to the company and willing to go the extra mile for it. Their high commitment may be due in part to the practice of actively soliciting employee input, acting on employee suggestions, and giving people enough freedom and variety in their jobs to make their work interesting. The company also has a very generous profit-sharing plan, the first ever established by an airline. Southwest's senior management would be the first to say that they have benefited enormously from empowering people at all levels of the company. As Herb Kelleher, the founder and ex-CEO of Southwest saw it, employees on the front lines are the ones who know how things should be done: "They're the ones who make things happen, not us. The people out there are the experts. Before you implement an idea that has been generated in the office, you should always take it to the field and ask for their criticisms."[14]

Another CEO who is a believer in consulting with others at all levels is Bill Ford, Henry Ford's grandson, who took over from Jacques Nasser as the CEO of the demoralized auto giant in 2001. He has taken Ford of Europe's success at reducing costs and improving quality as his "blueprint" for the revitalization of North American Ford. In pursuing his challenging but highly necessary goals of cutting costs, increasing the efficiency of manufacturing processes, speeding the design and development process, and restoring both quality and excitement to the company's products, Ford continually consults with people at all levels of the company. He selected a team of strong senior executives, whose opinions and ideas he openly relies on, but he also actively solicits opinions and feedback from managers many layers below him in the hierarchy, and even from assembly-line workers. In his view, one of the company's chief problems in the past was the isolation of its top executives, and that is something he is definitely changing. As James Padilla, group vice president of Ford North America, puts it, "He's not a traditional command-and-control automotive CEO."[15] It is not yet certain that his attempts to restore Ford to its former glory can succeed, but if they fail it will not be for lack of listening.

## Keep Lines of Communication Open

A common denominator for understanding and meeting the different types of leadership challenges is effective communication among leaders themselves and between leaders and other members of the organization. If leaders at all levels are to play an active role and make good decisions, they need to understand the organization's objectives, priorities, and strategies. We saw earlier how important communication was in the turnaround at Nissan and how Bill Ford and others have made it a policy to communicate with employees at all levels of the company. Two-way communication across levels is needed to ensure that people not only understand what is expected of them but are committed to doing it.[16,17]

According to a recent study of nearly thirteen thousand workers, less than half of all employees surveyed understood the steps their companies were taking to reach new business goals or how what they did was related to achieving those goals. Watson Wyatt, the consulting firm that conducted the study, concluded that this confusion among employees is likely to make it more difficult for companies to recover from any protracted slumps that may occur. They found that three-year total returns to shareholders are three times higher at companies where employees understand corporate objectives and the ways in which their jobs contribute to achieving them.[18]

There are many things leaders can do to encourage and facilitate effective communication. Written and e-mail communication about challenges and strategies can serve a very useful purpose, but there is no real substitute for face-to-face interaction. This type of communication may take place on an ad-hoc basis, or there may be formal programs in place to ensure that it occurs. Several of the direct leadership behaviors described in earlier chapters are relevant for improving communication about important issues. A number of the management programs described in earlier chapters also emphasize the open exchange of ideas and information.

In some cases it is useful to hold regular forums to discuss issues and changes. At Procter & Gamble's Indian subsidiary, there are regular sessions with the CEO, where employees are free to raise questions on organizational changes, express their concerns about their roles and the business, and have the CEO and directors reply immediately. Since it is an open forum (which is known as "Let's Talk"), any and all questions are allowed. One employee might ask about a hard-core business issue, while another might have a suggestion about the design of a new facility. In fact, the final layout of the new headquarters was largely an outcome of the discussions at "Let's Talk" sessions. Questions can also be submitted anonymously, but as employees learn that there are no repercussions when they question senior management's decisions, anonymity becomes less and less necessary. "P&G has found that opening lines of communication focuses employees' energy towards positive output and away from corridor talk. The 'Let's Talk' open sessions are increasing employee feedback on business choices and company policies, helping to deliver a more meaningful face to the external world, and even boosting employee morale," says Anthony Rose, senior manager of public affairs.[19]

Efforts to improve two-way communication can also be a more informal process, as when leaders walk around in their departments or on the factory floor, or otherwise make themselves available to employees. At Southwest Airlines there is a straightforward "open-door" policy whereby any employee is free to air concerns and ideas with everyone from the mechanics to the CEO at any time. At Pfizer, openness is a cultural value emphasized by CEO Henry McKinnell, who encourages all the company's employees, even temps, to talk to him about their concerns and any complaints they may have. Moreover, to make Pfizer employees feel more comfortable with raising concerns or bringing forward new ideas, the company enhanced its open-door policy to increase access to other senior managers as well. McKinnell does not pretend to have all the answers and is willing to admit when he does not know the best way to deal with a problem.[20]

Keeping the lines of communication open is especially important when leaders have to make unpopular decisions. People need to know why a controversial decision was made or why they are being asked to do things that seem inconsistent with organization goals. They need to understand the balance that is being sought, why sacrifices now will be worth it in the long run, and how their concerns are being addressed. As CEO of Nissan, Ghosn communicated almost relentlessly with employees. It has been said that he "recognizes the benefits of communication like perhaps no other business leader in the world."[21] He made innumerable whistle-stop tours of factories and dealerships to communicate his vision of the new Nissan, answer questions, and solicit ideas. This non-hierarchical approach both charmed and energized employees, who quickly became his greatest fans. Former skeptics in the business press were forced to acknowledge that what had looked like an impossible task—changing the entrenched culture of a traditional Japanese company—had been carried out successfully.[22]

### Use Reward Systems to Support Multiple Objectives

The reward system in an organization can be designed to support multiple objectives and help leaders deal with all three types of challenges. As we saw in Chapters 4, 6, and 8, reward and recognition programs can help to improve efficiency, innovation, and human relations by showing individuals and teams that their efforts are valued and appreciated. The reward system is also a major determinant of an organization's ability to attract and retain highly competent employees. There are numerous types of programs, and the structure of the program is only limited by one's imagination.

At First Maryland Bancorp (now Allfirst Financial), a "Brainstorm" program was designed to generate ideas for increasing revenues or decreasing expenses. Rewards were promised to all individuals or teams whose ideas were adopted during the three months in which the program was conducted. Of the roughly $3 million that the program cost, $2 million was spent on rewards. Examples of the innovative ideas for achieving efficiency include a proposal for more efficient ways to route telecommunications circuits and a proposal to reduce maintenance costs on computer equipment at branch banks. The savings achieved were almost eight times the cost of "Brainstorm." Moreover, according to senior vice president Brian King, the program also served as a learning experience for employees, one that yielded benefits beyond the immediate cost savings. King felt that by learning about the financial aspects of doing business, employees would be enabled to make better decisions about the use of resources.[23]

When major changes are made in an organization, it is essential for top management to ensure that the appraisal and reward systems are consistent with the objectives of the changes. When people are merely told that something is important, without being measured and rewarded in terms of how successfully they achieve it, they will more than likely continue as they have always done. Whatever the change that leaders are trying to implement, aligning HR systems with those goals is vital to effecting real culture change. A common mistake in trying to develop a more innovative culture, for example, is to continue punishing failure, which means that people will be reluctant to take the risks associated with innovation. The turnaround efforts at Nissan and at MetLife described earlier would have been much less successful if the appraisal and reward systems had remained the same.

### Encourage and Exemplify Leadership by Example

Leading by example is an important form of influence for leaders. One of the most effective things a leader can do is to serve as a role model for the kinds of behavior expected of employees. The examples set by leaders at any level can influence members of the organization at lower levels, and examples set by top executives can cascade down through the organization. A chief executive who uses scarce funds to build an ostentatious new headquarters building or to purchase a company jet for executives is not setting an example of controlling costs. A department head who always travels first-class and is known for taking clients out to lavish lunches is unlikely to inspire direct reports to prune their own expenses.

Take the case of American Airlines, whose senior executives asked for—and received—major concessions from its pilots and other staff, amounting to $1.62 billion in savings, during one of the ailing airline's recent financial crises. Union members were told that their cooperation was imperative if American was going to be saved from bankruptcy. Shortly afterward, however, those same employees learned that the senior managers who had demanded the concessions from them had just awarded themselves lavish retention bonuses in addition to a generous supplemental pension plan. The company president—Donald Carty—was due to receive $1.6 million under the new bonus plan if he stayed with American for another three years. Union members reconvened and voted to pull back from the cost-cutting agreement. The attempt to improve efficiency might have succeeded if senior management had been sensitive to the human issues and had set an example by making big sacrifices themselves. It was only after Carty resigned that the unions finally agreed to renegotiate.[24]

Ghosn's effectiveness at Nissan was partly a result of demonstrating the accountability he expected from all Nissan's other employees. When he took over as CEO, he pledged that he and his whole senior team would step down if Nissan failed to show a profit in 2000. It was an impressive demonstration of his own sincerity and commitment, and it made what he was asking of others seem more acceptable. Ghosn was modeling for his employees the kind of attitudes and behaviors he was demanding of them.

## Competencies for Effective Leadership

A number of *competencies* are relevant for flexible leadership. Competencies are skills that can be learned with sufficient opportunity for instruction and practice. This final section of the chapter describes some competencies found relevant in scholarly research on effective leaders. We will describe these competencies in terms of specific guidelines rather than abstract skills, and they are shown in Table 12.2.

### Table 12.2.  Competencies for Effective Leadership

- Maintain situational awareness
- Embrace systems thinking
- Focus on what is really important
- Maintain self-awareness
- Preserve personal integrity

## Maintain Situational Awareness

Situational awareness means understanding how external and internal events in the organization are relevant for the effectiveness of a leader. To understand the significance of a particular event or trend and to identify an appropriate response requires a good understanding of the external environment, but it also requires a good understanding of the organization and its processes and people. It will be difficult for a top executive to resolve a problem, initiate a change, or inspire commitment without a clear understanding of the shared values and beliefs that make up the organization culture, the prior events and decisions that determine how the organization got to where it is now, the impact proposed changes could have on work processes and customers, and the political processes that affect major decisions. To become more situationally aware, it is necessary to actively probe beneath surface appearances to learn about prior events, power relationships, interpersonal relationships, informal processes, hidden agendas, and the attitudes and feelings of the people who will be involved in a decision or affected by it.[25]

Behaviors such as internal and external monitoring are relevant for improving situational awareness, but to obtain up-to-date information about relevant events, it is usually necessary to develop an extensive network of contacts inside and outside of the organization. These contacts can provide information that is not available from formal communications or from the regular information systems. Network members can also be a source of assistance and political support for a leader. Effective leaders use different parts of their network for different purposes and extend the network as needed to accomplish a particular objective.[26,27]

Networks are developed in a variety of ways, such as (1) talking with people before, during, and after meetings, ceremonies, and social events in the organization; (2) serving on special committees, interest groups, and task forces; (3) joining civic groups, advisory boards, and social clubs; and (4) attending workshops, trade shows, and meetings of professional associations. Cooperative relationships are established and maintained by showing respect and positive regard, offering unconditional favors (e.g., passing on useful information, offering to help with a problem), keeping in touch, and showing appreciation for favors received, especially those requiring a significant effort on the part of the person doing the favor. The process of networking is a perpetual activity, because old relationships need to be maintained and new ones established as people in key positions change, the organization changes, and the external environment changes.

Situational awareness also involves understanding the needs and feelings of people whose support and cooperation are needed to accomplish a leader's objectives. The ability to understand a person's emotions is one aspect of "emotional intelligence."[28,29] Empathy for the needs and feelings of others helps a leader to develop cooperative interpersonal relationships and influence people successfully. A leader who understands the hopes and dreams of others is better able to arouse their enthusiasm and optimism for a proposed activity or change.

Consider what happened when two brokerage companies merged, creating redundant jobs in each division. One division manager called his people together and gave a gloomy speech that emphasized the number of people who would soon be fired. This manager was too worried about his own fate to consider that his direct reports were also concerned about their future. Division performance declined as many competent but demoralized people left to take jobs in other companies. In contrast, the manager of another division explained why the merger was necessary, and he promised to keep people informed and to treat everyone fairly. This manager knew what his people were feeling, and he acknowledged their fears and tried to build confidence. As a result, his best people stayed, and his division remained as productive as before.[30]

### Embrace Systems Thinking

Understanding the factors that determine organizational performance in a particular situation requires the use of "systems thinking."[31] It is important to understand that complex problems often have multiple causes, which may include actions taken earlier to solve other problems. In large systems such as organizations, actions invariably have multiple outcomes, including unintended side-effects. Changes often have delayed effects that tend to obscure the real nature of the relationship. A change in one part of a system will eventually affect other parts of it, and reactions to the change may cancel out the effects. An example is when a manager downsizes the workforce to reduce costs, but pressure to maintain the same output requires expensive overtime and use of consultants (including some of the same people who were downsized), thereby negating any cost savings.

Another common phenomenon is a reinforcing cycle wherein small changes grow into much bigger changes that may or may not be desirable. For example, after a change made to improve processes in one organizational unit is successful, other units are encouraged to imitate it, resulting in more benefits than initially expected. A negative example is the following: rationing is introduced to conserve a resource; to avoid a temporary shortage people rush to stock up on it, thereby causing even greater shortages.

When making decisions or diagnosing the cause of problems, it is essential to understand how the different parts of the organization are interrelated. Even when the immediate objective is to deal with one type of challenge, such as improving efficiency, leaders need to consider the likely consequences for other performance determinants and the possibility that any immediate benefits will be nullified by later events as the effects of a decision or change eventually ripple through the system. While strategic thinking about these issues is clearly more important for high-level leaders than for lower-level leaders, it is relevant for leaders at all levels.

An example of how a leader can encourage systems thinking to improve problem solving can be found at Ford during the design of a new model car. The project manager found that the engineers who designed the air conditioning, the headlights, the power seats, and the CD player were all working independently, and when used simultaneously these devices would drain the car battery. In previous cases of this type, the engineers from different departments would argue about who should make the design sacrifices to deal with a problem. Eventually their boss would have to tell one department to make the sacrifice, and the engineers in that department would feel like losers. In this case, however, the project manager asked the engineers to take a broader systems perspective when trying to understand the nature of the problem. Working together as a cooperative team, they were able to come up with an integrative "win-win" solution that satisfied everyone and saved considerable time in the design process. The solution was to increase the idle speed slightly in order to increase the battery charge.[32]

### Focus on What Is Really Important

Most people in leadership positions are faced with relentless pressure to deal with immediate problems and respond to requests for assistance, direction, or authorization. It is easy to become overloaded with activities and obligations, many of which are not relevant for attaining key objectives. Effective leaders are more proactive in their behavior; their actions are guided by clear objectives and priorities. Even though much of their daily activity is in response to immediate problems and requests, they attempt to identify necessary activities and plan time for them.

In the extensive practitioner-oriented literature on time management, there is considerable agreement about the importance of planning daily and weekly activities in advance. However, it is not feasible to plan in advance exactly how each minute of the day will be spent. The unpredictable nature of the environment makes it essential to view chance encounters, interruptions, and unscheduled meetings initiated by others not just as intrusions on scheduled activities, but rather as opportunities to gain important information, discover problems, influence others, and move forward on implementation of plans and informal agendas. Obligations that might otherwise be time wasters, such as required attendance at some meetings and ceremonial occasions, can be turned to one's advantage. Thus, even when reacting to unforeseen events, the behavior of effective leaders is guided by their objectives and priorities.[33,34]

Leaders who become too preoccupied with reacting to day-to-day problems have no time left for the reflective planning that would help them to avoid many of the problems or for the contingency planning that would help them cope better with unavoidable problems. Therefore, it is desirable to set aside some time on a regular basis for reflective analysis and planning. Listen to Antonia Bryson, a deputy commissioner in New York City's Department of Environmental Protection: "What happens in government is that you always tend to get caught up in crises. But it's helpful to sit back at the end of every week and ask, 'Is this part of my long-term plan of what I want to accomplish while I am in this job?' The higher up you go, the more you have to constantly examine how you are setting your own priorities. Are you going to the right meetings? Are you going to too many meetings? Are you using your staff members effectively to make sure you yourself are spending time on the right things and accomplishing what you want to get accomplished?"[35]

### Maintain Self-Awareness

In addition to situational awareness, effective leaders also develop good self-awareness. The ability to understand one's own emotions and motives is another aspect of "emotional intelligence," and it is relevant for leadership effectiveness in many ways.[36,37] It can help leaders solve complex problems, make better decisions, adapt their behavior to the situation, and manage crises. The ability to understand one's own needs and likely emotional reactions to events facilitates information processing and decision making in stressful situations and it helps one maintain optimism and enthusiasm about a project or mission in the face of obstacles and setbacks.

Self-awareness also includes a good understanding of one's own abilities and behavior. It is difficult to learn from experience without a clear awareness of your behavior and its influence on others.

Understanding of strengths makes it easier for a leader to build on them and become more effective. Understanding of weaknesses makes it easier to correct them or make them irrelevant. A popular approach to assess skills and behavior is with the use of multi-source feedback programs (sometimes called "360-degree feedback"). In these programs, managers can compare how they perceive themselves with the way they are perceived by subordinates, peers, and bosses. An assessment center or an executive coach can also provide useful information about a leader's skills and behavior.

Goleman, Boyatzis, and McKee[38] describe a senior manager at a northern European telecommunications company who became more effective after improving her self-awareness. Whenever she felt stressed, she tended to communicate poorly and take over the work of her direct reports. However, she was unable to understand why she was struggling at work. Through coaching she was urged to focus on her key values and aspirations and to consider how those ideals could become part of her everyday life. This experience helped her to see the missing elements of her emotional style and to better understand the impact of her behavior on others.

### Preserve Personal Integrity

Personal integrity is related to success or failure as a leader. Without integrity, a leader is unlikely to retain the trust, loyalty, and support of people whose cooperation is essential. Integrity means that a person is honest, ethical, and trustworthy. One important indicator of integrity is keeping promises and honoring commitments. Another indicator of integrity is the extent to which a leader's behavior is consistent with values articulated repeatedly to other people. A third indicator of integrity is taking responsibility for one's actions and decisions. Leaders will appear weak, undependable, and dishonest if they make a decision, then deny responsibility when it is unsuccessful.

Some of the biggest corporate scandals in recent years involved the self-serving actions of top executives who treated the company as their private fiefdom.[39] For example, prosecutors have accused Tyco's former chief executive officer, Dennis Kozlowski, and former chief financial officer, Mark Swartz, of running a criminal enterprise within Tyco's executive suite. The two executives were charged with thirty-eight felony counts for pilfering $170 million directly from the company and for pocketing an additional $430 million through tainted sales of stock. Other recent examples of companies with scandals involving unethical leadership include Enron, Adelphia, and HealthSouth.[40]

A lack of integrity will eventually have negative consequences for individual leaders as well as for the organization. Longitudinal studies at the Center for Creative Leadership found that managers with high integrity had more successful careers, and that lack of integrity was common among managers whose careers derailed after an initial period of rapid advancement.[41] An important aspect of integrity is the extent to which a leader fulfills the responsibility of service and loyalty to the organization and its members. People will lose trust in a leader who has exploited or manipulated them in pursuit of self-interest. Ethical leaders give higher priority to the needs of followers and constituents than to their own personal wealth and career advancement. They are willing to take calculated risks to benefit the organization, but they avoid decisions that will seriously endanger the organization and the people who depend on it.

The importance of integrity is continually emphasized at companies such as Valero Energy, Dell Computer Corp., Pitney Bowes Inc., Southwest Airlines, Darden Restaurants Inc., Microchip Technology, National Geographic Society, and Tellabs. FedEx stresses to its employees that it will not tolerate impropriety of any kind, and the company moves quickly when there is wrongdoing. When any type of illegal activity is reported, internal security officials conduct a thorough investigation. Recently, two employees were caught embezzling funds with the help of outsiders. They were fired and turned over to the authorities for prosecution.[42]

Pitney Bowes, a leading office machine manufacturer, has a similar philosophy about ethics. "The company's trust and integrity are an important brand set of the company," says Michael J. Critelli, chairman and chief executive officer. "I will go a very long way in not compromising on that value." Critelli continually reinforces the ethics message through videos and voice mail, and he personally responds to employees' email within a couple of weeks. Critelli also holds at least fifteen town hall meetings with employees every year. Senior management goes out of its way to mix with employees and respond to their questions. In addition, he has a strict policy that requires any executive who wants to sell company stock to clear it through him. The company also has a very strict policy about avoiding loans and financial dealings with directors.[43]

## Conclusions: The Essence of Flexible Leadership

Flexible leadership involves knowing what to do, how to do it, and when to do it. Being a flexible leader requires more than the use of a particular set of behaviors, programs, or strategies. Considerable ingenuity and cooperation are required to juggle the sometimes difficult tradeoffs. Strategic thinking skills, interpersonal skills, and knowledge of the culture and core competencies of the company are all relevant for flexible leaders. To identify challenges and determine appropriate actions requires an analysis of relevant information from the internal and external environments. Formal and informal systems must be in place to ensure that high-quality information is collected and available to leaders who need it.

To meet leadership challenges successfully, all leaders in an organization must work together in a coordinated way. Flexible leadership does not mean that each leader is free to focus only on challenges for his or her primary area of responsibility, without concern for other parts of the organization. Leadership practices used by leaders at different levels must be compatible with each other and with the overall strategy of the organization. To be useful, formal programs and management systems must be supported and implemented by the leaders at each level and within each subunit. Finally, meeting the multiple challenges successfully requires widespread support and involvement by everyone who must make things happen in an organization, including employees not in formal leadership positions. Even though enhancing human relations and resources has been treated as a distinct challenge, its importance should never be underestimated. In a time of increasing competition, dynamic change, and global interdependencies, the skills and commitment of the company's leaders and members will strongly determine its survival and prosperity.

# Notes

## Chapter 1: The Nature of Effective Leadership

1  CNN Money. http://money.cnn.com
2  MSN Money. www.msn.com
3  Bowen, B.D., & Headley, D.E. (2003). Airline quarterly ratings. Wichita, KS: W. Frank Barton School of Business.
4  Mehta, S.N. (2002, April 15). Pat Russo's Lucent vision. *Fortune*, p. 126.
5  Reed, S., & Arndt, M. (2003, February 10). Work your magic, Herr Dormann. *Business Week*, p. 46.
6  Norton, L.P. (2001, November 19). Meet Mr. Nissan. *Barron's*, p. 17.
7  Laing, J.R. (2000, July 3). Fixer-upper: Can Jamie Dimon restore Bank One's lost luster? *Barron's*, p. 21.
8  Campbell, S. (2000, March 13). Ingram Micro's future lies in new CEO's hands—Foster care. *Computer Reseller News*, p. 116.
9  Kovar, J.F. (1999, November 15). The king of storage. *Computer Reseller News*, p. 143.
10  Goldstein, L. (1999, September 27). Prada goes shopping. *Fortune*, p. 207.
11  Meindl, J.R., Ehrlich, S.B., & Dukerich, J.M. (1985). The romance of leadership. *Administrative Science Quarterly, 30,* 78–102.
12  Finkelstein, S. (2003). *Why smart executives fail.* New York: Portfolio.
13  Keenan, F., & Brady, D. (2002, March 22). How soft-touch CEOs get hard results. *Business Week Online*.

14 Davenport, T.O. (1999, December). Human capital: Employees want a return on their investment, and they expect managers to help them get it. *Management Review*, p. 37.

15 "People Skills Now Seen As Essential." *Africa News Service*, April 22, 2002.

16 Leadership is in the genes. (2002, July). *IIE Solutions*, p. 66.

17 Ambrosini, D. (2002, June 21). Yale survey says U.S. business leaders doubt boards of directors. *Connecticut Post*.

18 Bass, B.M. (1990). *Handbook of leadership: A survey of theory and research*. New York: The Free Press.

19 Yukl, G. (2002). *Leadership in organizations* (5th ed.). Upper Saddle River, NJ: Prentice Hall.

20 Bennis, W.G., & Nanus, B. (1985). *Leaders: The strategies for taking charge*. New York: Harper & Row.

21 Collins, J. (2001). *Good to great*. New York: HarperBusiness.

22 CEOs make up half of corporate reputations. (2000, June 12). *Investor Relations Business*.

23 Revell, J. (2002, November 18). Should you bet on the CEO? *Fortune*, p. 189.

24 Ibid.

25 Creswell, J. (2002, November 25). Will Martha walk? Probably. *Fortune*, p. 121.

26 Norris, F., & Treaster, J.B. (2002, Oct. 4). Conseco's troubles outlast reign of a would-be savior. *The New York Times*, p. C2.

27 Bennis, W.G., & Nanus, B. (1985). *Leaders: The strategies for taking charge*. New York: Harper & Row.

28 Zaleznik, A. (1977). Managers and leaders: Are they different? *Harvard Business Review*, 55(5), 67–78.

29 Hickman, C.F. (1990). *Mind of a manager, soul of a leader*. New York: John Wiley & Sons.

30 Kotter, J.P. (1988). *The leadership factor*. New York: The Free Press.

31 Rost, J.C. (1991). *Leadership for the twenty-first century*. Westport, CT: Greenwood.

32 Mintzberg, H. (1973). *The nature of managerial work.* New York: Harper & Row.
33 Kotter, J.P. (1990). *A force for change: How leadership differs from management.* New York: The Free Press
34 Ibid.
35 Yukl, G. (2002). *Leadership in organizations* (5th ed.). Upper Saddle River, NJ: Prentice Hall.
36 Blake, R.R., & Mouton, J.S. (1964). *The managerial grid.* Houston, TX: Gulf.
37 Fleishman, E.A. (1953). The description of supervisory behavior. *Personnel Psychology, 37,* 1–6.
38 Ekvall, G., & Arvonen, J. (1991). Change-centered leadership: An extension of the two-dimensional model. *Scandinavian Journal of Management, 7,* 17–26.
39 Yukl, G. (1997). *Effective leadership behavior: A new taxonomy and model.* Paper presented at the Eastern Academy of Management International Meetings, Dublin, Ireland.
40 Yukl, G., Gordon, A., & Taber, T. (2002). A hierarchical taxonomy of leadership behavior: Integrating a half century of behavior research. *Journal of Leadership and Organizational Studies, 9,* 15–32.
41 Katz, D., & Kahn, R.L. (1978). *The social psychology of organizations* (2nd ed.). New York: John Wiley & Sons.
42 Tushman, M.L., & Romanelli, E. (1985). Organizational evolution: A metamorphosis model of convergence and reorientation. In L.L. Cummings & B.M. Staw (Eds.), *Research in organizational behavior, Vol. 7.* Greenwich, CT: JAI Press.
43 Beer, M., & Nohria, N. (2000, May-June). Cracking the code of change. *Harvard Business Review.*
44 Kotter, J.P. (1996). *Leading change.* Boston, MA: Harvard Business School Press.
45 Nadler, D. A., Shaw, R.B., Walton, A.E., & Associates (1995). *Discontinuous change: Leading organizational transformation.* San Francisco, Jossey-Bass.
46 Miller, D. (1990). *The Icarus paradox.* New York: HarperCollins.

47 Prahalad, C.K., & Hamel, G. (1990, May/June). The core competence of the corporation. *Harvard Business Review*, 79–91.
48 Wall, S.J., & Wall, S.R. (1995). *The new strategists: Creating leaders at all levels*. New York: The Free Press.
49 Boal, K., & Hooijberg, R. (2000). Strategic leadership: Moving on. *Leadership Quarterly, 11*, 515–549.
50 Osborn, R.N., Hunt, J.G., & Jauch, L.R. (2002). Toward a contextual theory of leadership. *Leadership Quarterly, 13*, 797–837.
51 Quinn, R.E. (1988). *Beyond rational management: Mastering the paradoxes and competing demands of high performance*. San Francisco: Jossey-Bass.
52 Zaccaro, S.J. (2001). *The nature of executive leadership*. Washington, DC: American Psychological Association.
53 Kim, H., & Yukl, G. (1995). Relationships of self-reported and subordinate-reported leadership behaviors to managerial effectiveness and advancement. *Leadership Quarterly, 6*, 361–377.
54 Yukl, G., & Lepsinger, R. (1991). An integrating taxonomy of managerial behavior: Implications for improving managerial effectiveness. In J.W. Jones, B.D. Steffy, and D.W. Bray (Eds.), *Applying psychology in business: The manager's handbook*. Lexington, MA: Lexington Press.
55 Yukl, G.A., & Nemeroff, W. (1979). Identification and measurement of specific categories of leadership behavior: A progress report. In J.G. Hunt & L.L. Larson (Eds.), *Crosscurrents in leadership*. Carbondale, IL: Southern Illinois University Press.
56 Yukl, G., Wall, S., & Lepsinger, R. (1990). Preliminary report on validation of the managerial practices survey. In K.E. Clark & M.B. Clark (Eds.), *Measures of leadership*. West Orange, NJ: Leadership Library of America.
57 Yukl, G., Gordon, A., & Taber, T. (2002). A hierarchical taxonomy of leadership behavior: Integrating a half century of behavior research. *Journal of Leadership and Organizational Studies, 9*, 15–32.

## Chapter 2: The Challenge of Improving Efficiency and Process Reliability

1  Garten, J.E. (2000, December 18). The war for better quality is far from won. *Business Week*, p. 32.

2  Ibid.

3  Mayne, E. (2002, December 1). Greek tragedy? *Ward's Auto World*.

4  Ramirez, D., Jr. (2002, October 4). Ford to put gas tank guards on police cars. *Fort Worth Star-Telegram*.

5  Nicolazzo, R.E. (2001, May). The power of public opinion. *Risk Management*, p. 41.

6  Cosco recalls 1 million high chairs. (2001, January) *Home Accents Today*, p. S16.

7  Recent Consumer Product Safety Commission product recalls. (2001, September 24). *Home Textiles Today*, p. S76.

8  CPSC Recall List. (2000, October). *Home Accents Today*, p. S67.

9  Fishman, C. (2001, April). "But wait, you promised." *Fast Company*, p. 110.

10  Zemke, R. (2002, July). The customer service evolution. *Training*, p. 44.

11  Stires, D. (2002, September 30). Fast food, slow service. *Fortune*, p. 38.

12  Grimes, Brad. (2002, December). You call this service? *PC World*, p. 143.

13  Armstrong, L., Ihlwan, M., & Kerwin, K. (2001, December 17). Chung Mong Koo successfully managing change in image and quality. *Business Week*, p. 16.

14  Demos, D., & Dinkin, L. (2002, November 5). Productivity metrics not just for factories. *American Banker*, p. 11A.

15  Loren, G. (2002, December). In praise of pragmatic leadership. *Harvard Management Update*, p. 3.

16  Muczyk, J.P., & Adler, T. (2002, Fall). An attempt at a consensus regarding formal leadership. *Journal of Leadership & Organizational Studies*, p. 2.

17 Salter, C. (2002, July). Crash course. *Fast Company*, p. 42.

18 Ibid.

29 Ibid.

20 Govidarajan, V., & Gupta, A.K. (2001, July). Strategic innovation: A conceptual road map. *Business Horizons*, p. 3.

21 Maney, K. (2003, January 20). Dell business model turns to muscle as rivals struggle. *USA Today*, p. 1B.

22 Brelis, M. (2000, November 6). Unconventional business strategy makes Southwest Airlines a model for success. *The Boston Globe*.

23 Donnelly, S.B., (2002, Oct. 28). One airline's magic: How does Southwest soar above its money-losing rivals? Its employees work harder and smarter in return for job security and a share of the profits. *Time*, p. 45.

24 Torbenson, E.& Marta, S. (2003, June 19). Southwest has high-tech strategy for future. *The Dallas Morning News*.

25 Success of Wal-Mart reaches unprecedented heights 40 years after founding. (2002, July 2). *Arkansas Democrat-Gazette*.

26 O'Keefe, B. (2002, May 13). Meet your new neighborhood grocer. *Fortune*.

27 Hatfield, B. (2002, February 21). Girl has second transplant after error. *The America's Intelligence Wire*.

28 Morgan, O. (2003, March 2). Nuclear safety risks exposed. *The Observer* (London, England), p. 1.

29 Migoya, D. (2002, September 19). ConAgra already had list of health violations before beef recall. *The Denver Post*.

## Chapter 3: Leadership Behaviors to Enhance Efficiency and Process Reliability

1 Campbell, A. (1999, April). Tailored, not benchmarked. *Harvard Business Review*, 77(2), 41.

2 Yukl, G. (2002). *Leadership in organizations* (5th ed.). Englewood Cliffs, NJ: Prentice Hall.

3 Armstrong, L., Ihlwan, M., & Kerwin, K. (2001, December 17). Chung Mong Koo successfully managing change in image and quality. *Business Week*, p. 16.

4  Working with workers. (2002, July 1). *PR Week* (US), p. 15.
5  Paine, L.S. (1994, March/April). Managing for organizational integrity. *Harvard Business Review*, p. 106.
6  Chew, L. (1995). Lessons from lesson. *IFCI Institute*. http:// risk.ifci.ch/137570.htm.
7  *Times* reporter who resigned leaves long trail of deception. (2003, May 11). *The New York Times*, p. A1.
8  Peters, T.J., & Austin, N. (1985). *A passion for excellence: The leadership difference*. New York: Random House.
9  Armstrong, L., Ihlwan, M., & Kerwin, K. (2001, December 17). Chung Mong Koo successfully managing change in image and quality. *Business Week*, p. 16.
10 Yukl, G., Wall, S., & Lepsinger, R. (1990). Preliminary report on validation of the managerial practices survey. In K.E. Clark & M.B. Clark (Eds.) *Measures of leadership* (pp. 223–238). West Orange, NJ: Leadership Library of America.
11 Peters, T.J., & Austin, N. (1985). *A passion for excellence: The leadership difference*. New York: Random House.
12 Stewart, R. (1976). *Contrasts in management*. Maidenhead, Berkshire, England: McGraw-Hill UK.
13 Yukl, G. (2002). *Leadership in organizations* (5th ed.). Englewood Cliffs, NJ: Prentice Hall
14 Iisenberg, D.J. (1984). How senior managers think. *Harvard Business Review*, 62(6), 81.
15 Kepner, C., & Tregoe, B. (1965). *The rational manager*. New York: McGraw-Hill.

### Chapter 4: Programs and Management Systems for Improving Efficiency and Process Reliability

1  Hammer, M., & Champy, J. (1993). *Reengineering the corporation: A manifesto for business revolution*. New York: Harper & Row.
2  London, S.S. (2002, July 15). When quality is not enough. *The Financial Times*, p. 9.
3  Pender, L. (2001, May 15). Faster, cheaper ERP. *CIO*, p. 124.
4  Earls, A.R. (2002, Spring). Integrating ERP can overcome CRM limits. *Software Magazine*, p. 29.

5 Rigby, D.K., Reichheld, F.F., & Schefter, P. (2002, February). Avoid the perils of CRM. *Harvard Business Review.*

6 Hall, E.A., & Rosenthal, J. (1994). How to make reengineering work. *McKinsey Quarterly,* Issue 2.

7 Hill, S., Wilkinson, A., Mohrman, S.A., Tenkasi, R., Lawler-Lakhe, R.R., & Mohanty, R.P. (1995, September/October). Understanding TQM in service systems. *International Journal of Quality & Reliability Management,* p. 139.

8 Lakhe, R.R., & Mohanty, R.P. (1995, September/October). Understanding TQM in service systems. *International Journal of Quality & Reliability Management,* p. 139.

9 A quality circle nets a nice round figure. (1995, July). *Supervisory Management.*

10 Ellis, K. (2001, December). Mastering Six Sigma. *Training,* p. 30.

11 Challener, C. (2002, September 9). Quality initiatives: Six Sigma at work in the chemical industry. *Chemical Market Reporter,* p. 20.

12 London, S.S. (2002, July 15). When quality is not enough. *The Financial Times,* p. 9.

13 Beer, M., & Nohria, N. (2000, May/June). Cracking the code of change. *Harvard Business Review.*

14 Smith, D., & Blakeslee, J. (2002, September). The new strategic Six Sigma. *Training & Development.*

15 Freeman, S.J., & Cameron, K.S. (1993). Organizational downsizing: A convergence and reorganizational framework. *Organization Science,* 4(3), 10–29.

16 Band, D.C., & Tustin, C.M. (1995, December). Strategic downsizing. *Management Decision,* p. 36.

17 Making companies efficient: The year downsizing grew up. (1996, December 21). *The Economist,* p. 97.

18 Turner, F. (2000, September 29). History of downsizing imparts lessons. *Business First-Columbus,* p. A38.

19 Quinn, J.B., & Hilmer, F.G. (1994, Summer). Strategic outsourcing. *Sloan Management Review.*

20 Quinn, J.B., & Hilmer, F.G. (1994, Summer). Strategic out-sourcing. *Sloan Management Review.*

21 Bryne, J.A. (1996, April 1). Has outsourcing gone too far? *Business Week.*

22 Quinn, J.B., & Hilmer, F.G. (1994, Summer). Strategic out-sourcing. *Sloan Management Review.*

23 The outing of outsourcing. (1995, November 25). *The Economist*, p. 57.

24 Levinson, H. (1970, July/August). Management by whose objectives? *Harvard Business Review*, p. 125.

25 Jewett, D. (2003, May 12). GM wants to tailor plant equip-ment to region. *Automotive News*, p. 48.

26 Foss, B. (2003, May 21). Airlines eye standardized carrier fleet. *The Seattle Times*, p. E2.

27 Shervanti, T., & Zerillo, P.C. (1997, January/February). The albatross of product innovation. *Business Horizons*, p. 56.

28 Grimaldi, L. (2000, October). Program notes. *Meetings & Conventions*, p. 22.

29 Oldenburg, D. (2002, October). ROI incentives tools for mea-suring excellence. *HR Magazine*, p. 70.

30 Kerr, S. (1975). On the folly of rewarding A. while hoping for B. *Academy of Management Journal*, 18, 769–783.

## Chapter 5: The Challenge of Adapting to the External Environment

1 Hamel, G. (2003, Winter). Innovation as a deep capability. *Leader to Leader.*

2 Carofano, J. (2002, December 2). Style channels; producing a shoe for seemingly every category imaginable, Skechers' design team stays in perpetual motion. *Footwear News*, p. 67.

3 Ahles, A. (2002, June 25). Innovation, strategy boost Samsung's share of cell phone market. *Fort Worth Star-Telegram.*

4 Watts, R.M. (2002, May). Strategies for market disruptions. *Journal of Business Strategy*, p. 19.

5. Ibid.

6 Stires, D. (2002, September 30). Fast food, slow service. *Fortune*, p. 38.

7 Trachtenberg, J.A. (1996, June 28). How Philips flubbed its U.S. introduction of electronic product. *Wall Street Journal. Europe*, p. 1.

8 Feldman, J.M. (2002, September). The king of the hill evolves. *Air Transport World*, p. 36.

9 Ibid.

10 Peltz, J.F. (2002, October 6). Southwest still soaring as other airlines stall. *Los Angeles Times*, p. C-1.

11 Harvey, F. (2003, August 6). Warrior wields new weapon from armory. *The Financial Times*, p. 4.

12 Evers, J. (2003, January 10). CES: Dell to sell PCs at airport kiosks. *InfoWorld.com*.

13 Woll, J. Not all adaptive organizations are alike. *Perspective on business innovation, Issue 9: The adaptive imperative*. Cap Gemini Ernst & Young Center for Business Innovation.

14 Eisenberg, D. (2003, January 20). There's a new way to think Big Blue. *Time*, p. 48.

15 Meller, G., & Kao, J. (2002, July/August). Setting the stage for innovative action. *Physician Executive*, p. 24.

16 McLagan, P.A. (2002, November). Change leadership today. *Training & Development*, p. 26.

17 Christiansen, C. (2003). *The innovator's dilemma*. New York: HarperBusiness.

18 Spence, B. (2003, August 11). The new spin on innovation. *The Financial Times*.

19 Gilbert, J. (1995, July/August). Profiting from innovation: Inventors and adopters. *Industrial Management*, p. 28.

20 Horibe, F. (2002, March). The most dangerous gap. CMA *Management*, p. 48.

21 Bolton, M.K. (1993, Winter). Imitation verses innovation: Lessons to be learned from the Japanese. *Organizational Dynamics*, p. 30.

22  Gilbert, C. & Bower, J.L. (2002, May). Disruptive change: When trying harder is part of the problem. *Harvard Business Review.*

23  Curry, S.R. (2003, April). Product imperfect. *Potentials*, p. 28.

24  Tice, C. (2001, May 11). Webvan biz plan never had a chance to deliver. *Puget Sound Business Journal*, p. 7.

25  Wall, S.J., & Wall, S.R. (1995). *The new strategists: Creating leaders at all levels.* New York: The Free Press.

26  Collins, J. (2001). *Good to great.* New York: HarperBusiness.

27  Finkelstein, S. (2003). Why smart executives fail. New York: Portfolio.

28  Eisenstein, P.A. (2003, January 14). How Ford Motor Co. got back on track. *CIO Insight.*

29  Prahalad, C.K., & Ramaswamy, V. (2000, January). Co-opting customer competence. *Harvard Business Review*, p. 79.

30  Schneider, D.M., & Goldwasser, C. (1998, March). Be a model leader of change. *Management Review*, p. 41.

**Chapter 6: Leader Behaviors to Enhance Adaptation**

1  Wall, S.J., & Wall, S.R. (1995). *The new strategists: Creating leaders at all levels.* New York: The Free Press.

2  Katzenbach, J.R. (1996, Winter). Real change. *The McKinsey Quarterly*, 1, 148(1).

3  Miller, C.C., & Cardinal, L.B. (1994). Strategic planning and firm performance: A synthesis of more than two decades of research. *Academy of Management Journal*, 37, 1649–1665.

4  Prahalad, C.K., & Hamel, G. (1990, May/June). The core competencies of the corporation. *Harvard Business Review*, p. 79.

5  Huey, J. (1995, April 17). Eisner explains everything. *Fortune, 131*(7), 44 (12)

6  Fusaro, D. (1988, May 30). New DeVilbiss poised for growth. *Metalworking News*, 15, p. 12.

7  Wall, S.J., & Wall, S.R. (1995). *The new strategists: Creating leaders at all levels.* New York: The Free Press.

8  Bennis, W.G., & Nanus, B.(1997). *Leaders: Strategies for taking charge.* New York: HarperBusiness.

9 Hamel, G. (2003, Winter). Innovation as a deep capability. *Leader to Leader*, No. 27.

10 Anders, G. (2002, March). How Intel puts innovation inside. *Fast Company*, (56), p. 122.

11 Hatten, K. & Rosenthal, S. (2000, September/October). Creating knowledge through experiments. *Knowledge Management Review*.

12 Katzenbach, J.R. (1996, Winter). Real change. *The McKinsey Quarterly, 1*, 148(1).

13 Kouzes, J. & Posner, B. (1995). *Achieving credibility: The key to effective leadership*. Nightingale-Conant Corp.

14 Pellet, J. (2002, June). Leading the creative charge. *Chief Executive*, p. S6.

15 Sutton, R.I. (2002, January). When ignorance is bliss. *Industrial Management, 44*(1), 8 (6)

16 Filipczak, B. (1997, May). It takes all kinds: Creativity in the work force. *Training, 34*(5) 32.

17 Galagan, P.A. (2002, July). Delta force. *Training & Development,* 56(7), 20 (12).

18 O'Dell, C., & Grayson, J.C. (2001, July 16). Identifying and transferring internal best practices. Knowledge Management, White Paper.

19 Warner, F. (2002, August). In a word, Toyota drives for innovation. *Fast Company*, p. 36.

## Chapter 7: Programs, Systems, and Strategies for Enhancing Adaptation

1 Pryor, A. K., & Shays, M. (1993, Spring). Growing the business with intrepreneurs. *Business Quarterly, v57* n3 p. 42 (8).

2 Ibid.

3 Slywotsky, A., &Wise, R. (2003, April). Double-digit growth in no-growth times. *Fast Company*, p. 66.

4 Hamel, G., & Skarzynski, P. (2001, November). Innovation: the new route to wealth. *Journal of Accountancy, v192,* i5, p. 65 (4).

5 Lakin, S. (2001, March/April). BT's approach to ideas management. *Knowledge Management Review.*

6 Delbridge, R., & Lowe, J. (1995). The process of benchmarking: a study from the automotive industry. *International Journal of Operations & Production Management, 15* i4.

7 Goldwasser, C. (1995, June). Benchmarking: People make the process. *Management Review.*

8 Bogan, C., & Callahan, D. (2001, March). Benchmarking in rapid time. *Industrial Management,* p. 28.

9 Murdock, A. (1997, November). Lateral benchmarking or what formula one taught an airline. *Management Today,* p. 64 (4).

10 Dervitsiotis, K. N. (2000, July). Benchmarking and business paradigm shifts. *Total Quality Management.*

11 Peters, T.J., & Waterman, R.H., Jr. (1982). *In search of excellence: Lessons from America's best-run companies.* New York: Harper & Row.

12 Peters, T.J., & Austin, N. (1985). *A passion for excellence: The leadership difference.* New York: Random House.

13 Joyce, W., Nohria, N., & Roberson, B. (2003). *What really works: The 4 + 2 formula for sustained business success.* New York: HarperBusiness.

14 Billington, J. (1998, July). Customer driven innovation. *Harvard Management Update, 3*(7).

15 Seybold, P.B. (2001, May). Get inside the lives of your customers. *Harvard Business Review.*

16 O'Dell, C., Grayson, J.C. (2001, July 16). Identifying and transferring internal best practices. Knowledge Management, White Paper.

17 Greco, S. (1998, April). Where great ideas come from. *Inc.,* p. 76.

18 Casison, J. (2001, June). Power to the people human resource forum: Employee motivation. *Incentive.*

19 Vogelstein, F. (2003, May 26). Mighty amazon. *Fortune.*

20 Woll, J. Not all adaptive organizations are alike, perspective on business. *Innovation, Issue 9:* The Adaptive Imperative, Cap Gemini Ernst & Young Center for Business Innovation.

21 O'Dell, C., Grayson, J.C. (2001, July 16). Identifying and transferring internal best practices. Knowledge Management, White Paper.

22 Barth, S. (2000, October). KM horror stories, *Knowledge Management.*

23 Ibid.

24 Barth, S. (2001, April). Learning from mistakes. *Knowledge Management.*

25 Hargadon, A., & Sutton, R. I. (2000, May). Building an innovative factory. *Harvard Business Review,* p. 157.

26 Dobbs, K. (2000, January). Simple moments of learning. *Training, (37)* i1 p. 52.

27 Hargadon, A., & Sutton, R. I. (2000, May). Building an innovative factory. *Harvard Business Review,* p. 157.

28 Ford, R. C., & Randolph W. A. (1992). Cross-functional structures: A review and integration of matrix organizations and project management. *Journal of Management,* 18, 267–294.

29 George, J. M., & Jones, G. R. (1996). *Understanding and managing organizational behavior.* Reading, MA: Addison-Wesley.

30 Hoskisson, R.E., Hitt, M.A., & Ireland, R.D. (2004). *Competing for advantage.* Cincinnati, OH: Thompson South-Western.

31 Joyce, W., Nohria, N., & Robertson, B. (2003). *What really works: The 4 + 2 formula for sustained business success.* New York: HarperBusiness.

32 Finkelstein, S. (2003). *Why smart executives fail.* New York: Portfolio, Penguin Group.

33 Jensen, M.C. (1988). Takeovers: Their causes and consequences. *Journal of Economic Perspectives,* 1(2), 21–48.

34 Rappaport, A., & Sirower, M.L. (1999). *Harvard Business Review,* 77(6), 147–158.

35 Finkelstein, S. (2003). *Why smart executives fail.* New York: Portfolio, Penguin Group.

36  Hitt, M.A., Ireland, R.D., Harrison, J.S., & Best, A. (1998). Attributes of successful and unsuccessful acquisitions of U.S. firms. *British Journal of Management, 9*, 91–114.

37  Joyce, W., Nohria, N., & Robertson, B. (2003). *What really works: The 4 + 2 formula for sustained business success.* New York: HarperBusiness.

38  Lessons learned from mergers and acquisitions: best practices in workforce integration. (1999). Philadelphia, PA: Right Management Consultants.

39  Creating values though mergers and acquisitions: Preliminary executive report. (2003). Philadelphia, PA: Right Management Consultants.

40  Hoskisson, R.E., Hitt, M.A., & Ireland, R.D. (2004). *Competing for advantage.* Cincinnati, OH: Thompson South-Western.

41  Ibid.

42  Kroll, L. (2001, May 21). Procter & Gamble. *Forbes Best of the Web*, 90.

43  Ulfelder, S. (2001, July/August). Partners in profit. *computerworld.com*, 24–28.

44  Ibid.

45  Hoskisson, R.E., Hitt, M.A., & Ireland, R.D. (2004). *Competing for advantage.* Cincinnati, OH: Thompson South-Western.

46  Hutheesing, N. (2001, May 21) Marital blisters. *Forbes Best of the Web*, 30.

### Chapter 8: The Challenge of Managing Human Resources

1  Byrne, J.A. (2003, August). How to lead now: Getting extraordinary performance when you can't pay for it. *Fast Company*, (73), p. 62 (6).

2  Rucci, A.J., Kirn, S.P., & Quinn, R.T. (1998, January/February). The employee-customer-profit chain at Sears. *Harvard Business Review*.

3  Welber, M. (2003, May). In a league of its own. *Workforce*, 82(50), 34 (4).

4  Butcher, S. (2003, April 27). Stampede out of banking gath-
   ers pace. *Financial News*, p. NA.
5  Lee, L., & Thornton, E. (2002, June 3). Schwab vs. Wall Street:
   With the big firms rocked by scandal, Schwab is going after their
   disgruntled—and rich—clients. *Business Week*, Issue 3785, p. 64.
6  Stone, A. (2003, May 22). Schwab's challenge: Keep climb-
   ing. *Business Week Online*.
7  Leonard, B. (2001, May). Turnover at the top. *HR Magazine*,
   46(5), 46.
8  Greengard, S. (2002, March). Moving forward with reverse
   mentoring. *Workforce*, 81(30), 15.
9  Larson, M. (1997, January 13). Corporate culture is Southwest's
   edge. *Business Journal Serving Greater Sacramento*, 13(43), 30.
10 Freiberg, K., & Freiberg, J. (1998). *Nuts! Southwest Airlines'
   crazy recipe for business and personal success*. New York: Bantam
   Doubleday.
11 Cox, B. (2002, May 16). Southwest Airlines attributes profitability to treating customers, workers well. *Fort Worth Star-
   Telegram*.
12 Brathwaite, S.T. (2002, July/August). Denny's: A diversity
   success story. *Franchising World*, 34(5), 28 (2)
13 Zirlin, L. (2000, June 15). Woe is Denny's. *Restaurants &
   Institutions*, 110(16), 20.
14 Stamps, D. (1996, July) Going nowhere: Culture change at
   the postal service fizzles. *Training*, 33(7), 26 (8).
15 Gelber, A. (2002, August 4). Workers wage war on overtime.
   *The Standard Times*.
16 People brand: The employment imperative: A research report.
   (2000). Philadelphia, PA: Right Management Consultants.
17 Prewitt, E. (1999). How to keep your company's star employees. *Harvard Management Update*.

### Chapter 9: Leader Behaviors for Enhancing Human Resources

1  Bass, B.M. (1990). *Handbook of leadership: A survey of theory
   and research*. New York: The Free Press.

2 Yukl, G. (2002). *Leadership in organizations* (5th ed.). Englewood Cliffs, NJ: Prentice Hall.

3 Eden, D. (1992, Winter). Leadership and expectations: Pygmalion effects and other self-fulfilling prophesies in organizations. *Leadership Quarterly, 3*(4), 271–305.

4 Byrne, J.A. (2003, August). How to lead now: Getting extraordinary performance when you can't pay for it. *Fast Company*, p. 62.

5 LaBarre, P. (2001, August). Marcus Buckingham thinks your boss has an attitude problem. *Fast Company*, p. 88.

6 Greaves, D. (2003, September). Interview with Daniel Greaves.

7 Weiser, C.R. (1994, July). Best practice in customer relations. *Consumer Policy Review*.

8 Nelson, B. (2001, May 25). Worker ideas can improve the bottom line. *Business First-Columbus*, p. A21.

9 Byrne, J.A. (2003, August). How to lead now: Getting extraordinary performance when you can't pay for it. *Fast Company*, p. 62.

### Chapter 10: Programs and Management Systems for Enhancing Human Resources

1 Gale, S.F. (2001, June). Bringing good leaders to light. *Training*, p. 38.

2 Short takes. (2002, January/February). *Journal of Business Strategy*, p. 3.

3 Sonnenfeld, J.A., & Khurana, R. (2002, July 30). Fishing for CEOs in your own backyard. *Wall Street Journal*.

4 Klien, S.A. (2003, March 17). CEO departs struggling Mount Sinai Hospital. *Crain's Chicago Business*, p. 4.

5 Gogoi, P. (2003, April 21). Arch support. *Business Week*, p. 52.

6 Gale, S.F. (2001, June). Bringing good leaders to light. *Training*, p. 38.

7 Ibid.

8 Burton, J. (1999, October). Dana Corp.: Succeeding at succession. *Chief Executive*, p. 38.

9 Barbian, J. (2002, May). The road best traveled. *Training*, p. 38.
10 Ibid.
11 Warner, F. (2002, April). Inside Intel's mentoring movement. *Fast Company*.
12 Simon, R. (2003, July 30). Companies get stingy with stock options. *Wall Street Journal*.
13 Bencivenga, D. (1997, February). Employee-owners help bolster the bottom line. *HR Magazine*, p. 78.
14 Stamps, D. (1996, March). A piece of the action. *Training*, p. 64.
15 Ibid.
16 Lee, C. (1994, July). Open-book management. *Training*, p. 21.
17 Ibid.
18 Sims, H. (1995). *Business without bosses*. New York: John Wiley & Sons.
19 Dumaine, B. (1994, September 5). The trouble with teams. *Fortune*, p. 86.
20 Elmuti, D. (1996, March/April). Sustaining high performance through self-managed work teams. *Industrial Management*, p. 4.
21 Hackman, J. R. (1986). The psychology of self-management in organizations. In M. S. Pollack & R. S. Perloff (Eds.), *Psychology and work: Productivity, change, and employment* (pp. 89–136). Washington, DC: American Psychological Association.
22 Lawler, E. E. (1986). *High involvement management*. San Francisco: Jossey-Bass.
23 Sims, H. (1995). *Business without bosses*. New York: John Wiley & Sons.
24 Hosford, C. (2003, May). AFLAC's advantage. *Incentive*, p. 26.
25 Yukl, G. (1989) *Leadership in organizations* (2nd ed.) Englewood Cliffs, NJ: Prentice Hall.
26 The opportunity to honor companies that care. (2001, September 14). *The Business Journal* (Raleigh, NC), p. 7A.
27 Salter, C. (2002, July). Crash course. *Fast Company*, p. 42.

28  Campanelli, J.A. (2003, February). Good first impression. *Inside Business*, p. 53.

29  Do I know you? (1999, October 15). *Inc.*, p. 208.

## Chapter 11: Multiple Challenges and Tradeoffs for Leaders

1  Simons, J. (2003, April 14). King of the pill. *Fortune*, p. 94.

2  Mayne, E. (2002, December 1). Greek tragedy? *Ward's Auto World*.

3  Eisenstein, P.A. (2003, January 14). How Ford Motor Co. got back on track. *CIO Insight*.

4  Miller, D. (1990) *The Icarus paradox*. New York: HarperCollins.

5  Foust, D. (2003, January 17). The GE way isn't working at Home Depot. *Business Week Online*.

6  Mathews, S. (2003). About Home Depot, *Bloomberg News*.

7  Stratford, S. (1997, May 12). Levi's as ye sew, so shall ye reap. *Fortune*.

8  Harvey, F. (2003, August 6). Warrior wields new weapon from armory. *The Financial Times*, p. 4.

9  Imberman, W. (2001, November/December). Why engineers strike: The Boeing story. *Business Horizons*.

10  Bischoff, G. (2003, August 18). Frustrated union attacks Verizon in the pocketbook. *Telephony*.

11  Munk, N. (1999, April 12). How Levi trashed a great American brand. *Fortune*.

12  Slywotzky, A., & Wise, R. (2003, March/April). The dangers of product driven success. *Journal of Business Strategy*.

13  Fields, G., & Wilkes, J.R. (2003, June 30). The ex-files: FBI's new focus places big burden on local police. *The Wall Street Journal*, p. A1.

14  Taylor, A., III. (2002, February 18). Nissan's turnaround artist: Carlos Ghosn is giving Japan a lesson in how to compete. *Fortune International*, p. 34.

15  MetLife chief's constant is change. (2002, June 3). *Insurance Chronicle*, p. 1.

16 Hillman, J. (2001, December 11). MetLife's cultural transformation increases productivity. A.M. *Best Newswire*.

17 Block, P. (1993). *Stewardship: Choosing service over self-interest*. San Francisco: Berrett-Koehler.

18 Greenleaf, R.K. (1977). *Servant leadership: A journey into the nature of legitimate power and greatness*. New York: Paulist Press.

19 Sharp-Paine, L. (1994, March/April). Managing for organizational integrity. *Harvard Business Review*, pp. 106–117.

20 Nielsen, R.P. (1989). Changing unethical organizational behavior. *Academy of Management Executive*, 3(2), 123–130.

21 Collins, J. (2001). *Good to great*. New York: HarperBusiness.

22 Collins, J.C., & Porras, J.I. (1997). *Built to last: Successful habits of visionary companies*. New York: HarperBusiness.

23 Finkelstein, S. (2003). *Why smart executives fail*. New York: Portfolio.

24 Nee, E. (1998, May 4). Reboot. Turning around Wang Laboratories. *Forbes*, p. 136.

25 Bray, H. (1999, May 6). Netherlands' Getronics NV to buy Massachusetts-based Wang Global. *The Boston Globe*.

26 Horibe, F. (2002, March). The most dangerous gap. *CMA Management*, p. 48.

27 Kazan, D. (2001, April 16). CEO failures can help us avoid our own mistakes. *Westchester County Business Journal*, p. 10.

**Chapter 12: The Path to Flexible Leadership**

1 Collins, J.C., & Porras, J.I. (1997). *Built to last: Successful habits of visionary companies*. New York: HarperBusiness.

2 Ibid.

3 Ibid.

4 McCall, M.W., Jr. (1998). *High flyers: Developing the next generation of leaders*. Boston: Harvard Business School Press.

5 McCall, M.W., Jr., Lombardo, M.M., & Morrison, A. (1988). *The lessons of experience*. Lexington, MA: Lexington Books.

6  Vicere, A.A., & Fulmer, R.M. (1997). *Leadership by design*. Boston: Harvard Business School Press.

7  Joyce, W., Nohria, N., & Roberson, B. (2003). *What really works: The 4 + 2 formula for sustaining business success*. New York: HarperBusiness.

8  McCall, M.W., Jr. (1998). *High flyers: Developing the next generation of leaders*. Boston: Harvard Business School Press.

9  Joyce, W., Nohria, N., & Roberson, B. (2003). *What really works: The 4 + 2 formula for sustaining business success*. New York: HarperBusiness.

10  Collins, J. (2001). *Good to great*. New York: HarperBusiness.

11  Joyce, W., Nohria, N., & Roberson, B. (2003). *What really works: The 4 + 2 formula for sustaining business success*. New York: HarperBusiness.

12  Peters, T.J. (1987). *Thriving on chaos*. New York: HarperCollins.

13  Peters, T.J., & Austin, N. (1985). *A passion for excellence: The leadership difference*. New York: Random House.

14  Lee, W.G. (1994, Autumn). A conversation with Herb Kelleher. *Organizational Dynamics*.

15  Morris, B. (2002, November 18). Can Ford save Ford? *Fortune*, p. 52.

16  Collins, J. (2001). *Good to great*. New York: HarperBusiness.

17  Peters, T.J., & Austin, N. (1985). *A passion for excellence: The leadership difference*. New York: Random House.

18  Taub, S. (2002, September 11). Dazed and confused. *CFO.com*.

19  Singh, Na. (2001, October 5). P&G gets the formula right. *Financial Express*.

20  Conlin, M., & Kerwin, K. (2002, November 11). CEO coaches. *Business Week*, p. 98.

21  Cowell, A. (2003, February 9). N-I-S-S-A-N: Rah! Rah! Rah! *The New York Times*.

22  Taylor, A., III. (2002, February 18). Nissan's turnaround artist. *Fortune International*, p. 34.

23  Nelson, B. (2002, March). Making employee suggestions count. *ABA Banking Journal*, p. 12.

24  Goo Kehaulani, S. (2003, April 25). American Airlines ousts CEO Carty amid labor uproar. *Seattle Times*.

25  Schein, E.H. (1992). *Organizational culture and leadership* (2nd ed.). San Francisco: Jossey-Bass.

26  Kaplan, R.E. (1984, Spring). Trade routes: The manager's network of relationships. *Organizational Dynamics*, pp. 37–52.

27  Kotter, J.P. (1982). *The general managers*. New York: The Free Press.

28  Goleman, D. (1995). *Emotional intelligence: Why is it more than IQ?* New York: Bantam Books.

29  Mayer, J.D., & Salovey, P. (1995). Emotional intelligence and the construction and regulation of feelings. *Applied and Preventive Psychology, 4,* 197–208.

30  Goleman, D. (1998, November/December). What makes a leader? *Harvard Business Review*, p. 93.

31  Senge, P.M. (1990). *The fifth discipline: The art and practice of the learning organization*. New York: Doubleday.

32  Dumaine, B. (1994, September 5). The trouble with teams. *Fortune*, p. 86.

33  Kotter, J.P. (1982). *The general managers*. New York: The Free Press.

34  Mintzberg, H. (1973). *The nature of managerial work*. New York: Harper & Row.

35  Haas, R.N. (1994). *The power to persuade: How to be effective in an unruly organization*. Boston: Houghton-Mifflin.

36  Goleman, D. (1995). *Emotional intelligence: Why is it more than IQ?* New York: Bantam Books.

37  Mayer, J.D., & Salovey, P. (1995). Emotional intelligence and the construction and regulation of feelings. *Applied and Preventive Psychology, 4,* 197–208.

38  Goleman, D., Boyatzis, R., & McKee, A. (2001, December). Primal leadership. *Harvard Business Review, 79*.

39  Finkelstein, S. (2003). *Why smart executives fail*. New York: Portfolio.

40 Bianco, A., Byrnes, N., Symonds, W., with Polek, David. (2002, December 2). The rise and fall of Dennis Kozlowski. *Business Week*. i3813, p. 64.

41 McCall, M.W., Jr., Lombardo, M.M., & Morrison, A. (1988). *The lessons of experience*. Lexington, MA: Lexington Books.

42 Blank, D. (2003, February). A matter of ethics. *Internal Auditor*, (60) i1, p. 26 (6).

43 Ibid.

# Index

**A**

Ackerman, R., 27
ACSI (American Customer Satisfaction Index), 28
Action planning, 42–43t
Adaptation: conditions affecting importance of, 82–84; examples of failures, 84–87; examples of successful, 87–89; organizational growth/competitiveness through, 81–82; reasons for success or failure, 89–96; tradeoff between efficiency vs., 194–197; tradeoff between human relations vs., 199–201. *See also* Innovation
Adaptation enhancement: building support for change for, 109t–111; encouraging innovative thinking for, 115–117, 116t; envisioning change for, 106–108, 107t; facilitating collective learning for, 97, 118t–120; implementing change for, 111–115, 114t; leadership behaviors for, 99–121, 106–121; monitoring the environment for, 99–102, 100t; practices for, 130–133; programs for, 123–130; relationships among change-oriented behaviors, 120–121; strategic planning for, 102–106, 104t; strategies for, 135–140; structural forms to facilitate, 133–135; ways to facilitate, 96–98
Adaptation enhancement programs: external benchmarking, 125–127; intrepreneurship programs, 123–125; reward and recognition programs, 129–130; for understanding customers, 127–129
Adaptation enhancement strategies: mergers and acquisitions, 135–138; strategic alliances, 138–140

Adaptation enhancement systems, 131–133
Adaptation failures: AT&T, 84; Lucent, 85; McDonald's, 85–86; Phillips, 86–87
Adaptation successes: Dell Computers, 88; IBM, 89, 203; Maxygen, 88–89; Southwest Airlines, 87–88
Adaptation success/failure factors: failure to implement innovations, 91; inadequate assessment of the market, 92–93; inadequate support by top management, 96; lack of innovative ideas, 90–91; poor strategic fit, 93–94; poor timing in implementing innovations, 91–92; resistance to change, 94–96
Adelphia, 235
Adelphie, 220
AFLAC, 187
AFLAC Employee Appreciation Week, 187
After-action review, 130
Akili Systems Group, 190
Allfirst Financial, 226
Amazon.com "Just Do It" program, 130
American Airlines, 227–228
*American Banker,* 29
American Business School, 28
American Express, 89, 126
AMP Inc., 119, 129
Analytical Sciences Inc., 188
Andersen Corporation, 110–111
Anderson, B. H., 133
Apple Computer, 91
Applegate, L., 70
Aramark, 157
Armstrong, C. M., 8, 84
ASTD study, 180

AT&T, 8, 84
Autodesk, 128

**B**

Bain & Co., 31
Banknorth Group "Stupid Rules" contest, 116
Barings Bank, 53
Barrett, C., 87–88
BE (British Energy), 36
Beckman Instruments, 137
Beer, M., 67
Behavior theory, 7
Belazi, O., 152
Bell, C., 181
Benchmarking, 125–127
Benmosche, R., 206
Bennett, C., 111
Bertelli, P., 3, 4
Best Buy, 73, 133, 160
Bezos, J., 130
Blair, J., 53–54
Blakeslee, J., 67
Blanchard, K., 160
Boeing, 198–199
Bonaparte, A., 128
Booz Allen Hamilton, 29
Bordelon, C., 129
Born leader myth, 6–7
Bossidy, L., 28
Bowmar, 91
Boyatzis, R., 234
BPI (business process improvement), 63–64
Breen, E., 8
British Airways, 171
BT (British Telephone), 125
BT Ideas program, 125
Burch, R., 172–173
Burger King, 73, 85
Burson-Marsteller, 7
*Business Week*, 5
Buzzsaw.com, 128–129

**C**

Canon, 105
Cantalupo, J., 176
Capital One "test and learn" approach, 130–131
Career counseling, 164
Carry, D., 228

Casio, 105
Catalyst, 180
CD-I (Phillips), 86–87
Celebrity leader myth, 7–9
Center for Creative Leadership, 180, 235
Center for Effective Organizations (USC), 29
Ceremonies, 172
"Challenges in Managing High Potential Employees" study (2000), 176
Chambers, J., 118
Change: adaptation and envisioning, 106–108, 107t; balancing stability vs., 211–214; building support for, 109t–111; implementing, 111–115, 112t; performance determinants and, 201–203; resistance to, 94–96, 213
Change agents, 113–115
Change-oriented behaviors: building support for change, 109t–111; encouraging innovative thinking, 115–117, 116t; envisioning change, 106–108, 107t; facilitating collective learning, 118t–120; implementing change, 111–115, 112t; monitoring the environment, 99–102, 100t; relationships among, 120–121; strategic planning, 102–106, 104t
Charan, R., 28
Charles Schwab, 146–147, 200
Christensen, C., 91
Chrysler, 6
Chung Mong Koo, 29, 57
CIA (Central Intelligence Agency), 214
Cisco, 118
Clarifying roles/objectives: described, 45; examples of effective/ineffective, 47–49; goals setting and, 49–51; guidelines for clarifying objectives, 50t; guidelines for clarifying work roles/responsibilities, 45t–46; importance of, 46–47; reasons for inadequate, 47
Cleco Power "Ideas for Excellence" program, 129
Coaching, 163–164
Collective learning: facilitating, 118t–120; as organization culture value, 97; practices of, 130–131
Collins, J., 29, 220
Commerce Bank's Commerce University, 189

Communication: effective leadership and, 223–226; open-door policies and, 225–226
Compaq, 100
Competition: adaptation importance relative to, 83–84; adaptation to keep pace with, 81; strategic planning to gain advantage over, 102–106, 104t
Competitive strategy, Dell and Southwest examples of, 1–3
ConAgra, 36
Conseco, 8
Consulting leadership behavior, 166–169, 167t
Core competencies, 105
Core ideology, 218–220
Corning Inc., 27
Corporate Leadership Council study (2000), 176
Cost reduction programs: downsizing, 68; focus of, 67–68; outsourcing, 69–70
Critelli, M. J., 236
CRM (customer relationship management), 65
Cross-functional teams, 134–135
Customers: encouraging innovative thinking to better serve, 115–117, 116t; monitoring environment to learn about, 99–102, 100t; programs for understanding, 127–129

**D**

Dana Corp., 177–178
Darden Restaurants Inc., 235
Davis, J., 119
De Beers, 69–70
Delegation/empowering, 169t–171
Dell Computers: adaptation success by, 88; effective empowerment at, 171; effective leadership of, 1–3; efficiency vs. human relations tradeoff by, 198; high efficiency/process reliability of, 32; integrity emphasized at, 235
Dell sale kiosks, 88
Deloitte & Touche, 70
Delta Airlines, 68
Denny's, 150–151
Deutsche Telekom, 139
Developing practices, 162–166, 163t
Development Dimensions International, 176
DeVilbiss Company, 105–106

Devlin, G., 100–101
Direct leader behavior: change-oriented, 15; overview of, 14–16, 15t; relations-oriented, 15–16; task-oriented, 14–15
Dow Chemical Company, 44
Downsizing, 68
DPR Construction, 75
Dunlap, A., 8
DuPont, 128
Dyno Nobel, 165–166

**E**

Eaton, B., 6
Education assistance programs, 179–180
Effective leadership: build capable leadership at all levels for, 220–221; build commitment to core ideology for, 218–220; competencies for, 228t–236; encouraging/exemplifying leadership by example, 227–228; good management required for, 30; guidelines listed for, 217–218t; involving/empowering people at all levels, 221–223; keep lines of communication open for, 223–226; using reward systems to support multiple objectives, 226–227. See also Flexible leadership model; Leadership
Effective leadership competencies: embrace systems thinking, 230–232; focus on what is really important, 232–233; listed, 228t; maintain self-awareness, 233–234; maintain situational awareness, 229–230; preserve personal integrity, 234–236
Efficiency: conditions affecting, 34–36; leadership behaviors to enhance, 39–62; management systems/structural forms to improve, 70–74; organization which exemplify, 30–34; quality and process improvement programs and, 63–70; recognition/reward systems to improve, 74–76; tradeoff between adaptation vs., 194–197; tradeoff between human relations vs., 197–199; ways to improve, 36–37
Efficiency examples: Dell Computers, 32; Southwest Airlines, 32–33; Sterling Autobody Centers, 30–31; Wal-Mart, 34
Eisner, M., 105
Ellerbe Becket and Skidmore, 129
Emerging Workforce study, 180

Emotional intelligence, 233
Employee benefit programs, 187
Employee development programs: mentoring programs, 180–181; skill assessment and feedback programs, 178–179; training and education assistance programs, 179–180
Employee ownership programs, 182–183
Empowering leadership behavior, 169t–171
Empowerment: balancing control vs., 214–215; monitoring while allowing, 52–53; as part of effective leadership, 221–223
Empowerment programs: described, 181–182; employee ownership programs, 182–183; open-book management, 183–184; self-managed teams, 184–185
Enron, 220, 235
Environment: adaptation enhanced by monitoring the, 99–102, 100t; adaptation to external, 81–98
ERP (enterprise resource planning), 65
ESOP (employee stock-ownership plan), 182–183
*Execution: The Discipline of Getting Things Done* (Bossidy and Charan), 28
External benchmarking, 125–127

**F**

Fairbank, R., 131
FBI (Federal Bureau of Information), 203, 214
Federal Express (FedEx), 139, 235
Feedback programs, 178–179
Firestone, 28
First Maryland Bancorp "Brainstorm" program, 226
Fisher, G., 92
Flexible leadership model: on balancing competing demands/tradeoffs, 18–19; essence of, 236–237; origins of, 19–22; overview of, 11–13fig, 15; three key propositions of, 21. *See also* Effective leadership; Leadership
Florida Power and Light, 126
Ford, B., 94, 223
Ford, H., 223
Ford Motor, 27–28, 93–94, 194–195, 223
Ford North America, 223
France Telecom, 139, 140
Functional specialization, 73–74

**G**

Gallo, 69
Gallup Organization, 6
GameChanger initiative (Royal Dutch/Shell), 124–125
The Gap, 73
Gatorade, 136–137
GE Capital, 8
GE Capital Fleet Services, 65
GE (General Electric), 67, 68, 148, 177
GE Medical Systems, 148
Gelsinger, P., 110
Getronics NV, 213
Ghosn, C., 204, 205–206, 225–226, 228
Global One, 139–140
GM (General Motors), 47–48, 73, 131
Goal setting, 49–51
Goleman, D., 234
Gonzalez, R., 160
Goodyear, 28
Grain Processing Corporation, 66
Gramm-Leach-Bliley Act (1999), 202
Great Plains, 186
Greaves, D., 165–166
Greenberg, J., 85, 86
Greenfield Online, 93
Group identity symbols, 172

**H**

Haas, R., 197
Hallmark Cards, 135
Hamel, G., 108
Harbour Report, 195
Harris, S., 47–48
*Harvard Business Review*, 94
*Harvard Management Update*, 29
Hastings Center, 36
Haylon, B., 31
HealthSouth, 235
Heroic leader myth, 4–6
Hershey, 64
Hewlett-Packard, 100, 128, 220
Hill, V., 189
Home Depot, 30, 195–197
Honda, 105
Human capital, 143
Human relations: tradeoff between adaptation vs., 199–201; tradeoff between efficiency vs., 197–199
Human relations enhancement: employee development programs for, 178–181; empowerment programs for, 181–185;

human resources planning systems for, 175–178; orientation and team-building programs for, 189–190; quality of work life programs for, 187–188; recognition, award, and benefit programs for, 185–187

Human resource enhancement: consulting behavior for, 166–169, 167t; developing behavior for, 162–166, 163t; empowering behavior for, 169t–171; recognizing behavior for, 158–162, 159t; relationships among behaviors for, 173–174; supporting behavior for, 155–158, 156t; team building behavior for, 171–173, 172t

Human resource management: conditions affecting importance of, 144–146; examples of good human relations in, 147–150; examples of human relations problems in, 150–152; implications of strategy for, 146–147; leadership behaviors for, 155–174; ways to improve relations and, 152–153

Human resource planning systems, 175–178

Human resources (good examples of): General Electric, 148; Pitney Bowes, 149–150; Southwest Airlines, 149

Human resources (poor examples of): Denny's, 150–151; Radio Shack, 152; U.S. Postal Service, 151

Hyundai Motor Co., 29, 46, 57

**I**

Iacocca, L., 6

IBM: adaptation success by, 89, 203; knowledge management systems of, 132; On-Demand Computing program of, 69

Ideo Tech Boxes, 134

IMA Inc., 64

Immelt, J., 148

Incentive programs, 74–76

Initiation rituals, 172

Innovation: adaptation failure due to failed implementation of, 91; adaptation failure due to lack of, 90–91; adaptation failure due to timing of implementing, 91–92; advantages of promoting, 81–82; balancing stability vs. changes of, 211–214; facilitated by leaders, 97–98; structural forms to facilitate, 133–135. See also Adaptation

Innovative thinking, 115–117, 116t

The Innovator's Dilemma (Christensen), 91

Integrity, 234–236

Intel, 110

Intrepreneurship programs, 123–125

Iridium, 92

**J**

Jacobi, P., 201

Jager, D., 213

James, G., 201

J.D. Power & Associate, 29

Jetway Systems, 171

Jo-Ann Stores, 189

John Deere, 66

Johnson Controls, 124

Journal of Leadership & Organizational Studies, 29

JPMorgan Chase, 69, 89

**K**

Kelleher, H., 149, 222

Kim Sang Kwon, 46

King, B., 226

Knowledge management systems, 131–133

Kodak, 67, 92

Korncavage, D., 183

Kotter, J. P., 9, 10

Kozlowski, D., 235

KPMG, 139

**L**

Leaders: as change agents, 113–115; collective learning facilitated by, 97, 118t–120; influence on organizational culture by, 97; innovation facilitation by, 97–98; myth of managers and, 9–10. See also Managers

Leadership: examining nature of effective, 1–3; failure to support adaptation, 96; indirect, 16–18; performance determinants of, 14, 17t–18t; quality of, 2–3; three types of direct, 14–16, 15t. See also Effective leadership; Flexible leadership model

Leadership behaviors: clarifying roles and objectives, 45t–51; to enhance adaptation, 99–121; to enhance efficiency, 39–62; for enhancing human resources, 155–174; monitoring operations and performance, 51–58; operational planning, 39–45; people-oriented, 15t, 20–21; relationships among the, 60–61; solving operational problems, 58–60, 59t; task-oriented, 15t, 20–21

Leadership tradeoffs: adaptation vs. human relations, 199–201; additional examples of, 207–215; among three performance determinants, 193–201; efficiency vs. adaptation, 194–197; efficiency vs. human relations, 197–199; examples of effective balancing of, 203–207; handling changes in performance determinants, 201–203

Leadership tradeoffs examples: control vs. empowerment, 214–215; MetLife experience, 206–207; Nissan experience, 204–206; short-term vs. long-term objectives, 210–211; stability vs. change, 211–214; stakeholders demands and expectations, 208–210

Leaderships fact & myth: born leader, 6–7; celebrity leader, 7–9; of easy answers, 10–11; heroic leader, 4–6; on leaders and managers, 9–10; newspaper headlines exemplifying, 3–4

Leeson, N., 53

Levi Strauss & Co., 197–198, 201

L.L. Bean, 126

Lombardi, V., 147–148

Lowe's, 196

Lucent, 85

**M**

McDonald's: "Made for You" project, 85–86; mystery shoppers hired by, 28; poor human resource planning by, 176; standardization used by, 73

McDonald's Hamburger University, 189

McDonald's USA, 85

McKee, A., 234

McKinnell, H., 109–110, 225

McKinsey re-engineering research, 65

McNeill, J., 30–31

McNerney, J., 148

Management systems: described, 70; functional specialization, 73–74; knowledge management systems, 131–133; open-book, 183–184; performance management, 71; TQM (total quality management), 63, 65–66. See also Structural forms

Managers: effective leadership as requiring good, 30; myths on leaders and, 9–10. See also Leaders

Maxygen, 88–89

MBO (Management by Objectives), 71

Mentoring programs, 180–181

Merck, 220

Mergers and acquisitions, 135–138

MetLife (Metropolitan Life Insurance Company), 206–207

Micro, Ingram, 3, 4

Microchip Technology, 235

Moares, J., 36

Mobil, 111

Monitoring operations/performance: described, 51–52; empowerment and, 52–53; examples of effective and ineffective, 53–54; guidelines for monitoring operations, 54t–55; guidelines for monitoring performance, 55–58, 56t; prior performance/performance of similar units standards for, 55

Morcott, S. "Woody," 177–178

Motorola, 92

Mount Sinai Hospital, 176

Murray, T., 36

Myth of born leader, 6–7

Myth of celebrity leader, 7–9

Myth of easy answers, 10–11

Myth of heroic leader, 4–6

Myth of leaders and managers, 9–10

**N**

Naitonal Geographic Society, 235

Nakamura, S., 205

Nardelli, B., 196

Nasser, J., 93–94, 194–195

New York Times, 53–54

Nissan, 94, 204–206, 228

Nokia, 108

**O**

"One Pitney Bowes" philosophy, 149–150

Open communication, 223–226

Open-book management, 183–184

Operational planning: action plan tool used during, 42–43t; different levels of, 43–45; ensuring compatibility during, 41–42; guidelines for, 42t; systematic approach to, 40–41

Operational problems. See Solving operational problems

Organizational culture: collective learning as part of, 97; core ideology of, 218–220; influence of leaders on, 97; open-door policy as part of, 225
Orientation programs, 189–190
Outsourcing, 69–70
Owings & Merrill, 129

**P**

Padilla, J., 223
Palmisano, S., 89
PARC (Palo Alto Research Center), 91
Parker, J., 149
Participative leadership, 166–169, 167t
*PC World* survey, 28
Pelaez, R., 157
People-oriented behavior: direct leadership and, 15t; meta-category of, 20–21
Performance determinants: described, 14; handling changes in, 201–203; programs, management systems, structural forms influencing, 17t–18t; tradeoffs among the three, 193–201
Performance management, 71
Performance Research Associates, 181
Persistence Software, 190
Pfizer: building support for change at, 109–110; flextime program of, 188; Master's Group of, 172–173; openness valued at, 225; R&D budget of, 194
Pharmacia, 109
Phillips, 86–87
Pillsbury, 132
Pitney Bowes, 149–150, 235, 236
Planned opportunism approach, 89
Polaroid, 67
Porras, J., 220
Preserving personal integrity, 234–236
PriceWaterhouseCoopers, 67
Process reliability: conditions affecting, 34–36; examples of, 30–34; programs and management systems for improving, 63–77; ways to improve, 36–37
Process reliability examples: Dell Computers, 32; Southwest Airlines, 32–33; Sterling Autobody Centers, 30–31; Wal-Mart, 34
Procter & Gamble: "Let's Talk" sessions of, 224–225; resistance to change experienced at, 213; strategic alliances used by, 139

**Q**

Quaker Oats Company, 136–137
Quality of leadership, 2–3
Quality of work life programs, 187–188
Quality/process improvement programs: BPI (business process improvement), 63–64; re-engineering, 64–65; Six Sigma, 37, 63, 66–67; TQM (total quality management), 63, 65–66

**R**

Radio Shack, 152
Re-engineering, 64–65
Recognition/reward programs: described, 74–75; employee benefit programs, 187; enhancing adaptation through, 129–130; examples of, 75, 185–187; improving productivity/process reliability with, 75–76; multiple objectives supported by, 226–227
Recognizing leadership behavior, 158–162, 159t
Reflexite Technology Corporation, 183
Renault, 204
Resistance to change, 94–96, 213
Rex Healthcare, 188
Right Management Consultants, 137–138, 152
ROA (return on assets), 2, 12
ROI (return on investment), 2
Royal Dutch/Shell GameChanger initiative (1996), 124–125
Russo, P., 3, 4

**S**

Samsung, 83
Schwab Private Client, 147
Sears, Roebuck & Company, 48, 143
Self-awareness, 233–234
Self-managed teams, 184–185
September 11, 2001, 87, 147, 149, 203
Serentec, 188
Short-term vs. long-term objectives, 210–211
Siddiqui, H., 66
Situational awareness, 229–230
Six Sigma, 37, 63, 66–67
Skechers, 83
Skill assessment program, 178–179
Smith, D., 67
SmithKline, 137
Snapple, 136–137

Solving operational problems: guidelines for, 59t–60; process of, 58–59; research on crisis management and, 59
Sony, 92, 220
Southwest Airlines: adaptation success by, 87–88; benchmarking used by, 126; effective leadership of, 1–3; empowerment encouraged at, 222–223; good management of human resources at, 149; high efficiency/process reliability of, 32–34; integrity emphasized at, 235; "open door" policy at, 225
Spherion, 180
Springfield ReManufacturing Corp., 184
Sprint, 139
Stability vs. change, 211–214
Stack, J., 184
Stakeholder demands/expectations, 208–210
Standard operating procedures, 71–72
Standardized facilities and equipment, 73
Sterling Autobody Centers, 30–31
Stewart, M., 8
Strategic alliances, 138–140
Strategic fit, 93–94
Strategic planning, 102–106, 104t
Structural forms: to facilitate innovation, 133–135; standardized facilities and equipment, 73; work rules and standard operating procedures, 71–72. See also Management systems
Sulzberger, A., Jr., 54
Sunbeam, 7–8
Supportive leadership behavior, 155–158, 159t
Swartz, M., 235
Systems thinking, 230–232

T

Target, 196–197
Task-oriented behavior: direct leadership and, 15t; meta-category of, 20–21
Team building leadership, 171–173, 172t
Team-building programs, 189–190
Teams: cross-functional, 134–135; self-managed, 184–185
Telecommunications Act (1996), 85
Tellabs, 235
Thompson, B., 31
Thompson, R., 189
3M: core ideology of, 220; Microreplication Technology Center of, 116–117

360-degree feedback, 234
Top management. See Leadership
Toyota's "Oobeya" approach, 119
TQM (total quality management), 63, 65–66
Tradeoffs. See Leadership tradeoffs
Training programs, 179–180
Triarc, 137
Tyco, 129, 220, 235
Tyco International, 8

U

UBS, 167
Union Pacific's "Idea Works" program, 129–130
University of Pennsylvania study, 143
University of Southern California, 29
U.S. Postal Service, 139, 151

V

Valero Energy, 235
Verizon, 199
Videotape Beta format, 92

W

Wal-Mart, 34, 93, 131
Walt Disney: as Buzzsaw.com client, 128; core competencies and adaptation of, 105; employee orientation/training programs of, 189
Wang, A., 213
Wang Laboratories, 213
Weber, L., 206–207
Webvan Group Inc., 93
Welch, J., 67, 148
Wellpoint Health Network, 177
Wendt, G., 8
Wendy's, 85
Wolfe, K., 64
Work rules, 71–72
WorldCom, 220
Wyatt, W., 224

X

Xerox, 67, 91, 126

Y

Yale School of Management, 6
Yoshida, T., 119